HOPE
BLOOMS

HOPE BLOOMS

Organ Donation, the Rose Parade®, and *Our Journey to Save Lives*

BRYAN STEWART

Advantage®

Published by Advantage, Charleston, South Carolina.
Member of Advantage Media Group.

ADVANTAGE is a registered trademark, and the Advantage colophon is a trademark of Advantage Media Group, Inc.

Printed in the United States of America.

10 9 8 7 6 5 4 3 2 1

ISBN: 978-1-59932-948-2
LCCN: 2018932492

Cover and layout design by Melanie Cloth.
Back cover photo by Scott Weersing.
Jacket photo by Kate Moore.

This publication is designed to provide accurate and authoritative information in regard to the subject matter covered. It is sold with the understanding that the publisher is not engaged in rendering legal, accounting, or other professional services. If legal advice or other expert assistance is required, the services of a competent professional person should be sought.

Advantage Media Group is proud to be a part of the Tree Neutral® program. Tree Neutral offsets the number of trees consumed in the production and printing of this book by taking proactive steps such as planting trees in direct proportion to the number of trees used to print books. To learn more about Tree Neutral, please visit **www.treeneutral.com**.

Advantage Media Group is a publisher of business, self-improvement, and professional development books and online learning. We help entrepreneurs, business leaders, and professionals share their Stories, Passion, and Knowledge to help others Learn & Grow. Do you have a manuscript or book idea that you would like us to consider for publishing? Please visit **advantagefamily.com** or call **1.866.775.1696**.

This book is dedicated to the Donate Life community.

TABLE OF CONTENTS

PART THREE | THE GREAT LEAP FORWARD

PART FOUR | JUST IMAGINE

ACKNOWLEDGEMENTS

This book would not be possible without the ongoing Donate Life Rose Parade Float campaign that inspired it and the many people who contributed their support, expertise, and heart to our collective effort.

I am grateful to Gary and Lois Foxen, Karen Libs, Tom Mone, Cheryl Bode, Gloria Bohrer, Esther-Marie Carmichael, Tenaya Wallace, Thomas Asfeldt, Laurie Wolowic, Kevin Monroe, Rivian Bell, Kathleen Hostert, Kari Kozuki, and Ginny McBride for their vision and pioneering contributions.

For their important contributions over the years, I thank Glenn Abercrombie, Lisa Bernfeld, Dave Bosch, Stu Brower, Jackie and Jack Colleran, Christina Courtney, John Dean, David Fleming, Mary Ganikos, Aaron Gilchrist, Stephanie Jansky, Kari Kozuki, Glenn Matsuki, Debbie Morgan, Ken Moritsugu, Dave Pittman, Renee Rhodes, Paula Symons, Ron Taubman, Mike and Mimi Thompson, and Amy Waterman.

For their leadership at the Rose Palace and Rosemont Pavilion, I thank Andrew McBride, Tina Vanderhorst, Dan Sandoval, Vicky Nguyen, Debbie Martin, Joy Weller, Bob Bruno, and Gee Wong. The beauty of floragraphs owes much to the skill and guidance of Lynne, Lindsay, and Katherine Frutchey, Martha Alonso, Pam Charron, Leslie Leath, Stephanie McMackin, Lisa Rhodes, Judy Smith, and Adam Teller.

I thank the thousands who met our call for volunteers, including Matt Barbagallo, Beverly Bliss, Jeff Boner, Mona and Sara Castro, Tim Crompton, Pam and Bruce Endo, Liz Fox, Brook Hanson, Amber Heidrich, Bryan Herring, Dave Hollon, Craig, Nicole and Justin Hostert, Lois Hubbs, George and Diane Linares, Liz Fox, Holly Miyagawa, Rosemary, Arlene, Stephanie and Vanessa Rodriguez, Daniel Ronco, Tammy Rusznak, Kathy Snow, Mason Sommers and the Golden Girls: Norma Hostert, Shirley Douthit, Cora Johnson, Sharyn Miller, Cheryl Thorpe, and Fidelma Brach.

For their dedication each holiday season, I thank OneLegacy colleagues, including Stephanie Schmitz, Erika Ospina Awad, Lacey Wood, Annie Kure, Iva Cook, Sandra Madera, Monica Padlo, Ann Wennerberg, Kari Williams, Margaret Wylie, Jaime Campbell, Sonia Navarro, Simera Nichols, Ralph Sutton, Heidi Aguiar, Jeff Fleming, Michelle Post, Anna Binder, Luz Diaz, Flora Leos, and Deborah Tanner.

For amplifying our message in the media, I thank Elena de la Cruz, Sabrina Ho, Dahiana Kast, Vanessa Van Nguyen, Paula Valle Castañon, Debra Stolberg, Randa Lipman, Jennifer Moe, Scott Weersing, Chris Chavira, Luis Ramirez, Chris Sariego, Jan Ramage, Leanna Flecky, William and Michelle Chen, Neil Van Harte, Robert Ballo, and Griff Partington.

For their generous guidance and partnership, I thank Phoenix Decorating Co., including Bill, Gretchen, Chris and Lyn Lofthouse, Sean McMinimy, Cynthia McMinimy, Jim Jennings, Larry Palmer, Brian Dancel, Misty Harlan, Yona Richman, Sean Quinn, Craig Singer, Bill Arcudi, Mark Yoshikawa, Adolfo Garcia, Mark Paulson, Jaime Arrevillaga, Jenard De Castro, Eva Monroy, and Melody Martinez.

I thank the staff and volunteers of the Pasadena Tournament of Roses, including David Eads, Bill Flinn, Jeff Allen, Heidi Hoff, Monique Sims, Jeannette Collier, Rick Jackson, Bob Miller, Pam McNeely, and Laura Farber.

Within the sponsoring organizations listed in the appendix are champions to whom I am grateful for their support: Martha Anderson, Darlene Aymerich, Debra Bordreaux, Tim Brown, Kim Charles, Suzanne Conrad, Tom Cycyota, Sue Dunn (and her parents Jim and Betty), Jennifer Gelman, Elisse Glennon, Walter Graham, Susan Gunderson, Jacki Harris, Lori Hartman, Kirsten Heintz, Mike Hudson, Julie Humeston, Sara Pace Jones, Rusty Kelly, Rob Linderer, Norman Lyon, Gina Matarazzo, Cathy Olmo, Jeff Orlowski, Vicky Owen, Marcia Penido, Marilyn Pongonis, Lauren Quinn, Bob Rigney, Sharon Ross, Joe Roth, Marcia Schoenfeld, Paul Schwab, Pamela Shute, Cindy Sjilstrom, Jeanette Slakey, Candy Smith, Merry Smith, Lisa Stocks, Kim Van Frank, Phyllis Weber, Frank Wilton, Charlene Zettel, and OneLegacy's board of directors, led by Dr. Robert Mendez.

I thank the thousands of participants who shared their stories with the world, including those who profoundly affected my experience: Patricia Abdullah, Lily and Brian Allen, Leiauna Anderson, Kari and Erica Barlament, Milt and Janet Bemis, Jose and Maria Bueno, Jennifer and Victor Choe, Louis Dachis, David and Rick Eckstein, Reg, Maggie and Eleanor Green, Kacey and Patrick Johnson, Steve and Tish Jokela, Mike Jones, Valen Keefer, Chris Klug, Peter and Frances Kupczak, Larry and Vivian Lefferts, Matt and Matty Logelin, Ann Lopez, Lori Malkin, Indra and Zulma Michaca, Eric Miller, Kim Morsching, Philip Palmer, Arnold and Eva Perez, Jayne and Peter Stanyon, Todd and Tara Storch, Eunice Sutton, Hooshang Torabi, Bethany and Kieran Vogel, and Kelly Wright.

Over the course of writing the book, I thank Deb Raupp, Esther-Marie Carmichael, Debbie Frank, and Christina Courtney for helping me shape the story; Daniel Allen, Michael Roth, Joe, Christina, and Jo'vonne for their welcoming smiles at Coffee Bean; Randy Bernstein and Alan Rothenberg for their support; Sarah Gray, Reg Green, Samera Arkel and Aaron Gilchrist for their guidance; and the team at Advantage|ForbesBooks, including Adam Witty, Keith Kopcsak, Tracy Pelham and the editorial team: Eland Mann, Adam Vlach, Melanie Cloth, Laura Rashley, Saara Khalil, and Andy Gilliom.

And I thank Sophia Stewart and Darlene Mininni for supporting my dedication to the Donate Life mission.

PROLOGUE

Donate Life's float entry emerged from Rosemont Pavilion for judging and the attendant dress rehearsal for the pageantry to come the following morning. Thousands of blooms exploded into color as they saw sunlight for the first time. Dozens of sponsors and volunteers feverishly sprayed the roses, carnations, mums, and irises to counter temperatures in the eighties. In less than twenty-four hours, the conclusion of the 2012 Rose Parade® would give the flowers permission to wilt.

Two dozen transplant recipients, living donors, and donor family members, each in their parade day attire, circled the float, contemplating where on the deck they would be seated on New Year's Day. Donor families surveyed six giant floral clocks to find their loved one's floragraph among the seventy-two memorials to givers of life.

A Phoenix Decorating Co. cherry-picker approached the float's camera side, coming to a stop within reaching distance of the only part of the structure not yet covered with organic materials: the twelve o'clock position on the middle clock. The space was designated for Christina-Taylor Green, the nine-year-old girl shot and killed at Rep. Gabrielle Giffords's constituent event in Tucson less than a year earlier.

Carefully and with quiet deliberation, John Green climbed the ladder and applied his daughter's oval portrait to the clock, making it whole. The hundreds who had gathered below offered a tearful ovation both in reverence to the young cornea donor and in celebration of their own courage in the face of adversity.

We hailed from big cities, small towns, and dozens of states from coast to coast, representing the extraordinary diversity that defines America. Here, steps away from the historic Rose Bowl Stadium, none of those differences mattered. There were no fault lines. In less than two days, our pilgrims to Pasadena had come together as one. Honoring one another united us.

PART ONE

GENESIS

1

GARY'S LETTER

*I have been so moved about getting my transplant and
have seen what a tremendous difference it made to my
life that I want to pay back society for this gift.*

—GARY FOXEN, 2003

KAREN TOOK TWO STEPS INTO my office and
handed me a letter.

"Bryan, we need to do this," she said.

Delivered in her trademark East Texas accent, Karen's voice had
a conviction that you typically heard in political speeches or predic-
tions of victory, but rarely in day-to-day conversation. In this case,
though, there was no ego on the line—only a resolute belief in a
powerful vision, its potential to help people, and our ability to bring
it to life.

That vision had been on Karen's mind for seven months, ever
since a letter from Gary Foxen of Orange, California, first came
across her desk. Gary had spent much of his lengthy career as a traffic
engineer with the Automobile Club of Southern California. While
he deeply enjoyed the nature of his day-to-day work, the holiday

season added special meaning for Gary and his coworkers as they volunteered to decorate the Auto Club's float entry in the Rose Parade. For more than a decade, Gary found himself uplifted by the collaboration, creativity, and community spirit surrounding the international event.

Gary's life took a drastic turn, however, when his lungs, ravaged by years of smoking, began to fail. Eventually, his condition deteriorated to the point where only a lung transplant would extend his life beyond a few months. Fortunately for Gary, the family of a woman who died in a sudden accident granted permission for her organs to be recovered for transplant. One of her lungs turned out to be a match for Gary, and in June 1999, his wait for a transplant ended with a positive outcome.

Once many transplant recipients have recovered from the procedure, they often find themselves transformed by their experience. Primal questions emerge: *Why am I still alive? In what ways have I changed? How do I thank and honor the person and family who saved my life?* For some, the desire to "give back" leads them to volunteer and share their story with others. For Gary, it inspired a vision he shared in an April 17, 2001, letter to Dr. Robert Mendez, board chairman at OneLegacy, the nonprofit, federally designated organ procurement organization (OPO) serving the seven-county Los Angeles area. The letter read:

I am one of those whose life was saved by receiving a new lung at UCLA in 1999. It truly has made me a new person and I will forever be indebted to the family that made me the object of their generosity. I have been trying to find a way to repay society for this wonderful gift and I believe I have a good idea on how to do that.

The thought I have is for the entry of a float in the Rose Parade, decorated by organ recipients and their loved ones, celebrating the gift of life and honoring the families who have shown their unselfish dedication to the well-being of others. The exposure would put a more human face on the somewhat abstract subject, and completing a project of this sort would certainly generate a feeling of accomplishment for those involved.

Mendez passed the correspondence to Karen Libs, who at the time was the executive assistant to OneLegacy's chief executive officer, Tom Mone. Tom agreed with Karen's assertion that the idea was a good one, but he felt the Pasadena Tournament of Roses—well-known for their conservative adherence to tradition—would deem organ donation "too much of a downer" to approve the cause's participation in an event known as "America's New Year Celebration®."

In 2001, the organ donation authorization rate in the United States was just a few points above 50 percent; that is, under circumstances where organ donation was a possibility, consent was granted just over half the time. In the greater Los Angeles area, the rate was even lower, with less than half of opportunities going forward.

Among the many factors contributing to such low authorization rates, it was not unusual for hospital staff to block organ donation professionals they perceived as "vultures" or "ambulance chasers" who would only cause further pain to traumatized families if they requested their consent for donation. Some organ procurement coordinators even saw themselves in this light, so it was understandable to think that public and professional audiences alike would not be ready to accept organ donation in such an uplifting setting as the Rose Parade.

Like Karen, I saw things differently from the moment she handed me Gary's letter on my first day on the job as OneLegacy's marketing director. I had already been exposed to the organization and the field through a branding project that Tom commissioned with my previous employer, Siegel+Gale. Through the five-month engagement, I came to believe that organ donation needed to—and could—be repositioned as something overwhelmingly positive, thus motivating millions of people to commit to be donors.

All too often, the decision whether to donate is made under the most difficult of circumstances: after a loved one has suffered a major head injury resulting in brain death—irreversible brain damage causing the end of independent respiration, clinically regarded as indicative of death. Such circumstances are extremely rare—less than 1 percent of all deaths—and historically preceded about half the time by a hemorrhage or other bleeding in the brain, a quarter of the time by motor vehicle accidents, and otherwise by some other head trauma. In such cases, maintaining the brain-dead patient on a ventilator preserves the possibility of donating organs to patients on the national transplant waiting list.

Families are often unaware of their loved one's wishes at the time they are approached with the opportunity to donate. Uncertainty at such a highly emotional time can lead families to default to a decline, resulting in deaths of transplant candidates. Furthermore, research showed that more than one-third of families declining to donate on their loved ones' behalf later wished they had consented to organ donation or questioned their original refusal.[1]

I sensed an opportunity to help families avoid even greater uncertainty under such traumatic circumstances.

Could it be the sight of an evocative Rose Parade float entry could motivate millions of families to discuss their donation wishes ahead of time? Might the vision of grateful transplant recipients motivate people to sign up in states with donor registries? Would the visible presence of our community in such a positive context help reposition organ donation from being about death to being about life?

Those were the possibilities that came to mind as I read Gary's letter. Karen was right: we needed to do this. But we were just two people, and there was no doubt that a Rose Parade float entry would take a village. Fortunately, we had a few things going for us.

First, Tom had a penchant for boldness, so I had confidence that he and OneLegacy would be supportive of a solid plan. Second, as the largest OPO in the country, the organization was positioned to marshal the resources that would be needed to make the most of the opportunity. And third, my college and professional experience—rooted in events, entertainment, marketing, and communications—illuminated a clear path forward. But never could I have imagined the beauty, goodwill, and enduring impact that emerged over twelve years of inspired, sustained, and shared purpose.

2

IF WE BUILD IT ...

You're not just getting the opportunity to give a chance of life to another human being. You're giving this person back to his community, back to his family. That's a pretty remarkable thing.

—PATRICIA ABDULLAH,
living kidney donor (2004 rider)

ORGAN DONATION AND THE Rose Parade: at first glance, those concepts seem utterly disparate, or at least they did in the early 2000s. But I had seen firsthand the power of parades as a medium of communication.

Soon after arriving at UCLA, in 1984, I learned about the university's Homecoming Parade, an intermittent tradition since 1927 that capped a week of campus activities leading up to the football game with their crosstown rival, USC. The night before the game, thousands of students and alumni lined Westwood Boulevard all the way to Bruin Plaza to cheer two dozen parade floats representing a wide range of campus organizations, including the occasional residence hall.

UCLA's on-campus housing community served mainly as a springboard for first-year students to affiliate with fraternities, sororities, activities, and cultural organizations. For residents of the high-rises and suites who had not yet found their tribe, joining together to decorate a Homecoming Parade float seemed like a meaningful way to instill a sense of community. I saw that spirit come to life in the spring of 1985 when I founded Mock Rock, a lip-sync contest involving the four residence halls that ultimately had an eleven-year run.

The success of Mock Rock helped me secure $1,500 from the Rieber Hall activities fund and enlist the help of resident assistants Dan Rubanowitz and Tony Rael, whose carpentry experience was essential for constructing a wood frame to hold chicken wire and tissue paper in place. There were very few requirements outside of being roadworthy, but I was determined to stand out from the standard front-heavy design that came with a flatbed truck chassis. The solution: a long flatbed trailer pulled by an electric utility cart.

Our novel infrastructure and the parade theme, "Born to Be Bruins," fertilized a breakthrough concept: diaper-clad baby bears stacking alphabet blocks into a pyramid that read "GO UCLA" on each side. The blocks sat atop a classic red wagon, with the utility cart transformed into an old-fashioned locomotive. The whimsical characters—two teaming to lift the uppermost block, two cubs more riding a seesaw, one lounging with sunglasses and a drink, and another hanging off the back and kicking his legs in a desperate bid not to fall off—garnered Rieber's float the prestigious Animation Trophy.

While I had neither attended nor deliberately viewed the Rose Parade, my college experience left no doubt that its large, captive, and attentive audience provided a powerful messaging opportunity. As for our message, Gary's suggestion to put "a more human face on [a] somewhat abstract subject" had resonated with me from the outset of the Siegel+Gale branding project.

Tom hired Siegel+Gale to help the Southern California Organ Procurement Center (SCOPC), which recently merged with the UCLA-based OPO, create a new brand that would unify the organization and appeal to professional and public constituents alike. From a standing start, we had about six weeks to present a game-changing strategic branding opportunity that Tom and his management team had yet to identify themselves.

As I researched organ donation websites, the simple and sincere words of loss, longing, and pride that family members had posted in memory of children, parents, and siblings who had saved lives in their passing moved me to tears—not so much out of sadness, but rather at the combination of sorrow and inspiration that left me feeling deeply aware of what it meant to be human.

THE COMBINATION OF SORROW AND INSPIRATION LEFT ME FEELING DEEPLY AWARE OF WHAT IT MEANT TO BE HUMAN.

A week into the engagement, we brought SCOPC's leadership team together to gauge the organization's self-image. Following introductions, I looked across the table and asked the regional manager, Jim Trisch, to describe what the organization did.

"We respond to referrals from hospitals and ensure the timely recovery of organs for transplant," Jim replied.

While Jim was factually correct, it struck me that his answer was about the *what*, not the *so what*. My immediate reaction—*They do so much more than that!*—revealed the OPO's strategic opportunity: *give greater meaning to what organ donation makes possible, and it will transform how professionals and the public view the opportunity to donate life.*

Fast-forward one year, and it was clear to Karen—and now to me—that Gary's vision had the potential to realize that opportunity. By the next day, I had a detailed plan and framework inspired by, of all things, six years in sports marketing.

My experience running a pro beach volleyball league and contributing to Major League Soccer's inaugural season conditioned me to see a Rose Parade float as a collection of component parts that, when assembled, created a greater whole: two dozen sponsored riders aboard a fully decorated floral float, constructed from a design that dramatized the value of organ donation in a clearly understandable way. Each step would require people: a passionate, knowledgeable organizing committee to offer creative and practical guidance; sponsors to provide funding; a float builder to design, construct, and provide materials; volunteers to decorate; and riders to represent our community to a national audience.

The choice of whether to move forward came down to two questions: *Should we build it, and if we do, will they come?*

The Rose Parade seemed like a natural platform to promote organ donation. The third-most-watched entertainment event in the world was seen by seven hundred thousand spectators and upward of forty million US television viewers on multiple national and regional broadcast and cable networks, including ABC, CBS, NBC, Univision, Telemundo, HGTV, Travel Channel, Tribune, and RFD-TV. Naturally, to better understand the event, I attended the 2002 Rose Parade.

Making my way from the West San Fernando Valley, traffic to East Pasadena was surprisingly easy. After parking on a street a quarter-mile north of Colorado Boulevard, we walked to the grandstands situated three miles east of Old Town Pasadena. Scores of people—including entire families—had staked out prime viewing positions along the sidewalk by arriving before dawn or even the night before. From our seats on the south side of the street, the view was breathtaking as the rising sun illuminated the mountains surging along the north side of the San Gabriel Valley.

The crowd's anticipation was palpable as a stealth bomber flyover marked the eight o'clock start at the intersection of Orange Grove and Colorado Boulevards. About forty-five minutes later, choreographed motorcycles reached our location, clearing the way for the procession of a hundred parade entries. For two solid hours, each floral float, marching band, and equestrian unit received the audience's undivided attention. Entries that were especially creative, spectacular, or unusual were greeted with applause. On rare occasions—especially with presentations involving the military—an entry would earn a standing ovation. I saw the possibility that our float entries—with their meaningful purpose, expressive riders, evocative themes, and moving concepts—would at some point elicit such accolades.

Granted, the Rose Parade audience is not of a singular mindset. For every "parade geek" fascinated by the spectacle of a spirited procession, there is a "Grinch" who finds the whole thing a bit silly. But regardless of each spectator's position on the interest spectrum, and whether they were watching comfortably at home or had braved the early morning (or overnight) cold, they expected their investment of time and attention to be rewarded. (Years later, Sandy LaRouche—who from 1988 to 2007 appeared in St. Louis's First Night celebration as the Snow Queen—succinctly explained a parade audience's mindset: "When people watch a parade, they want to be charmed.")

Just as compelling as the size and eagerness of the audience was the nature of the event itself. Many of its components and themes dovetailed nicely with the idea of organ donation: the spirit of renewal, the use of organic materials, the omnipresence of blooming flowers, and a month-long lead-up during the season of giving. In addition, the unabashedly positive spirit surrounding the century-old tradition offered a halo effect that could help organ donation be seen in a similarly positive light.

Clearly, we had a powerful opportunity in front of us, but applying to be a float participant was no small matter. When evaluating our candidacy, the Tournament of Roses would surely take our financial health into account, and other than OneLegacy's seed funding, we couldn't be certain that our fragmented regional and national community would join the endeavor. While our entire field stood to benefit from the parade's national broadcasts, many organizations saw the Rose Parade as a strictly Southern California event. Securing sponsorship pledges required us to make a case beyond the parade and float; we had to convey what our participation could make possible.

First, our float participants could be the centerpiece of a national public relations campaign centered around a high-concept pitch to news outlets: transplant recipients and donor family members participating in the Rose Parade in memory of or gratitude for those who gave life in their passing. Second, the month-long lead-up to the New Year could motivate donation and transplantation organizations nationwide to collaborate on a promotional campaign for the first time.

Both possibilities required a leap of faith: we could neither guarantee media coverage, nor could we be certain that our fragmented community would congeal around a platform that was both untested and highly unconventional.

We could build it, but would they come?

3

... WILL THEY COME?

I had the opportunity to meet one of the recipients of Shannon's kidneys. We wrote back and forth for about two years, and then we met. What a wonderful feeling to know that this woman's life went on, as did Shannon's legacy.

—**DARLENE AYMERICH,**
donor mother (2004 rider)

BEFORE WE COULD BUILD ANYTHING, we had to agree to a timeline going forward. Our feeling of urgency to help waitlisted transplant candidates compelled us to consider applying in February for the 2003 Rose Parade. However, there were serious downsides to fast-tracking our application.

First, Tournament rules—not to mention common sense—stipulated that floats had to represent a legal entity. Since engaging our community was bound to take time, OneLegacy would likely be the participant of record, thus positioning our entry as a regional rather than national cause.

Second, the venture would be expensive—the float alone would cost more than $100,000—and other organizations would be reluctant to contribute to a "OneLegacy" entry. The nation's fifty-nine organ recovery organizations collaborated on clinical matters, but when it came to community outreach they prided themselves on their identities and independence.

Furthermore, time was not on our side. Entering a float in the Rose Parade was an enormous commitment, and considering our small staff and my other priorities, fourteen months wouldn't provide ample time to plan and execute the project.

Lastly, even if OneLegacy funded the project independently, leveraging the opportunity required broad support among community partners and volunteers, neither of which had been cultivated before or since the SCOPC-ROPA merger. Relationships with transplant centers were on a strictly functional level, and the only connection we had with people affected by transplant were six sets of dramatic before-and-after photos—slides, actually—illustrating severe abdominal and skeletal afflictions successfully treated through transplantation of donated organs and tissues.

Only one case study had any semblance of a narrative: Lily, who at age fourteen months received a liver transplant at UCLA in 1984. Community and hospital presentations concluding with Lily's 1989 kindergarten photo invariably ended with a question about her whereabouts. "We don't know," we would answer, "but our hope is that, like other transplant recipients, she has continued to thrive and will do so for decades to come."

Laying the foundation for an ongoing tradition required us to take our time, think nationally, and plan on debuting in the 2004 Rose Parade. At the time, domestic organ donation advocacy was spearheaded by the Coalition on Donation, a nonprofit organization founded in 1992 and based at the United Network for Organ Sharing (UNOS) in Richmond, Virginia. The term "coalition" in the nonprofit's name owed to the politics surrounding the organization's founding at a time when some of the field's leaders were not yet convinced of the value of a national platform. Collective promotional efforts had been limited to free public service announcements produced and distributed by the Ad Council, including a 1996 campaign featuring Michael Jordan.

At this foundational stage, the Coalition on Donation's support was essential to position the Rose Parade campaign as a national effort that could encourage OPOs and transplant centers to come aboard. Fortunately, OneLegacy's longtime communications director, Gloria Bohrer, was a Coalition board member. She set up an introductory phone call with Coalition executive director David Fleming, which I followed up with a formal proposal.

As the document stated, since "OneLegacy will receive the greatest benefit from the initiative," our OPO committed $75,000 toward the estimated cost of $140,000, all but $20,000 of which was earmarked for the float itself. Our request for the Coalition to contribute $20,000 cited the many ways that Rose Parade participation would benefit the cause:

- dramatize our mission in a relevant yet unexpected way, helping to promote a positive image for organ donation and transplantation

- reach a large, diverse audience of parade spectators, including many families

- demonstrate a highly visible community outreach effort to our partner hospitals and transplant centers, both within our region and nationwide

- potentially involve hundreds of donor families, recipients, partners, employees, and their families in the building of the float

- generate media interest throughout Southern California

- provide an opportunity to establish relationships with other parade sponsors and civic organizations, with the potential of creative nationwide workplace partnership programs

On April 9, Gloria shared the news we had been eagerly awaiting: the Coalition on Donation would "commit to raising the $20,000 we [were] requesting" through "an effort to secure a large corporate sponsor." Now that we were officially a national initiative, we looked ahead to the Association of Organ Procurement Organizations (AOPO) Annual Meeting, in June, which included sessions focused on clinical practices, hospital development, family services, and community outreach. Gloria secured a fifteen-minute presentation to the field's public relations and public education specialists—a make-or-break opportunity.

After orienting my counterparts to the overall vision and benefits of participation, I handed out information packets with commitment forms requesting $25 per organ donor recovered in 2002. At the time, organ transplant activity was the most reliable measure of an OPO's financial resources, as their business model revolved around the standard acquisition charges they received from Medicare (for kidneys) or transplant programs (for extra-renal organs) to recover costs associated with organ recovery. OPOs vary greatly in size; the largest coordinated more than three hundred organ donation cases per year, while others handled a tenth of that many. Our goal was to secure the support of OPOs accounting for one-third of the nation's organ donation activity.

After the business meeting, I focused on the Exhibit Hall, introducing myself and the project to as many vendors as possible. They ran the gamut of infrastructure and service providers required to facilitate organ donation with precision and timeliness on every single case, including software for managing the process from end to end, perfusion machines to "exercise" kidneys between recovery and transplant, and air couriers to transport organs quickly over long distances. Other exhibitors included tissue processors—which rely on OPOs for the recovery of tissue that they subsequently prepare for medical use—and biotech companies conducting laboratory research on organs that are not suitable for transplant.

It was a company in this last category that may well have saved the initiative from coming to a screeching halt before it ever got out of the gate. Making my rounds, I stopped at the booth of Vesta Therapeutics, a privately held company researching techniques for liver repair and regeneration. Their representative, Thomas Asfeldt, had spent eight years as a procurement coordinator and another two on a hospital's internal organ donation team prior to moving into research.

After hearing my pitch, Thomas signed a commitment form on the spot, pledging $2,500 to become the campaign's first sponsor outside of OneLegacy and the Coalition on Donation. He subsequently joined me for two hours of brainstorming about the campaign and the transformative effect it could have on our field.

As energizing as that conversation was, over the next couple of days there were no other takers. The lack of interest among our colleagues nationwide begged the question as to whether the campaign had a future at all. But in Thomas I had found the first true believer from outside our small circle. His vote of confidence offered a glimmer of hope that others would support the program in time, but the clock was ticking.

As July approached, we had three months to secure $65,000 in pledges—a checkpoint that would signal sufficient progress to establish an organizing committee, reserve funding in OneLegacy's 2003 budget, and prepare our application to the Tournament of Roses. As the weeks went by, our prospects were not looking good. Despite three days of quality face time at the AOPO meeting, no additional commitments had come forward by the end of August.

In the face of our disappointment, we considered that the lack of a response might have more to do with timing than lack of interest. Until Labor Day, new initiatives for the following year took a back seat to vacations and back-to-school preparations. We also acknowledged four other factors that likely contributed to the silence since the June unveiling.

First, I was new to the field, so my colleagues had no frame of reference to feel assured by my experience. Second, the concept of a national campaign was a novelty in a landscape that had only recently consolidated from more than one hundred OPOs to fewer than sixty. Third, in the minds of many OPOs, the Rose Parade was a regional event despite its national reach. And lastly, up to this point I had relied on printed materials, trusting that my colleagues would run the opportunity up the chain of command. While this softer approach was meant as a sign of respect, we had to yet communicate directly with many decision-makers.

I took the first two weeks of September to update our proposal and compile an email list of OPOs, affiliated organizations, and Los Angeles-area transplant centers. A document titled "2004 Rose Parade Initiative" provided information about the Tournament of

Roses, the opportunity and benefits of float participation, the general direction of our float design and theme, cost estimates, images of non-commercial float entries, and commitments to date, which by then also included the Musculoskeletal Transplant Foundation (now MTF Biologics).

On September 19, the first wave of forty-nine proposals went out to OPOs. A formal request for support and a form offered OPOs three commitment levels: $25 per organ donor recovered in 2001, $10 per organ donor recovered, or a fill-in-the-blank option. The proposal also included a project timeline noting our fast-approaching deadline of October 7 to reach $120,000 in overall commitments.

The response was immediate. The next morning, Washington (D.C.) Regional Transplant Consortium (WRTC) committed $2,050. I immediately emailed the forty-nine OPO prospects thanking WRTC for their commitment, hoping their quick response would motivate other OPOs to fast-track their deliberations as we headed into the weekend. I arrived in the office on Monday to a $1,500 commitment from Tampa-based LifeLink Foundation, which covered Western Florida, Georgia, and Puerto Rico. Again, I circulated an email publicly thanking them. Several hours later, Upstate New York Transplant Services (Untys) in Buffalo pledged $1,000, and by the end of the day another four OPOs—from Arkansas, Illinois, Indiana, and Orlando—replied with assurances that they would do their best to support the effort. The bandwagon effect was working!

Between September 24 and 27, I sent a second wave of twenty-eight proposals to suppliers and Los Angeles-area transplant centers. We asked for $2,500 from the former, while multi-organ and kidney transplant programs were asked to contribute $2,500 and $1,000, respectively. On September 26, American Medical Bill Review pledged $2,500.

The next week saw a flurry of new commitments from Allo-Source, the Denver-based tissue processor, and six OPOs: LifeQuest Organ Recovery Services (Northwest Florida), Organ Donor Center of Hawaii (now Legacy of Life Hawai'i), Gift of Hope Organ and Tissue Donor Network (Illinois), Transplant Resource Center (now Living Legacy Foundation) of Maryland, Golden State (now Sierra) Donor Services (Sacramento, CA), and Life Alliance Organ Recovery Agency (Southeast Florida). By October 10, we surpassed $125,000 in total pledges.

On October 15, I spoke to Gary for the first time. I can only surmise that the reason we had yet to communicate directly was that I wanted our first conversation to deliver the best possible news, which it did: with $145,000 in commitments from twenty-seven organizations, we were ready to launch an organizing committee, with Gary as a charter member.

4

PHOENIX

*In memory of our dear son. Because of his cornea donation,
a lady who had been blind for forty years can see!*

—**ROSE DEDICATION** from Kentucky, 2009

AFTER TWELVE MONTHS OF concerted effort, we
were ready to shift our focus from fundraising to execution. Our
first order of business was choosing a float builder. While several
municipal floats were self-built, most float participants contracted
with a company specializing in the design, construction, and decoration of the Rose Parade's iconic floral floats.

Fiesta Parade Floats was renowned for lush, richly detailed
creations designed by the late Raul Rodriguez. Of the ten to twelve
floats they were contracted to build each year, about three-quarters
were among the parade's twenty-four award-winning entries. From
our standpoint, however, Fiesta had a major drawback: they were
based fifteen miles east of Pasadena. From the outset, we presumed
our lodging, decorating, and ancillary events would all be centralized in Pasadena so we could offer our guests convenience and an
immersive experience.

Thus, there was only one option: Phoenix Decorating Co., builder of the Auto Club floats Gary had decorated for a dozen years. Based less than a mile south of Old Town Pasadena, Phoenix built about 40 percent of the Rose Parade's floats each year. The family-run business had a reputation for producing well-engineered, reliable structures at an affordable cost. Although Phoenix was our choice by default, our first visit to their headquarters in late November made it clear that we had found our home.

As we pulled into the parking lot, a large exterior sign topped by the Phoenix Decorating logo declared that we had arrived at the Rose Palace. If not for my knowledge of the majestic craftwork applied within its walls, the moniker would have been quite the misnomer for an unremarkable gray warehouse. The family's patriarch, Bill Lofthouse, warmly welcomed me, Karen, Gary, and OneLegacy's director of corporate development, Cheryl Bode. Bill's expressive face, full head of hair, and neatly trimmed mustache and beard accentuated the rhythmic vocal cadence of an enthusiastic salesman. He exuded an authority, benevolence, and charm that surely engendered great loyalty from his employees and customers alike.

As we sat in a conference room surrounded by hand-drawn, brilliantly colored renderings, Bill educated us about the unique process of designing and building a Rose Parade float. The designer was the key player in the process, bringing tremendous skill and years of experience to the challenge of organizing appealing visual elements into a three-dimensional space, known colloquially as the "shoebox." Floats typically came in three standard lengths—thirty-five, fifty-five, and seventy feet—and were more than seventeen feet in width. Structures greater than eighteen feet tall—"over height" in Rose Parade lexicon—were outfitted with hydraulics and other mechanical components so that they could navigate underneath a freeway overpass at the end of the parade route.

Budget largely dictated the float's size and types of organic materials that were required by rule to cover every visible surface. Fresh flowers were vibrant but expensive, while dry materials—beans, grains, seeds, and dried petals—economically added color and texture. The number and distribution of standing and seated riders also influenced the designer's approach to a series of renderings that gradually evolved from rough pencil sketches to increasingly detailed black-and-white line drawings, then finally to three-quarter-view, full-color conceptual renderings.

Beyond technical considerations, of course, was the creative concept. We hadn't given much thought to the visual story we would use to introduce our cause to tens of millions of parade spectators and viewers, but we knew what it needed to accomplish. While some floats were spectacular or whimsical, we sought to elicit a visceral emotional response that, in turn, would inspire people to be donors.

As we toured the Rose Palace, fiery Phoenix Decorating logos adorned the black windbreakers of workers readying for the start of decorating two weeks hence. Two floats were still in the process of having their wood, fabric, and foam surfaces painted so materials could be applied in a manner akin to color-by-number. More than a dozen

WE SOUGHT TO ELICIT A VISCERAL EMOTIONAL RESPONSE THAT, IN TURN, WOULD INSPIRE PEOPLE TO BE DONORS.

other floats ready for decorating were stored at Rosemont Pavilion, a city-owned storage and decorating facility located within sight of the Rose Bowl Stadium marquee.

Having been oriented to float design and construction, the next step in our education was to experience decorating firsthand. After Christmas, the decorating schedule expanded from eight-hour shifts to double shifts running from eight o'clock in the morning to eleven o'clock at night. We arrived the evening of December 28th, when five full days of "dry decorating" transitioned to "floral decorating" and the placement of live flowers on the floats.

Parked immediately inside the entrance to the Rose Palace was the Farmers Insurance float, typically among the parade's largest. To the left, facing each other across a center aisle, were another ten floats representing a cross-section of float participants, including The Lutheran Hour, Ronald McDonald Charities, Eastman Kodak, Optimist International, and the cities of Los Angeles and Glendale. Each float was easily distinguished by elements dramatizing their chosen theme: whimsical characters, startlingly realistic animals, mythical creatures, well-known buildings and landmarks, and exotic landscapes. Along the perimeter walls were skeletal remnants of floats past—dinosaur heads, butterflies, railroad tracks—awaiting resurrection in future years.

Hundreds of volunteers filled the barn, with many were stationed at communal tables rhythmically cutting statice and strawflower into small flakes that fell into trays originally used for merchandising canned goods or beer. The remaining volunteers applied materials to the structures. Some covered large white areas with rice or coconut, while others defined features or added texture by meticulously placing split peas and beans one by one. Agile decorators wedged themselves into odd positions to access hard-to-reach areas, climbed up scaffolding and sat on narrow planks to work on upper components. Scores of volunteers wore matching sweatshirts identifying themselves as "Petal Pushers," a group of more than four thousand volunteers organized by the Lutheran Laymen's League. For decades they had decorated The Lutheran Hour Ministries float and several others.

Leading the volunteers were crew chiefs attired in green jackets, all of them part-time employees brought in each December to apply their years of decorating experience to guide the entries to completion. Female crew chiefs outnumbered men, and most were in their forties and above. Several chiefs were in their early twenties, and one whose experience began at age twelve was still in her teens.

Each float was assigned a crew chief and at least one assistant crew chief to manage the decorating process. They had a wide range of duties: planning the sequence of elements to be decorated, training volunteers on techniques for cutting or applying materials, monitoring people on scaffolding to ensure their safety, and sending runners to replenish glue and materials. Phoenix employees attired in black T-shirts and jackets moved scaffolding, filled glue containers, staffed the storehouse of dry materials, and managed the flower tent.

Amid the whirlwind of activity around us, Bill Lofthouse answered my questions. I had recently given thought to the theme and design for our inaugural float. It made sense for us to use the parade theme as our guidepost, as doing so would not only be seen as a sign of respect for the Tournament's storytelling framework, but it would also focus our creative exploration. After all, the raw emotional power of organ donation could take us in any number of directions, and achieving consensus on a strict timeline would be essential to our success.

The Tournament typically doesn't reveal the theme for a parade until the preceding January or February. But since the next year's floats had to go into production starting in February, Bill had inside knowledge of the announcement to come. However, he was sworn to secrecy, so he couldn't share the theme prior to the public announcement.

I pleaded for any kind of guidance, and seeing how anxious I was, Bill generously offered me a hint. "Music," he said, catching me off guard. "Hmm. Music," I replied, not anticipating the theme would be so specific. After a few seconds, he said it again. "Music." I nodded, letting it sink in. We shared a long glance, trading trust on his part for appreciation on mine. Then he repeated it one more time. "Music." Bill was no doubt amused by the puzzled expression on my face, which said, "Why on earth do you keep repeating that? I got it the first time." Only after the Tournament's announcement weeks later did I come to realize that Bill, without violating his covenant, had revealed the theme of the 2004 Rose Parade: "Music Music Music."

Into the increasingly frigid night, Karen and I watched all the elements—facility, scaffolding, floats, material, and people—come together as an orchestra. The sense of community that had inspired Gary made it easy to envision an organ donation-themed float in the Rose Palace. I imagined our staff and volunteers proudly participating with a deep sense of purpose: in memory of loved ones who had been donors in their passing, in gratitude for the extended life or improved quality of life that transplanted organs, corneas, and tissue made possible, and as a meaningful expression of professional pride. Our regional and national community was ready to be activated— that is, if the Tournament of Roses accepted our application.

5

CROSSING THE BRIDGE

*Anna is the strongest and most optimistic fourteen-year-old girl I
know. She has been waiting for twenty months for a new heart but
rarely lets it get her down. She is an inspiration to everyone she meets.*

—**ROSE DEDICATION** from Texas, 2013

IN BETWEEN OUR TWO VISITS TO the Rose
Palace, our core team—Tom, Karen, Gloria, Cheryl, community
programs supervisor Tenaya Wallace, and myself—met on December
11th to lay the groundwork for the next thirteen months. Topics
included a project timeline, opportunities to leverage our investment
regionally and nationally, and a committee structure that would
engage partners nationwide. Tenaya updated us on the volunteer
program she had been developing during her first six weeks at
OneLegacy. We also focused on the one hurdle upon which all of our
plans hinged: our float participant application.

Despite our progress, we felt no assurance that our application would be accepted. We had no contact with the Tournament
of Roses, and Bill Lofthouse had given us only cryptic insight into
the evaluation process. In addition, my interactions at schools and

hospitals over the last six months had exposed me to the discomfort both the public and healthcare professionals commonly felt about organ donation. Perhaps Tom's original instinct that we would be too much of a downer for the Tournament's comfort might be a decisive factor after all.

I felt the need to make an utterly compelling case the Tournament couldn't refuse. On December 17th, I hand-delivered our application to their Tournament House headquarters with a detailed cover letter explaining our organization, life-saving mission, and what we hoped to contribute to the event:

The Rose Parade represents for [the Coalition on Donation] a unique opportunity to further our goal of making organ and tissue donation a universally accepted and celebrated act of giving. The inspiring, life-affirming aspects of donation and transplantation are especially suited to be dramatized via a floral parade float.

With respect to our float sponsorship, we do not plan to be a one-time participant. Rather, our vision is that the Rose Parade will become an annual, time-honored tradition among all Coalition on Donation members as well as the millions of people who have been personally touched by donation and transplantation.

By accepting our float application, the Float Entries Committee will not only help the Coalition on Donation send an emotional and positive message about the benefits of donation, but the Tournament of Roses will also gain an ideal partner with the ability to harness the enthusiastic participation, goodwill, and promotional support of hundreds of thousands of donor families, transplant recipients, and healthcare professionals nationwide. In doing so, lives will be saved.

The importance of our pledge to be "an ideal partner" to the Tournament of Roses cannot be overstated. We promised to not only extract as many benefits as possible from our participation, but to deliver value back to the Tournament and the many organizations in its orbit. It placed us in a "spirit of service" mindset that dovetailed nicely with our life-saving mission—and would hopefully position us as a positive addition to the parade lineup.

Throughout January, Bill Lofthouse assured us that things were on track, but we weren't taking anything for granted. I was neither encouraged nor discouraged by a phone call I received from a Float Entries Committee member in February. To my surprise, he didn't ask a single question about whether our cause was a fit for the Rose Parade. His inquiries focused instead on our financial resources.

As I came to learn, several one-time-only float participants had reneged on the 20 percent balance due to their float builders after the parade. Given our dozens of financial contributors, the Tournament needed assurances that we would stand behind our financial commitments. I assured them that while the float would be entered on behalf of the Coalition on Donation, OneLegacy would be the responsible party. The Tournament's concerns were underscored by a second, brief phone call from the same committee member, who once again asked about our finances. I assured him that we were in it for the long haul.

Despite the uncertainty, we had no time to waste. As we moved full-speed ahead, John Dean of the Coalition on Donation accompanied his plaudits for our efforts with some sage advice in an email:

It has been our experience from the past in implementing national campaigns and projects that unless there is a buy-in and a sense of responsibility from the membership (in this case, financial contributors) from day one, the chances of failure and frustration are greatly magnified. As OneLegacy and the coalition are the two major financial supporters of this project, we must take great care in seeing that there is a process in place that insures each partner will have the opportunity to contribute ideas and have a fair say in our efforts.

John's words of caution were well taken and timely. Without sacrificing momentum, we needed to involve our partners in a meaningful way. Fortunately, our core team had recently laid the foundation for an organizing committee that would provide oversight and specialized attention to key operational areas: design and decoration, partner relations, public relations, marketing programs, volunteers, parade day, and administration.

While I focused on partner relations, public relations, and administration, Karen was especially well-suited for heading up the Design and Decoration Committee. Not only did she bring the heart that inspired her to see the project's potential from the outset, but she also had an extensive art background. After being nationally recognized for her art talents in high school and majoring in art at North Texas State University, she had worked as an interior designer in the Dallas area for five years.

On March 6, 2003, the Coalition on Donation Rose Parade Float Committee met for the first time via conference call. In addition to Tom, Karen, Gary, and myself, charter members included John Dean, Dave Bosch of Gift of Hope, Esther-Marie Carmichael of the Centers for Medicare and Medicaid Services, Kathy Giery of LifeQuest, heart recipient Glenn Matsuki of Cedars-Sinai, and donor mother Jayne Miller of MTF.

The committee was brought up to speed on creative development, which had already been under way for eight weeks. The creative process needed to be truly collaborative, as a deep emotional connection to the theme and design would propel our community's interest in promoting and attending the event.

The first week of January, I had circulated the first draft of a "float design brief," a tool that drew inspiration from strategy and creative briefs commonplace at advertising and branding agencies. A week later, I sent a second draft to the Coalition on Donation and other external contacts who had expressed an interest in the endeavor. Toward the end of month, we sent Phoenix a final float design brief to help them develop "a distinct and memorable float design" with several key attributes:

- sends a positive message about the choice to be a donor

- celebrates the value of one's life

- inspires a visceral emotional response among the parade audience

- portrays the emotional relationship between donors, donor families, and transplant recipients

- features donor family members and transplant recipients riding on the float

- incorporates animation in a tasteful and subtle fashion, if at all

- does not overuse common icons for donation, such as hearts, doves, butterflies, and hands

The brief also included a full page of brainstormed themes, songs, and visual elements to inspire the designer. While the design briefs and committee meetings allowed for robust input and feedback among all concerned, Karen and I worked directly with Phoenix to ensure they received focused guidance.

Early on, our creative thinking congealed around a metaphor that could serve as an accessible, evocative way of introducing the intrinsic value of our mission: a bridge. Fundamentally, organ donation was a bridge between death and life, grief and hope, illness and recovery. It also had the practical advantages of fitting the float's "shoebox" dimensions perfectly and carrying a lot of people. Such a strong visual centerpiece demanded a worthy theme.

Parade rules prohibited the participant's product or service from being included in the theme. For example, Kodak could not use "cameras" or "film" in their theme, but could refer to their uses or benefits, such as "movies" or "memories." Likewise, although we were prohibited from using a clause like "organ and tissue donation," the emotional nature of our mission gave us a world of options. Among the eight theme ideas we suggested in the design brief, two included *symphony*—a metaphor not only relevant to the parade theme, but an apt description of the coordination, skill, and beauty endemic to donation and transplantation.

In the interest of focusing Phoenix's creative efforts, we suggested they start with concepts centered around a bridge, with an underlying "symphony" theme. With four months until our planned June

1 unveiling of the theme and design at the Coalition on Donation annual meeting, we figured we had time to start with six to ten designs, choose two or three for refinement, then come to a consensus on a final concept. It would take three to four weeks to transform the final color sketch into a detailed, full-color, publication-ready rendering, so it was in our best interest to come to a final decision by the first week of May.

No sketches had been presented by our March 6 committee meeting, but knowing Phoenix was hard at work, we didn't worry. However, when our April 3 committee meeting arrived without any creative, it was clear we needed to accelerate the process. With Bill's approval, Karen and I escalated our involvement by working directly with the designer, Dave Pittman.

Dave had designed dozens of Rose Parade floats, drawing upon his interest in art history and experience with the Orange Bowl Parade in Miami and America's Thanksgiving Parade in downtown Detroit, Michigan. Having worked with Fortune 100 companies, professional sports teams, and international nonprofit organizations, Dave was highly collaborative and eager to support our mission.

Within two weeks, we reviewed two black-and-white sketches, each featuring a classic stone bridge over water and surrounded by lush landscaping. One was Greco-Roman in appearance, open to the sky with cherub statues at the four corners. The second had more of a French feel, with three cast-iron gazebos running the length of the bridge. The French bridge seemed to have some potential, so we asked Dave to add color to help us better visualize the finished product. Within a week he had prepared four color treatments, with varying combinations of gazebos (green vs. white), pathways (white vs. red paving stones), space underneath (open vs. largely closed), and water features (geese vs. rowboats).

Karen and I agreed that we had made tremendous progress, but as we prepared to share our options with the committee on May 1, we disagreed on how close we were to the finish line. With only five weeks until the unveiling, Karen was understandably anxious to bring months of development to a conclusion, but it was my view that we weren't quite there yet. The stone bridges looked heavy, and the elegant gazebos topped by floral sprays evoked a wedding or funeral. Unfortunately, neither of us had any specific ideas for improvement, our mutual frustration was palpable.

Talking with Dave about our impasse, I saw a path. "Forget we ever mentioned a bridge," I said. "What would a 'symphony of life' look like?" Within two days, Dave presented a color sketch with a radical, abstract concept: two explosions of color, each on its own "island" connected by a ten-foot arc of energy between them. The concept was daring, provocative, and a welcome contrast to the stoic designs we had seen to date.

The next day, our committee discussed the two options. The classic bridge impressed us as noble and uplifting, with the potential to be an award-winner. However, it was neither contemporary nor dynamic. The abstract design was hailed as bold and colorful, but it lacked reverence and wouldn't be intuitively associated with organ donation.

Our committee advanced the classic bridge to the refinement stage, with guidance to add color, contemporize key elements, and replace the riders' formal wear with everyday attire. However, the true breakthrough came out of Tom Mone's suggestion of the Japanese bridge from Claude Monet's water garden at Giverny, combined with guidance to incorporate the energy from Dave's abstract concept. Within ten days, Dave's work was complete, with "A Symphony of Life" to be unveiled in one week's time.

6

BUILDING BLOCKS

*The hard times, the uncertainty, the illness, the transplant, my
probable shortened lifespan—they were all worth it, because it
ultimately gave us a life worth living, no matter what the duration.*

—**JERRY PROSE,**
heart recipient (2004 rider)

DURING THE THREE MONTHS leading up to the
unveiling, our partner roster had stalled at thirty, leaving us well
short of the broad participation needed to genuinely represent our
national community. However, we had every confidence that the
design would invite additional financial support and sponsorship of
float riders.

We projected a contingent of twenty riders, split between the
Los Angeles area and outside the area. We invited partners to sponsor
a donor family member or transplant recipient to ride, with no additional cost aside from hotel and travel expenses. Partners were also
encouraged to send representatives to connect with the mission,
network with colleagues, and escort their sponsored participants.

Anticipating a sizable number of guests, we had started addressing travel considerations well before the Tournament accepted our application. Unfortunately, by the end of February, the four major hotels in Pasadena were already full. Lodging in Arcadia and downtown Los Angeles was available, but without a clear idea of how many people would come, committing to a room block was out of the question. Since we didn't have the staff to handle individual travel arrangements, we ceded that responsibility to our partners.

Meanwhile, the volunteer force that would be essential for float decorating was coming together nicely. Throughout spring, Tenaya hosted nine orientation workshops, training 125 OneLegacy Ambassadors eager to share their stories and engage in community outreach. Training workshops and speaking engagements also served as informal auditions for the eventual selection of local float riders.

Our prospects for generating media coverage of our participation received a boost when OneLegacy hired JDI Communications as our year-round public relations agency. JDI principal Rivian Bell's decades of experience as a journalist and media strategist would contribute mightily to building our media relations framework. Meanwhile, raising the profile of our campaign among Coalition on Donation affiliates was supported by "Phil's List," an email distribution group facilitated by my counterpart from the Oklahoma Organ Sharing Network (now LifeShare of Oklahoma), Phil Van Stavern.

In addition to sending major announcements to the media and our field, we also needed to communicate directly and routinely with our growing ranks of partners. Mid-April saw the debut of our first email update, "On the March," its title inspired by a parade procession, a community moving in lockstep toward our New Year's Day destination, and the newsreel from *Citizen Kane*. Our communication channels were fully activated for the first time on May 1 as we issued a press release announcing the Coalition on Donation had been formally invited to join the 2004 Rose Parade.

During the last four weeks leading up to the unveiling, we circulated Rose Parade trademarks, style guidelines, and appropriate terminology to describe our involvement. Since the Tournament was sensitive to the term "sponsor" being used for anyone other than sponsors of the parade itself, the Coalition on Donation was considered a "parade participant" and our financial contributors were "partners."

For all our anticipation of the unveiling making a huge splash, the actual opportunities to do so were underwhelming. The Coalition on Donation merely offered an abbreviated presentation during an informal function. Nonetheless, between the heavy traffic in the exhibit hall and wide circulation of the unveiling press release, buzz was building.

The unveiling release established two conventions that would be central to creative development going forward. First, the float concept was described in concise, evocative language: "more than a dozen donor family members and transplant recipients walking together across a beautiful garden bridge. A trellis running the length of the bridge will support a variety of intertwining florals, while two rowboats under the bridge will carry recipients and families of their organ donors." If we couldn't succinctly describe the scene, it was too complicated an idea.

Second, our float theme was closely aligned with the parade theme. "To those who are touched by the process, organ and tissue donation shares many hallmarks of classical music's masterworks: profound, often divine inspiration, an intimate relationship between participants, and its essence as one of humanity's great achievements." The language was flowery, but we wanted to assure the Tournament that we respected their storytelling framework. Doing so also set a precedent for interpreting the parade theme through our humanist lens.

The unveiling release had an instant impact, with new partners coming aboard and longstanding supporters stepping up to send riders. For the previous eighteen months, our initiative had been focused on fundraising, infrastructure, and messaging. It was time to see what our campaign could make possible.

7

WHO WILL RIDE

*Our entry is so unique in its concept and idea, and
now we're going to tell the world about it today.*

—GENE BATTALY,
heart recipient (2004 rider)

FROM THE OUTSET, an article of faith driving our
efforts was a steadfast belief that our Rose Parade participation would
attract media interest in the weeks leading up to the event. In the
Los Angeles area, we trusted that the meaningful purpose behind our
float would make us and our riders stand out from a crowded field
of more than fifty entries. Outside the area, each rider's likely status
as the sole ambassador of their city, region, or state to America's New
Year Celebration would add to their newsworthiness.

Since our local riders wouldn't need flights or hotel accommoda-
tions, we took time to choose ten participants who would represent
a range of Los Angeles-area sub-regions and transplant centers.
Some would be selected from the ranks of our volunteer OneLegacy
Ambassadors, while transplant programs would have the opportunity to nominate patients with compelling stories.

There was a sense of great urgency, however, to identify the other half of our contingent. With each passing week, hotel rooms and flight reservations would be increasingly scarce and expensive. We had no idea how many partners would take advantage of the opportunity to sponsor a rider, but most fortuitously, exactly ten stepped forward to be float rider sponsors.

The first to respond was Unyts, which planned to send Darlene Aymerich, their community education specialist and family support counselor. Darlene would be riding in honor of her brother, to whom she donated a kidney, and in memory of her twenty-seven-year-old daughter, Shannon, who became an organ and tissue donor after being killed in a car accident.

Soon thereafter, Dave Bosch took on the responsibility of facilitating float rider sponsorships. The response was fast and furious. Within two weeks, Dave had received confirmations from tissue bank RTI Donor Services (Wisconsin, now RTI Surgical)) and eight more OPOs: Gift of Hope, Life Alliance (Colorado and Wyoming), Lifebanc (Northeast Ohio), LifeLine of Ohio (Southeast Ohio), LifeLink Foundation, Lifesharing (San Diego metro area), Mid-South Transplant Foundation (Western Tennessee, Eastern Arkansas, and Northern Mississippi), and the Nevada Donor Network.

We issued Float Rider Selection Guidelines to ensure participants were well-suited for the opportunity's high profile, time commitment, and physical demands:

- speaking to the media, including national television

- attending float judging on New Year's Eve

- arriving as early as six o'clock in the morning on New Year's Day for the parade lineup

- standing (with structural supports) for up to three hours for the entire length of the parade

Any donor family member, living donor, or recipient of organs, tissue, or corneas was qualified to represent our national community as a rider. In addition, per parade rules, all float riders were required to be twelve years of age or older. Our guidelines also noted that among the ten local float riders, special considerations would be made to ensure diversity of ethnicity and age among the overall contingent, as well as geographic diversity to ensure coverage in many of the region's media sub-markets.

Donation rates in African American, Asian/Pacific Islander, and Latino/Hispanic communities were markedly lower than in white communities, and the need for transplants in these communities outpaced their share of the population—dramatically so among African Americans, who represented 35 percent of the kidney transplant waiting list.[12] With so many participants coming from OneLegacy's service area, we could ensure proportional representation overall.

The rider selection process was underway as the float was tested twice for roadworthiness. In late June, the first test (known as "T1") allowed the Tournament's Float Entries Committee to observe the structural vehicle's structural soundness. Because our float was still in an early stage of construction, its infrastructure was visible: chassis, steel skeleton, engine, steering mechanism, spaces for the driver and navigator, and a fire extinguisher.

At the end of July, "A Symphony of Life" was fully constructed, painted, and ready for the second and final test. The driver and navigator were joined by twenty-two test riders responding to Tenaya's open call to the 160 OneLegacy Ambassadors she had trained to represent our cause at schools, city council meetings, festivals, and other community touchpoints. As with T1, the test originated at the Rose Palace, traveled a quarter-mile south on Raymond Avenue to Glenarm, then made a three-point turn for the return trip. As the float neared the Rose Palace, a Tournament official shouted, "Fire! Fire"—the signal for all of the riders to evacuate the float within forty-five seconds, the threshold for passing the safety test.

The post-unveiling surge of sponsorship commitments introduced the prospect of subsidizing two more at-large riders. One of the boats easily accommodated an additional person and, by T2, Phoenix generously added a new standing position on the bridge. When considering candidates for the two open slots, our attention immediately gravitated to two individuals whose spirited advocacy emanated from very different perspectives.

Dr. Kenneth P. Moritsugu, deputy surgeon general of the United States since 1998, was also a donor father and husband, having lost his wife, Donna, and daughter, Vikki, to automobile accidents in 1992 and 1996, respectively. In addition to serving as a board member of UNOS, the National Kidney Foundation and Washington Regional Transplant Consortium, Moritsugu has spoken at scores of donor remembrance ceremonies over the years. Attired in his formal dress uniform, his authoritative yet empathetic demeanor was a source of comfort for grieving families.

By contrast, Chris Klug wore his official uniform strictly on mountain slopes. Less than two years after receiving a liver transplant to treat primary sclerosing cholangitis, Klug won a bronze medal in the parallel giant slalom at the 2002 Winter Olympic Games in Salt Lake City, Utah. In the year since, he had become a much-sought-after inspirational speaker. Both Moritsugu and Klug gladly accepted our invitations to join us for our Rose Parade debut.

The first two riders selected to fill our local contingent shared a remarkable story tailor-made for media coverage. Mike Jones, forty-three, and Patricia Abdullah, fifty-five, had met at a personal development seminar in 2001. Mike informed his classmates that his attendance might be impacted by dialysis, which he had undergone three times a week for five years due to his impaired kidney function. As part of the program, Patricia, a grandmother of three, invited Mike to ask if she would give him one of her kidneys.

Testing at Cedars-Sinai revealed that the only way they could have been a better match would have been if they were identical twins. Throughout his subsequent years of advocacy, Mike summed up their story powerfully: "A Caucasian, Muslim woman donated a kidney to save the life of an African American, Christian man at a Jewish hospital."

Two other riders shared similar destinies across time and distance. The lives of Brittney Andrews, thirteen, and Sara Castro, twelve, had been intertwined since infancy when both received heart transplants at Loma Linda University Medical Center—Brittney at three months of age, Sara at only five weeks. Though Brittney lived in Colorado and Sara in California, their transplants three days apart placed them on the same semiannual checkup schedule, and through their twice-a-year reunions they forged a deep friendship.

Kari Barlament, by contrast, joined the community of donor families only within the previous six months. Kari, then four months pregnant, and her husband Eric were on an errand to choose furniture for their nursery. Driving on an icy road in northeastern Wisconsin, a car veered over the center line and hit them head-on. Eric was killed instantly. Miraculously, Kari and her unborn daughter survived, and Kari donated her husband's tissues in accordance with his prior wishes. Five months later, on September 5th, their daughter Erica was born on Eric's birthday.

For nearly two years, our float had been a construction project. With the announcement of our inaugural class of float riders, it gained a life of its own.

8

ON THE MARCH

*I truly believed it would be the national campaign for organ
and tissue donation if we could ever make it happen.*

—KAREN LIBS, 2003

ENTERING NOVEMBER, the table was set to execute
our inaugural campaign. The float was ready for decorating, travel
plans were confirmed, and fifty-five official partners had pledged
more than $180,000, exceeding our original goal by $40,000. The
surplus had allowed us to invite Chris Klug and Ken Moritsugu as
celebrity riders whose presence would underscore the importance of
the effort. Then, with a month to go until the first day of decorating,
we ran into a glitch.

Eighteen months before, in April 2002, the Coalition on
Donation had offered their official support with a commitment to
raise $20,000 through "an effort to secure a large corporate sponsor."
From that moment forward, I had presumed theirs was a firm
pledge of financial support, going so far as to mention it in scores of
proposals to prospective sponsors. After I sent the invoice, however,
the Coalition informed me that they had committed to *help us raise*

the funds, not to provide it outright. Translation: our budget was now short $20,000.

My disappointment was ultimately tempered by the benefits that attended the misunderstanding, not to mention OneLegacy generously filling the funding gap. The Coalition's early endorsement was the vote of confidence we needed to believe the Rose Parade initiative had any potential whatsoever. The fact that our float entry would carry the Coalition on Donation's name with their "Donate Life" logo made it representative of our entire field and, as such, an endeavor worth supporting.

Our broad partnership support was encouraging, but the most important test of the campaign's effectiveness would be the level of interest among news media. After all, our mission was to increase donation rates, and news stories had the potential to increase Rose Parade viewership or, at the very least, reach people who did not plan to tune in.

To generate news coverage, we prepared a media kit with our unveiling and rider press releases, a theme/design one-sheet, and Coalition on Donation fact sheet. Outside the Los Angeles area, we trusted our partners to be familiar with their media landscape and encouraged them to pitch early and often. In some parts of the country—especially in the Upper Midwest, Big Ten conference territory—the Rose Parade enjoyed mythical status, so the prospect of a city, region, or state being represented in the event could pique the media's interest weeks and even months before the New Year. RTI landed the campaign's first story on October 11, when WLUK-11, the Fox affiliate in Green Bay, Wisconsin, aired a story about Kari Barlament's deeply meaningful participation.

Closer to home, the surfeit of Los Angeles-area participants compelled a divide-and-conquer approach so as not to besiege news outlets with overlapping pitches. In mid-November, representatives from four transplant centers and the local National Kidney Foundation and American Liver Foundation chapters joined us for a Local PR Working Group planning session. After matching riders with their local newspapers, we identified print, TV, and radio outlets with whom each of us had relationships; unclaimed outlets were assigned to JDI Communications. Phoenix Decorating would triage media arriving at the Rose Palace for scheduled or ad hoc stories. We adjourned with the expectation that media interest would begin in earnest with the onset of float decorating in early December.

Decorating didn't require much in the way of preparation for most float participants. Phoenix Decorating supplied the facility, materials, and crew chiefs (aka "green jackets"), some of whom had cultivated a stable of highly experienced veterans who could be counted on to volunteer throughout the month. A steady supply of volunteers was also ensured, with most emanating from the Petal Pushers, high-school-based Kiwanis Key Clubs, or San Gabriel Valley residents for whom float decorating was an annual holiday tradition.

From the outset, we chose to supply our own volunteers. Starting in mid-September, Tenaya enlisted approximately fifty volunteers for each of fifteen decorating shifts. Full-day, nine-to-five decorating shifts were scheduled for the first three Saturdays and first Sunday of December, while the five days after Christmas would each have double shifts of six to eight hours each. To help fill the seven hundred volunteer slots, we offered our partners the opportunity to claim shifts in whole or in part. St. Joseph Hospital and UCLA Healthcare filled entire shifts, while the National Kidney Foundation, TRIO Ventura County/West Valley Chapter, and United Organ Transplant Association (UOTA) contributed smaller numbers. The last two decorating days were slated for float riders, sponsor representatives, and their guests.

On Saturday, December 6, our onsite team arrived at the Rose Palace for the first day of decorating. OneLegacy Hispanic communications coordinator Dahiana Kast joined Tenaya and Gary on the sidewalk to set up our tent, while Karen headed into the Rose Palace to discuss the decorating game plan with the green jackets. One of the most experienced Phoenix crew chiefs had suffered a broken leg in the weeks leading up to decorating, so the subsequent shift in personnel elevated one of our two assistant crew chiefs, Skip, to the top position for the first time.

I focused on making sure our supplies were in order. Gary secured the donation of a $500 gift card from Home Depot, allowing us to purchase essentials such as buckets, scissors, small brushes, and latex and leather gloves, plus five plastic chairs to supplement Phoenix's metal variety. In addition, I made a series of late-night runs to grocery stores to gather dozens of cardboard trays for materials and cuttings.

Shortly after eight o'clock in the morning, volunteers began arriving at the sidewalk fronting Raymond Avenue. Upon checking in at our tent, each was given a T-shirt featuring the Pasadena Tournament of Roses logo on the front and the Donate Life logo on the back. Hot beverages, bagels, and donuts kept our volunteers happy until the nine o'clock hour approached, at which time I climbed onto a thirty-inch wall and conducted a ten-minute orientation to ready them for the day. They were introduced to our team, the float design, Phoenix Decorating, and safety precautions: no food, beverages, or headphones inside the barn; watch your step and always have three points of contact when climbing ladders. After introducing Skip, we separated the volunteers by their four general roles: cutters to transform statice and strawflower petals into colored flakes, pasters to apply materials over large areas, climbers to decorate atop ladders or scaffolding, and runners to replenish materials and glue as needed.

Applying materials to the float required standing or crouching for lengthy periods of time, so agile volunteers were coveted for the most physically challenging assignments. Kevin Monroe, who had participated in the T2 float test, was volunteering in memory of his brother, Elliott, whose life was extended four years thanks to the kidney that Kevin had donated to him in 1998. Kevin's work as a safety specialist at ConocoPhillips refineries made him comfortable with heights, so over the first four decorating days he spent most of the time atop scaffolding, applying crushed white rice to the bridge. The material's tendency to clump complicated the huge assignment, but Kevin's steadiness and skill made the central element of our float utterly beautiful. Kevin's experience, skill, and empathy made him an anchor of our decorating team going forward.

Another first-year volunteer who made enduring contributions was Laurie Wolowic, whose brother donated organs and tissues in their native Illinois after falling off a ladder on Thanksgiving Day 2002. Laurie's experience with entertainment industry craft services—food and beverage provisions for on-set film crew members—sensitized her to similar needs for our decorating corps. As with Kevin, her enthusiasm, versatility, and personal connection later led to an invitation to join our organizing committee.

The second weekend of decorating got off to a good start, but halfway through the day, the domino effect caused by the loss of a key crew chief again reared its head. Our assistant crew chief, Christine, was reassigned to Farmers Insurance, leaving Skip as our sole green-jacket. Karen's role expanded dramatically, compelling her to draw upon her art experience to quickly learn the nuances of different materials so she could train volunteers on proper technique. Under the circumstances, having a dedicated group of mature and purpose-driven volunteers became an even greater asset.

On the media front, as of the first day of decorating we had yet to see a news story publish since the October piece in Wisconsin. We were encouraged, however, when *People* magazine took an interest in a story on Gary and his inspired vision becoming a reality. The magazine sent a photographer to capture him decorating with his wife, Lois, a supporter of his idea from the outset. At this early stage, the float was still quite barren, so the magazine asked for a photo of the finished float by their publication deadline, which unfortunately was the week before New Year's Day. *People* had no choice but to abandon the story, but the near-miss validated our belief that the media indeed saw us as special.

Out-of-area news coverage finally started picking up on the second day of decorating. Beginning Sunday, December 7, eleven stories ran over the next five days, including seven more on Kari Barlament. Paula Symons, Kari's liaison at RTI and an experienced journalist in her own right, placed stories in print, TV, and radio. Her success encouraged other partners to double down on their efforts over the final three weeks.

While another eleven out-of-area stories ran between December 17–25, coverage in the Los Angeles area was slow to materialize, with only one story in a minor daily paper before Christmas Eve. On that day, coverage by the 106,000-circulation *Ventura County Star* and the local Telemundo affiliate's evening news provided a glimmer of hope.

With only one week to go, we trusted that with Christmas in the rearview mirror and the media looking ahead to the New Year, local coverage would catch up to the activity that we were seeing across the country. But we needed more than just a few stories to emerge. Only a wave of coverage would prove the assumption that had motivated dozens of partners to come aboard: that in time, our participation in the Rose Parade could serve as a platform for a truly national campaign.

9

THE DONATE LIFE FLOAT

It is a symphony of life. Each of us has the opportunity to play our own note. Let's make sure that note is in harmony to make a symphony of life. Because that is truly the right thing to do.

—KEN MORITSUGU,

donor husband and father (2004 rider)

FOR MANY AMERICANS, the day after Christmas ushers in a half-speed work week. For those preparing for the Rose Parade, the inverse is true, and nowhere is this axiom more evident than at the float decorating places.

Upon our return to the Rose Palace, the relaxed atmosphere of the first three weekends gave way to double shifts that quickly accelerated to a feverish pace. By December 27, much of the dry decorating was completed: the bridge was blanketed with crushed rice and coconut, tree bark covered the snaking vines, and the underside of the bridge was a wall of onion seed. The last major dry project: simulating the planks of a wooden bridge with corn husks, each one mangled—flattened by a heated roller—and cut to a rectangular shape.

The morning of December 30, our riders came together for the first time at the Rose Palace, where they were immediately pressed into service in our race to complete the float in time for judging the following day. Water-filled vials with live flowers were carefully inserted into foam surfaces to ensure that scores of hands produced one seamless work of art. Our riders and guests had the best of intentions, but the spectacle and media activity made it hard for some of them to focus their attention on the important work at hand.

Decorating work was occasionally disrupted by television crews. On the morning of December 30, HGTV cleared out the front of the float for a pre-parade piece on riders Patricia Elizarraraz, Sharon Maupin, and Kari Barlament. In the afternoon, an area was prepared for Ryan Zinn to appear in a live satellite interview with the CBS affiliate from his hometown of Columbus, Ohio, one of twenty-two out-of-area media stories that ran the week after Christmas.

That day, we also welcomed an official photographer into our fold, as the schedule of events—decorating, reception, and the parade—precluded me from continuing to act in that capacity. Scott Weersing had impressed me during my tenure in pro beach volleyball. *If he can shoot athletes jumping in the sand, sun, and wind*, I thought, *then he'll have no problem with a float traveling two and a half miles an hour*. I soon learned that Scott had worked for the *Pasadena Star-News* for five years and was intricately familiar with the parade's parameters and sight lines.

Meanwhile, away from crowds and cameras, we carefully arranged first-time meetings between donor families and the recipients of their loved one's organs. Typically preceded by a series of exchanged letters facilitated by the OPO, such meetings are extremely rare: fewer than 1 percent of organ donor families meet a loved one's recipient. The rarity of first-time meetings stems largely from the emotional circumstances surrounding donation and transplantation, which can inhibit one or both parties from reaching out. Recipients often feel guilty— "someone died so that I could live"—or unable to adequately express their gratitude, which can keep even the most grateful recipient from writing a letter. As for donor families, the suddenness of death prior to most organ donations leaves many families traumatized to the point that, despite their pride for their loved one's life-saving gifts, they simply need to move on. Even when both parties are ready and willing to meet, timing and distance can be deterrents.

Fortunately for two of our riders, their journeys to Pasadena came at the right time. One of the kidneys donated by Darlene Aymerich's daughter in Upstate New York seven years prior was transplanted in Los Angeles. (Unlike extra-renal organs, kidneys can remain outside the body for more than twenty-four hours, making cross-country transport to ideally matched recipients possible.) When she learned she was going to Pasadena, Darlene asked OneLegacy to reach out to the recipient, who, alongside her husband and son, was able to thank Darlene in person.

For former Los Angeles native Gene Battaly, returning to the area from Tennessee made it possible for him to meet the daughter of Andy Vonch, whose heart saved Gene's life in 1995. Such occurrences were repeated in the years to come, with the esteem of the Rose Parade contributing to the willingness of the parties to meet and, on occasion, invite media to witness the profound connection.

The evening of December 30, our community came together for a reception at the Castle Green, a nationally registered historic monument faithfully restored to its original Victorian-era style. The formal program featured remarks by selected riders and an official Tournament of Roses welcome from the Rose Queen and Royal Court, who delighted the audience with an acapella version of "Ain't

No Mountain High Enough." The evening was capped by a formal inauguration of our "Class of 2004."

Meanwhile, a very different—and decidedly unplanned—drama was unfolding at the Rose Palace. Through the early afternoon, hundreds of decorators tended to the floats like bees on a hive as flats of vialed flowers competed with scaffolding for right-of-way down the main aisle. After the two o'clock hour, three-quarters of volunteers were excused to accommodate "working judging," a roughly ninety-minute span during which the judges make preliminary assessments of each float's award-worthiness.

At six o'clock, our crew chief stepped away from the float for another in a series of extended breaks that had become so routine that Karen adopted the catchphrase, "We've been skipped again!" Perhaps it was the string of sixteen-hour days, the lack of a trained assistant, or the seemingly insurmountable task ahead of him. For whatever reason, this time his break did not end. Our crew chief had walked off the job.

Karen responded to the crisis with resilience, calmly sizing up the work that remained. We had yet to start the deck—the foam-covered base of the float that carried at least four times as many flowers as had been placed thus far. Following a brief lesson from another crew chief on the art of filling a deck, Karen led the charge late into the night, with a skeleton crew of six volunteers, including Tom and Laurie, working until three o'clock in the morning.

The morning of New Year's Eve, a small crew of staff and sponsor representatives arrived at the Rose Palace at eight o'clock for two hours of final touches. Styrofoam flats, each holding 150 to 300 vialed flowers, were emptied, their blooms filling the deck to make it ever more lush and vibrant. Blue irises forming the waterway under the bridge were incited to open under the heat of blow dryers.

As we punched the final vials into the foam, the anticipation of Bill Lofthouse announcing the completion of our float over the PA system begged a question: what name should he credit? Although we were officially the Coalition on Donation, the inclusion of the Donate Life mark in their logo underscored the challenges with the organization's name. "Coalition" had a political bent, and without context, "donation" was easily interpreted as relating to fundraising.

In addition, OneLegacy had already adopted the Donate Life name and logo as a master brand for various public initiatives, and the state's OPOs had done the same with the Donate Life California organ and tissue donor registry. We had also seen the Donate Life brand start to gain traction nationwide since early 2003, when Elaine Berg, the executive director of the New York Organ Donor Network and then-president of AOPO, enlisted me to spearhead a task force focused on how the Donate Life mark could be effectively incorporated by OPOs.

That momentum, combined with the omnipresence of Donate Life branding on our volunteer shirts, answered the question for us. Karen walked to the Phoenix office to inform them we were ready to "call it." Within minutes, the unmistakable voice of Bill Lofthouse echoed throughout the Rose Palace: "May I have your attention. We have an announcement. The Donate Life float is now complete!"

10

A SYMPHONY OF LIFE

The diversity of faces underscored the universal appeal of the parade. Best of all was the good-natured reaction evident everywhere. You felt that everyone there wanted everyone else to enjoy themselves. It's something of a miracle, isn't it?

—REG GREEN,
donor father (2005 rider)

IN SURPRISINGLY SHORT ORDER, the building was cleared of material, trash, tables, chairs, tools, and equipment, transforming the once-bustling Rose Palace into a veritable float museum. Farmers Insurance was rolled into the driveway to accommodate its substantial height, clearing room for the others to be positioned evenly throughout the barn.

As word spread that the judges were on their way, riders boarded their respective floats for what was essentially a dress rehearsal for the parade. Most of them were dressed in closely coordinated attire; for historical scenes, period costumes were a given. If the presentation involved choreography, uniform outfits made sense.

In the interest of creating some degree of visual cohesion for our float, we suggested that our riders wear tops in any shade of blue and bottoms in khaki or a similarly light color. Fifteen of them largely followed our recommendation, and while they all looked poised and elegant, what made the most lasting impressions were the riders who chose to wear something deeply personal.

Sara and Brittany donned their World Transplant Games Team USA jackets. Ryan Zinn wore a bright red sweater out of loyalty to his hometown Ohio State Buckeyes. Fellow heart recipient Carissa Carmichael wore a full-length purple gown with a short black jacket, as for her the Rose Parade was the prom experience that she missed due to her declining health.

Another unique touch—and a profound one, at that—was the visibility of framed photos that several participants asked to carry with them. Three donor mothers brought photos of their children: Darlene (daughter Shannon), Barbara Lawrence (son Sean), and Cathy Perez (son Louis). Kari carried a portrait of her husband Eric, while Gene had a framed picture of his heart donor, Andy.

Dr. Moritsugu led the contingent, standing proudly at the front of the bridge in his crisp white US Navy dress uniform. On the right side of the float, Mike and Patricia shared a rowboat, while Chris Klug and fellow liver recipient Sharon Maupin stood side-by-side above the Coalition on Donation logo toward the rear. On the opposite side, three riders sat in a rowboat and two shared a bench. The rest of the riders stood along the length of the bridge, with fourteen-year-old heart recipient Dionne Brown foremost among them. From our vantage point about eighty feet away, "A Symphony of Life" looked breathtaking.

With the arrival of the judges, the Rose Palace came to a standstill, with movement and whispering dissuaded. Phoenix decorating staff and invited guests stood along the walls closest to the roll-up door. Bill Lofthouse welcomed the Tournament of Roses Judging Committee and the three judges, each of whom had credentials qualifying them to evaluate award criteria including creative design, artistic merit, floral craftsmanship and presentation, use of color, animation, thematic interpretation, and dramatic impact.

As the delegation approached the first float, a member of the judging committee rang a handheld brass bell. The anachronistic "ding-a-ling" of a school bell was at once strangely old-fashioned and charmingly appropriate. After Bill Lofthouse ad-libbed a thirty-second introduction, the engine started, music filled the air, and animated elements jumped to life. The riders began waving from their seated or standing positions as the judges adopted their own pace, making notes of memorable features and initiating brief conversations with riders. After the judges completed an orbit, a repeated ring of the brass bell signaled the end of the ritual, culminating with a warm ovation congratulating all contributors to the float's completion.

The sequence repeated one by one, bringing the judges ever closer to us. With only ten minutes to go until our turn, I shifted my attention to our float and shuddered: in the place where she had been standing moments ago, Dionne was sitting on the bridge, head bowed between her drawn-in knees. Two riders unclasped their safety straps and tried to help her up, but she was unable to stand.

The disruption amid the stillness of the barn magnified the crisis now unfolding before my eyes: a transplant recipient was suffering a health crisis. (As we would come to learn later, she had simply been suffering from heartburn following her breakfast of Flamin' Hot Cheetos and a Coke.) Protocol demanded that our staff not intercede from our sideline position, so all I could do was stand by and watch. Fortunately, a Phoenix staff member saw the commotion and helped

Dionne off the float. Kari Barlament, who had been standing behind Dionne, stepped forward to fill her spot. Suddenly all was calm, with the judges never knowing otherwise.

After Bill introduced us, a modern version of Pachelbel's "Canon in D" emerged from the loudspeakers installed inside the chassis. Music was an important element for every float entry, with the potential to convey emotion, punctuate a message, or, at the very least, energize the riders. Our committee had weighed a number of options, ranging from pop (Elton John's "Circle of Life") to an emotional mainstay of OneLegacy's donor remembrance ceremonies, "Nwahulwana." However, once the committee discovered that the Mozambican ballad was about the sadness of a woman's bar-hopping lifestyle, it was nixed.

With the percussive "Canon in D" acting as a metronome, Ken's smile and wave charmed everyone in his sightline. But it was Kari's presence at the bridge entrance that captivated us. Standing nearly six feet tall in a light blue sweater, her hair framed by a rose-accented headband, and holding a portrait of Eric, she communicated a confident but wistful pride that represented the essence of donor families beautifully. Knowing all that had transpired since the previous Christmas—the accident, Eric's death, Kari's recovery, Erica's birth, and being ushered into a media spotlight—made her poise that much more remarkable.

With the second ringing of the bell, our guests erupted into applause. The only person missing was Karen, who after the long night before had driven ninety miles to her home in Ojai and gone straight to sleep. She was barely awake when I called to let her know that Bill had something very special to give to her. When she returned later that afternoon with her family to see the finished float, Bill and his son, Chris, presented her with a coveted green jacket. As she recalled, "I felt like I had just won the Masters!"

The adrenaline of judging carried me through a sleepless New Year's Eve to a six o'clock in the morning rendezvous with our riders. We made our way to Orange Grove, where overnight all fifty-five floats had lined up in formation. Seeing "A Symphony of Life" outside the barn for the first time was surreal, with bright klieg lights adding a sense of eeriness.

The float's picture-perfect deck was interrupted by two open hatch doors: one toward the rear for driver Bill Arcudi, and another in the front for navigator Mark Yoshikawa. Communicating through wired headsets, Bill, operating the controls in complete darkness, would rely on Mark's guidance to maintain ideal speed and trajectory along the red center line running the entire length of the five-and-a-half-mile parade route.

Rivian and I escorted Mike and Patricia to KTLA-5's makeshift stage on the lawn of the Tournament House for an appearance on their pre-parade show. The story capped a week of intensive local media coverage, highlighted by placements in the region's four largest daily newspapers (*Los Angeles Times, Los Angeles Daily News, Press-Enterprise,* and *La Opinion*), four TV stations, and a front-page story in the New Year's Eve edition of the *Pasadena Star-News*, headlined "Celebrating Life's Symphony" and carrying a photo of Sharon decorating with her granddaughter Jordan.

Meeting us in the float formation area was Scott Weersing, whose odd choice of a white painter's jumpsuit, it turned out, allowed him to blend in with the Tournament's Parade Operations volunteers, ranging from ushers and scooter-riding float escorts attired in crisp two-piece suits (so-called "White Suiters") to "horse debris" pooper scoopers in decidedly more utilitarian gear..

While his presence on the first mile of the parade route was not officially authorized, in future years Scott was credentialed as a float participant. The images he captured were the most valuable and enduring artifacts of our first or any year. Among the iconic images that became a staple was the rider lineup. Moving the caution tape that circled our float, we rerouted the stream of passersby to capture the Class of 2004 in the morning light, standing proudly and together for one moment in time. Moments later they climbed aboard and took their positions, and after a final goodbye we headed for our grandstand seats.

Making its way northward on Orange Grove, "A Symphony of Life" crossed the official parade starting line at Green Street and traveled 350 feet to "media corner," where a forty-foot, multilevel tower served as the radial point for the route's one hundred-degree right turn onto Colorado Boulevard.

Situated south and east of the tower and its dozens of credentialed photographers were grandstands of forty-one rows, atop which sat a series of network broadcasting booths. The float's "camera side," brilliantly lit by the rising sun, received most of the on-screen time. Broadcast commentary relied heavily on fact sheets supplied by the float builders months prior. As they did for most of the float entries, the announcers did justice to our purpose, message, participants, creative elements, and botanical highlights.

Meanwhile, we had walked briskly to our seats on the north side of the parade route, as crossing the street would be difficult once the head of the parade passed by. Earlier in the fall, I was introduced to a group whose annual fundraiser revolved around selling grandstand seats fronting the north side of the AT&T building on East Colorado about three-quarters of a mile east of media corner. Our nearly three hundred guests filled about half the seats, which were sheltered by large oak trees and located within walking distance of all major hotels. Free parking, access to restrooms, and free coffee and donuts added to the appeal of the $40-a-seat price.

As "A Symphony of Life" passed by our grandstands in Old Town, the moment was fleeting. By the time we got a half-dozen names in—"Kari! Ryan! Patricia! Sara! Brittney! Eunice!"—we were left with the lingering image of teenage liver recipient Brent Axthelm, standing on the bridge toward the back, waving to his family until the trailing float blocked our sightline.

Our float forged onward for another four miles and one hundred minutes, offering a testament to courage and compassion dramatized by a beautiful bridge, authentic riders, and an urgent call to action: *Donate Life.*

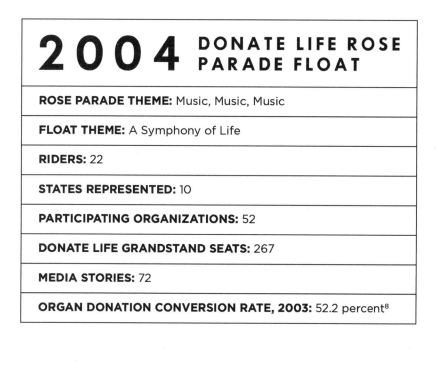

2004 DONATE LIFE ROSE PARADE FLOAT

ROSE PARADE THEME: Music, Music, Music	
FLOAT THEME: A Symphony of Life	
RIDERS: 22	
STATES REPRESENTED: 10	
PARTICIPATING ORGANIZATIONS: 52	
DONATE LIFE GRANDSTAND SEATS: 267	
MEDIA STORIES: 72	
ORGAN DONATION CONVERSION RATE, 2003: 52.2 percent[8]	

PART TWO

GROWING PAINS

11

COMING TOGETHER

We know a part of Nicky lives on in someone else and he made a difference in this world. Isn't that what we all want to do?

—**DONOR MOTHER** from New York, 2014

DURING OUR TWENTY-SIX-MONTH journey to the 2004 Rose Parade, we realized many of the possibilities that had inspired Gary's vision and driven our quest to bring it to life.

Contributing mightily to our success was the infrastructure we had put into place. Our media campaign was driven by coordinated PR working groups, press releases, fact sheets, and media training. Key implementation tools and processes—email lists, sponsorship proposals, an e-newsletter, website, timelines, seating diagrams, and itinerary spreadsheets—promised to drive campaign execution for the foreseeable future.

Progress came at a considerable personal cost, however. The four-month sustained effort by our OneLegacy operations team—myself, Karen, Tenaya, and Dahiana, who was now seven months pregnant—left us exhausted. The traditional holiday season had been an afterthought, consumed by an overriding imperative to bring our community together and support our lifesaving mission. Now that we knew what to expect from start to finish, I committed to better balancing work and family time as we looked ahead to our second campaign.

In fact, the 2005 Rose Parade had been in our sights for months. Thanks to early notification of the parade theme, "Celebrate Family," we got a head start on creative development. As a starting point, the committee decided to pair riders connected by blood, marriage, or a living donor transplant to dramatize how donation and transplantation strengthened families. Husbands and wives, parents and children, and siblings made for natural pairings, while living donors could involve friends who, through their experience, became like family.

Fundraising efforts were also well underway. Seeing how quickly organizations had stepped up to sponsor riders for our inaugural campaign, we structured our second-year packages to require a $5,000 contribution per rider. (For the purpose of establishing a per-rider benchmark, the second rider per pairing was considered a bonus.)

We immediately extended an invitation to Reg and Maggie Green, the world's most well-known donor parents. While driving through Italy with their two children in 1994, bandits mistaking the family for jewelers attempted a carjacking. As Reg accelerated, the men fired shots into the rear of the car. Reg, Maggie, and their four-year-old, Eleanor, were unharmed, but their seven-year-old, Nicholas, was mortally wounded.

When the Greens were informed at the hospital that their son was brain-dead, they immediately volunteered to donate his organs and corneas to Italians in need. Their generosity in the face of tragedy made international headlines and sparked the "Nicholas Effect," a threefold increase in Italian donation rates. The Greens immediately accepted our invitation.

At the committee's mid-January debrief meeting, we took an inventory of logistical shortcomings that emerged as we limped across the finish line. With so much of our time and energy focused on volunteers, decorating, media, and the reception, our riders got the short end of the stick. We were fortunate that sponsors stepped in to fill gaps—travel and post-parade transportation chief among them—but we needed to take ownership of our participants' experience.

Dr. Moritsugu recommended an orientation to allow the rider contingent to bond as a unit and receive coaching for the experience ahead. "Halfway through the parade, even I could feel exhausted," recalled the high-energy rear admiral. "Make it clear that this is a long-distance run, not a sprint." We also added a second, post-parade reception to reunite riders with our community, feed our guests at a time when most businesses opened late if at all, and bring the four days of activity to a proper close.

Coming out of the debrief, the adjustments to our game plan for the coming year paved the way for a smoother operation and improved guest experience in year two. However, the impact of these changes would pale in comparison to several developments that arose with the tides of evolution.

Throughout 2003, the fragmented national donation and transplant community took major steps toward achieving a more unified voice. Eleven months of collaborative work reached a climax with the January 7, 2004 announcement of a partnership between the AOPO and the Coalition on Donation. "All fifty-nine federally designated organ procurement organizations may now call themselves 'A Donate Life Organization,'" read the press release.

Later that month, our committee voted to formally change our parade participant identity to "Donate Life." Doing so required a variance from the Tournament of Roses, as their rules required all entrants to be named after organizations. The prominent visibility of the Donate Life logo throughout our inaugural campaign assured their approval, paving the way for the mid-March announcement of our return to the parade under the new moniker. "The Donate Life float has adopted as its namesake the call to action that makes life-saving transplantation possible," read the press release, which also announced our second-year rider sponsors: AlloSource, American Red Cross Transplant Services, California Transplant Donor Network (now Donor Network West), Coalition on Donation, Gift of Hope, MTF, NJ Sharing Network, OneLegacy, RTI, and Unyts.

Strides on the branding and fundraising front coincided with our pursuit of a partnership with another float participant, the Eastman Kodak Company. During our first year in the Rose Palace, our stall was adjacent to Kodak, which—through decades of parade participation—had earned a reputation for colorful, spectacular float entries befitting a brand synonymous with color photography. Even more meaningfully, the tagline accompanying the universally recognized Kodak logo—"Share Moments, Share Life"—naturally resonated with our community.

Early on, I noticed a startling contrast between our float's surplus of energized volunteers and Kodak's sparse, quiet crew. During shifts where we had more volunteers than we could handle, some generously stepped in to help the Kodak crew chiefs. Bill Lofthouse and I saw the potential for Donate Life to develop an operation similar to the Petal Pushers, whose support of four floats expanded their onsite visibility, attracted thousands of volunteers from across the country, and earned a financial contribution from Phoenix Decorating. However, motivating our volunteers to decorate another float was hardly a slam dunk; they needed to care about it.

Bill Lofthouse set the stage for putting our capabilities to the test by designing for Kodak a 2005 Rose Parade float tailor-made to appeal to our volunteers. Themed "Memory Lane," the concept featured a large photo album fronting a thirty-five-foot wood-railed stone bridge. The pages of the photo album featured photo-realistic portraits of people ("pictographs") to be decorated with grains, seeds, and other fine organic materials. Running the length of the bridge was a floral canopy filled with butterflies—a symbol often associated with organ donation—with most bearing pictographs on their wings.

Bill had put a lot of thought into the concept, but it would take more than a humanistic theme or symbolism to motivate our volunteers. "If we decorated their float, do you think Kodak would allow some of the portraits to depict organ and tissue donors?" I asked. He promised to do his best to make it happen.

Of course, a partnership with one of the world's most well-known brands would fall flat without a compelling float design of our own. The committee agreed that we should avoid overused symbols such as hearts, doves, butterflies, and hands. Our creative concept centered around a park setting that highlighted how simple everyday pleasures such as a picnic are celebratory for people touched by our cause.

Of the five concepts provided by Dave Pittman, two park scenes featured large wood and stone footbridges as central elements. Two more departed radically from our guidance: a fantastical lily garden with riders grouped into large flower blossoms, and an ornate candelabra that evoked a theme park ride from "Beauty and the Beast." The final sketch, a park scene with a fountain, bridge, gazebo, and tree, was our overwhelming favorite, mostly for its elegant distribution of our riders throughout the space. From beginning to end, it took only five weeks and one round of line drawings for us to go to color and have the final color rendering in hand—quite the contrast from our first year.

The unveiling of the 2005 Donate Life Rose Parade Float, "Many Families, One Gift," at the June Coalition on Donation meeting, while well-received, was also bittersweet, coming only weeks after Bill Lofthouse's wife, Gretchen, succumbed to a long illness. For nearly fifty years, Bill and Gretchen ran Phoenix Decorating side by side, with Gretchen's maternal demeanor a welcome presence during decorating season. Since she was unable to come to the Rose Palace the previous December, our team never had the pleasure of meeting her. Bill shared with us privately that in her passing Gretchen had been a cornea donor, filling us with added purpose as we began the six-month countdown to New Year's Day, 2005.

12

A GROWING FAMILY

Even the tiniest transplant, such as the tissue graft in
my clavicle, made a huge difference in my life. Thank
you so much for the gift you have given me.

—**ROSE DEDICATION** from Colorado, 2011

CAMPAIGN PLANNING unfolded at a brisk pace
throughout the first half of the year; the same could not be said for
fundraising efforts, which competed for attention with OneLegacy's
busy spring schedule: three donor remembrance ceremonies, a cross-
country ATV ride to promote organ donation, and a 5K at Cal State
Fullerton. Aside from our float rider sponsors, the average contribution of $1,250 required dozens more organizations to come aboard
to raise the last $55,000 demanded by our budget. The stakes were
high, and our prospects were not favorable.

As we continued to line up support, we were stunned by the
poignancy of AlloSource's chosen riders. It had been more than
five years since Kacey Ruegsegger was seriously wounded in the
Columbine High School shooting incident. She had been shot from
behind, leaving her right shoulder, thumb, and future shattered.

Thanks to the gift of bone and tissue prepared for medical application by AlloSource, Kacey avoided amputation and preserved her goal of a career in nursing. Kacey's five-mile journey alongside her sister, Britney, would reflect their shared experience over the last five years.

"Many Families, One Gift" was ready for decorating by late July, when two dozen of OneLegacy's Donate Life Ambassadors stood in for our float riders at T2. Seeing the fully-formed structure confirmed what I sensed during T1 the previous month: our sophomore float entry had the potential to be underwhelming. It wasn't a matter of the concept, which—from a creative and practical standpoint—carried the committee's full backing. As depicted in the float rendering, the park setting was lush, relatable, and supported our family-focused message. It was also affordable, fitting within our modest $125,000 budget.

Viewed on the street, however, it simply didn't have the strengths that made "A Symphony of Life" so compelling: a dominant focal point, colorful elements guiding the eye upward, and the energy of standing riders. In contrast, the park's four visual elements competed for attention, color was concentrated on the deck, and all but two of the twenty-three riders were seated.

Heading into August, only one $2,500 pledge had come in since the unveiling seven weeks prior. Redoubling fundraising efforts, I approached Astellas Pharma US, a first-year contributor of $1,500. Pharmaceutical companies had guidelines requiring that any support be earmarked for the direct support of patients, so we proposed they sponsor our volunteer decorators, many of whom were transplant recipients reliant on the company's immunosuppressive drugs. Buttressing our case was a decorating schedule that featured four shifts largely staffed by transplant centers—Cedars-Sinai, Loma Linda

University, St. Joseph Hospital, and UCLA—as well as groups from the region's two largest recipient support groups, TRIO and UOTA.

While Fujisawa considered our proposal, first-year float rider and new committee member Kari Barlament contributed $1,000 to the campaign in memory of her husband Eric—our first-ever individual and memorial gift. Sensing that others might find comfort in making memorial contributions, the committee designated a new support category, the Family Circle, to recognize monetary gifts made in memory of loved ones, in honor of donors, or in support of transplant recipients.

Within weeks, Astellas informed us that they had approved a $15,000 grant to support our volunteer operations. Later than week, the American Association of Tissue Banks (AATB) made a generous $5,000 contribution. The infusion couldn't have come at a better time, injecting newfound hope that the announcement of our riders would spark a final surge of pledges that would close our remaining $20,000 budget gap.

The Astellas grant coincided with the announcement of our Class of 2005:

- Lynn Allred, volunteer/PR coordinator at New Jersey Organ and Tissue Sharing Network, paired with her best friend and kidney donor, Tammy Schlesinger. (New Jersey)

- Nancy Eluskie, whose husband, Bob, in his passing, donated tissue that was transplanted into the knee of their nephew, fellow float rider Tim Eluskie. (Michigan)

- Father and son Derrick and DJ Floyd, who had become well-known in our field through the Coalition on Donation's "Empowering Testimonials" ad campaign. Receiving a kidney transplant had allowed Derrick to be the kind of father he had always wanted to be. (North Carolina)

- Susana Melesio and her mother Nimfa, whose liver transplant after fifteen years of sickness enabled her "to do everything I wish I had done in my life, including attending college." (Illinois)

- Chyrrel and Dick Mock, who volunteered for American Red Cross Transplantation Services in the aftermath of their sixteen-year-old daughter Anna's tissue donation after a fatal car accident. (Oklahoma)

- Cathy Olmo, community outreach coordinator at Donor Network West, and her daughter, Kelly, whose liver was transplanted just after her second birthday. (California)

- Sisters Mary Palmer and Deborah Quick, who donated the organs of their forty-five-year-old brother David and tissues of forty-three-year-old sister Nancy after their untimely deaths thirteen years apart. (New Jersey/New York)

- Liliana Quintanar, whose eighteenth birthday enabled her to donate a life-saving kidney to her identical twin sister and fellow float rider, Analia. (California)

- Kidney recipient Ellie Tomczak and her husband Dan, who was so grateful for the gift his wife received that he anonymously donated a kidney to a stranger. (New York)

As in our first year, our contingent was highly representative of the nation's ethnic diversity, counting thirteen white, four African American, four Hispanic/Latino, and two Asian riders among them. Their nearly even distribution into three age groups—twelve to thirty-nine, forty to forty-nine, and fifty-plus—added to their effectiveness as Donate Life ambassadors.

With the announcement of our riders, implementation moved into high gear. The first year's purely functional approach to an online presence evolved into a comprehensive section of OneLegacy's website featuring rider biographies, press releases, volunteer guidelines and signup forms, order forms for grandstand seats and Rose Bowl Game tickets, a photographic journal, art resources, and links to partners. In addition, we finalized plans for our promotional merchandise partner to sell official float pins, T-shirts, and sweatshirts through their website.

We had already assigned group decorating shifts to supply over half of the one thousand volunteers needed to decorate two floats. However, there was one problem: although Bill Lofthouse had been working behind the scenes for six months to lay the groundwork for our collaboration with Kodak, we had made no progress toward formalizing an arrangement. In mid-September, Bill finally gave me the green light to reach out to them.

From my participation in several national meetings, I had learned that "bold requests" are better received when preceded by "bold offers." Knowing that Kodak might be sensitive to sharing their brand equity, I focused my introductory letter of September 14 on the bold offer; the bold request would have to wait until they showed an openness to receiving one. I assured the Kodak manager that we were not asking for financial support, nor did we "seek to 'recruit' organ donors," as our approach was to "inspire people to choose to donate life." I appealed instead to what was in it for them: our desire

> **"BOLD REQUESTS" ARE BETTER RECEIVED WHEN PRECEDED BY "BOLD OFFERS."**

to help decorate the Kodak float with quality, and the potential for media coverage.

Nine days later, a reply from Kodak initiated a two-hour email exchange that began on an auspicious note:

> *We are excited that your members are going to assist Bill Lofthouse with the decorating of the Kodak float entry. However, you ... should not exploit the fact that your organization has any other arrangement with Kodak other than providing participants to decorate the float. Kodak does not have any additional funds to do any advertising or produce any other type of media support.*

Deducing that Kodak was expecting us to ask for monetary support, I assured them that our request was modest and meaningful:

> *[I]t has never been our intent to secure financial, advertising, or media support from Kodak. Our primary hope is that among the many people depicted on the butterfly wings ... images of organ donors would be included. These images would be neither prominent nor noticeable; they would simply blend in with all of the others.*

The response from Kodak was noncommittal:

> *Organ donors are not part of our strategy for this float as we want to recognize the diversity of the global population. I don't want anyone ... thinking that the Kodak float is going to represent past or present organ donors.*

Sensing a make-or-break opportunity, I carefully and respectfully addressed their concerns, assuring them that we would not "want the presence of organ donors among the images [to] lead one to believe that the Kodak float represented" our cause. That ours would be a small minority among dozens of images would "obscure the fact that they were present at all." I also pointed to our multicultural float rider contingent as evidence of our commitment to diversity.

With one final email, the manager gave Kodak's blessing.

I am sure that we can feature some of your donors in our selections but just didn't want to set the stage that all of our selections would represent donors.

On a personal note, he added:

I can assure you that as a card-carrying donor and also a person that would donate an organ to save the life of another that I am sensitive to your needs.

Over the next several months, those sentiments would contribute to a meaningful collaboration that would ultimately have a profound impact on the Donate Life Rose Parade Float's future.

13

FACES OF DONATION

You are the toughest and bravest little girl. To go through catastrophic kidney failure and transplant at your young age (eleven) is amazing. You are our hero. Love you more—Mommy and Daddy!

—ROSE DEDICATION from New York, 2013

ENTERING THE FOURTH quarter of 2004, we started fundraising for the 2006 Rose Parade. Six float rider sponsors committed within the first week, but any sense of accomplishment was muted by the sizable current-year deficit of approximately $20,000. Our only hope was that a funding request sent nearly a year prior to the Healthcare Resources and Services Administration (HRSA), a division of the US Department of Health and Human Services' Division of Transplantation, would come through.

With no assurances of a financial rescue, I was looking for any way to fund the campaign. Nine months prior, soon after "A Symphony of Life" returned from the Tournament's two-day post-parade float showcase, I returned to the Rose Palace to gather blooms from the deck with the intention of sending dried petals to the riders and sponsors. Given our yawning budget gap, there was no time like the present to put them to use. After sourcing four-ounce jars that would be affordable, elegant, and non-breakable, "Petals of Love" were made available for purchase.

While the petals generated only marginal interest, they inspired Linda Escobar, a volunteer, living donor, and staff member at Ronald Reagan UCLA Medical Center, to suggest selling roses to be placed on the 2005 float in the name of a donor, recipient, loved one, surgeon, or coordinator. "Maybe even Bob [Eubanks] and Stephanie [Edwards] could say ... that the roses in the garden are dedicated to donors," she wrote, offering to head the project. The idea of honoring people in such a meaningful way intrigued our committee, but with the campaign so far along, entertaining the concept would need to wait until after the New Year.

As Halloween approached, our expectations for exceeding first-year media coverage were measured, as the rider pairings left us with half as many stories to pitch, and only two local rider stories at that. However, we were starting to sense that our collaboration with Kodak might involve more than a cursory mention of our decorating support.

After Kodak originally affirmed the inclusion of donors' portraits on their float, OneLegacy aftercare coordinator Kari Kozuki identified candidate donor families. As she drew on a range of ethnicities and Southern California regions, two prerequisites were especially important. First, the families needed to be emotionally prepared for what would amount to a visual and emotional resurrection of their loved one for the duration of the holiday season. Second, the families would need to be comfortable in the media spotlight, a byproduct of being featured in one of the world's most-watched events. Kari also gave special consideration to families for whom the journey would aid in their grief process.

A face-to-face meeting in late October with Kodak's representatives cemented our relationship, allowing OneLegacy to inform eight donor families that their loved ones would be honored on the Kodak float in the 2005 Rose Parade. The committee had already decided to offer one of the portraits to Reg and Maggie Green in memory of their son Nicholas, whose donation had recently been the subject of a tenth-anniversary observance at UCLA Mattel Children's Hospital. To a person, the families of the other seven honorees—Christina Bueno, Kim Kimble Gast, Zenaida Aurellano Hoh, Tory Howe-Lynch, Stephen Jokela Jr., Richard LaRue, and Patricia Madera de Waldie—were deeply moved by the opportunity.

The day before the start of decorating, we issued a press release to formally announce the Donate Life-Kodak collaboration:

"Kodak was looking for an organization with similar values to help us decorate our float," said Robert W. Mayhue, Manager, Alliance Marketing, Eastman Kodak Company. "Kodak chose the Donate Life volunteers because we admire their organization and its purpose." In appreciation of the volunteers' decorating assistance, the Kodak float will depict eight Southern California organ donors among the scores of images that will appear on the wings of gigantic floral butterflies. Because the images will be depicted in flowers, they've been dubbed "floralgraphs" by Kodak.

Transforming photographs into photo-realistic organic portraits was technically challenging. Digital photography was in its infancy, so families provided actual or scanned hard copies. Every effort was made to color-correct, repair, and otherwise enhance the image using Adobe Photoshop. After enlarging the image to the portrait's finished size, a filter dramatically reduced the resolution and color contrast to ease decorating with grains, spices, and other fine materials in a manner akin to paint-by-number.

Given our lack of experience with this unique art form, once our donor families arrived on December 26, they would rely on Phoenix Decorating's creative professionals for guidance. The art department was led by Cynthia McMinimy, whose curiosity, eagerness to communicate, quirky sense of humor, and dedication to her craft were perfectly suited to her profession. Cynthia's team of detail artists would be stretched to help complete the fifty portraits under the watchful eyes of Mike and Mimi Thompson, a husband-and-wife team in their fifth year as Kodak's crew chiefs, and assistant crew chief, Carol Sager.

Karen arrived for the first day of decorating as our green-jacketed assistant crew chief, while committee members Esther-Marie Carmichael and Kevin Monroe—nicknamed "Rice Man" for his skill with the notoriously clumpy grain—began their monthlong Rose Palace residency. They and other key operations staff were easily spotted wearing jackets sporting the Donate Life brand's trademark light blue.

Assigned to welcome, register, and support seventy volunteers per shift were OneLegacy public education staff who had come aboard within the last year: communications assistant Simera Nichols and community development coordinators, Jaime Campbell (living donor to her uncle), Kathleen Hostert (living donor to her husband, Craig), and Alexis Vasilchak. Also donning blue jackets were Kari Kozuki and Lupe Hidalgo, whose expertise in donor family care was especially valuable to those volunteering in memory of their loved ones.

Now that we had a year under our belt, our team settled into a comfortable rhythm over the four days of dry decorating that preceded Christmas. As we had hoped, decorators assigned to "Memory Lane" seemed energized by Kodak's tribute to donors as they focused on the bridge, applying a combination of poppy seed, onion seed, and rice to the stonework. Donate Life float volunteers concentrated on the fountain (crushed walnut shells, sesame seeds), bridge (rice), gazebo (rice, corn husks), tree (kidney beans, yellow strawflower, dried yarrow branch), and eight lampposts (silverleaf, lunaria).

Having only two local rider families motivated us to treat every volunteer as a potential media story. Debra Stolberg of JDI Communications had some success pitching volunteer decorators to the general market, OneLegacy's Sabrina Ho made progress with Chinese outlets, and just before the holiday, Dahiana placed several Spanish-language stories about the Quintanar twins.

Placement of stories outside Southern California was handicapped by lack of experience, as six of the nine rider sponsors were first-timers. Prior to Christmas, the only notable progress was forged by Untys, where Delia Joslyn attracted coverage by positioning Dan and Ellie Tomczak as Buffalo's emissaries to the Rose Parade. After the holiday, Unyts again led the way by staging a sendoff event that received blanket media coverage in their service area.

Back in Pasadena, the arrival of our Kodak families set an entirely new tone for our team. We had welcomed scores of donor family members to float decorating, but until now none were tasked with something so visceral as essentially painting a portrait of their loved one.

Steve Jokela led a dozen family members into the Rose Palace to decorate the portrait of his son Stephen, who had died within the last two years. Two at a time, Stephen's family climbed a cherry-picker to access his floragraph, while on the opposite side, Kay LaRue decorated her son Richard's portrait at ground level. The butterfly-wing canvases were vertical, making the application of fine materials that much more daunting. Kay adopted an "airbrushing" technique by applying glue to her son's face, then "blowing kisses" of farina from her hand.

As media arrived at the Rose Palace—some in search of a story, others responding to JDI's relentless pitching—the Kodak and Donate Life floats became the center of activity. Over the final five days of the month, onsite support from our team and Kodak's PR agency managed a wave of interviews and photo opportunities that resulted in twenty-three local, thirty-five out-of-area, seven Spanish-language, and four Chinese-language stories. In addition, JDI's Debra Stolberg placed a story on the front page of *USA Today's* Life section, highlighted by color photos of the Green and LaRue families decorating their portraits. Our rider sponsors generated another thirty-five out-of-area stories, and the Donate Life float was the only one mentioned in an AP roundup published in seven newspapers.

The avalanche of media activity set an energetic tone throughout the final week of the campaign, when heightened emotions and the arrival of our guests would make anything possible—collaborations, connections, and, of course, moments of grace.

14

MANY FAMILIES, ONE GIFT

The crowds start small. Then they thicken, and the noise grows, and you realize for the first time that something very big is happening. Nothing, however, prepares you for the excitement and the stands reaching up to the sky as you round television corner.

—REG GREEN,
donor father (2005 rider)

SHORTLY AFTER ONBOARDING our volunteers the morning of December 26, Cynthia McMinimy approached me with a most delightful surprise. "We just realized that one of the Kodak butterflies doesn't have faces," she said. "Can we use a photo of your daughter?" Having said goodbye to my family that morning with the knowledge that I would see very little of them until after the New Year, Cynthia's offer was especially welcome. I was hoping it could bring a smile to my daughter's face after an abbreviated holiday celebration.

One of our newest committee members, however, cautioned me about accepting Cynthia's offer. Laurie, herself a donor sister, thought the opportunity should honor a donor. I appreciated her passionate advocacy of donor families, but with only a week remaining, rushing a donor family through such a public and emotional experience was impractical.

Donor family members were key contributors to our Rose Parade participation, and OneLegacy employees took great care to ensure they were properly supported at each touchpoint. Family Services staff organized decorating groups on December 26 and 27 to help families struggling with the absence of loved ones over the holidays. "Family of…" nametags were offered comfort and invited conversation between volunteers. Volunteer orientation for donor family decorating shifts had a unique tone, with friendly banter waived in favor of sincerity and shared remembrance.

With the arrival of our guests, the plan for four days of events went into motion. At the first-ever Float Rider Orientation on December 29, each participant took turns introducing themselves to one another and our staff before a briefing on decorating, judging, and the parade. Deborah and Mary were not aware of the opportunity to carry framed portraits of their siblings, so I assured them that we would prepare them by New Year's Day.

The next morning our volunteer operations and decorating teams rolled out the red carpet as we welcomed our riders and partners to the Rose Palace. OneLegacy transplant coordinator Melissa Friedman made an appearance as her alter ego, Tagalong the Clown, adding to the festivity of the sunny day. Inside the barn, volunteers attended to large, barren sections of the deck, auguring a long day and night ahead to be ready for the next day's judging.

Meanwhile, Dahiana, Lupe, and I accompanied the parents of Stephen Jokela and Christina Bueno to the Kodak Queen's Brunch, an annual gathering of Rose Queens from years past. Attendees were touched by the acknowledgement of the floragraph honorees at a pre-event press conference and during the program. Steve and Tish Jokela were delighted to meet 1941 Rose Queen Sally Stanton Rubsamen, a Pasadena legend who became a mathematician at Caltech and enjoyed a long career at the Jet Propulsion Laboratory.

Later that day, I received the best possible news: HRSA had approved our year-old request for a $20,000 grant, closing the budget gap that had haunted me for months. Our financial integrity for the year assured, I headed into the evening reception with my spirits high.

Following a cocktail hour, 250 guests filled the Castle Green ballroom to capacity. Emcee Kari Barlament welcomed the 2005 Rose Queen and Royal Court, who in turn presented to each of the eight Kodak donor families a memory box containing hand-written notes from the young women. Remarks by four rider families—the Greens, Floyds, Melesios, and Ruegseggers—were punctuated by Tony Galla's acoustic performance of our official song, "Give A Little Bit." The evening's highlight, however, was not listed in the program.

As Kacey and Britney returned to their seats, Kacey was asked to return to the podium for a special presentation. As she approached, her boyfriend Patrick quietly trailed behind, then veered to a curtain to retrieve a guitar we had bought for him. Stepping onto the stage, his serenade of Damien Rice's "The Blower's Daughter" filled the room. As Kacey took it all in, her facial expressions took us on her emotional journey: shocked, overwhelmed, deeply moved.

Patrick stopped mid-song and professed his wish to spend the rest of his life with Kacey. Setting the guitar down, he dropped to a knee, opened a jewelry box, and asked for her hand in marriage. Her acceptance prompted a rapturous ovation as they returned to their seats, with Patrick's arm raised in triumph.

As I stepped to the podium to continue the program, I was hardly alone in struggling to compose myself. Looking out at the audience, I saw my daughter looking back at me with the widest eyes I'd ever seen. "Yes, Sophia," I assured her. "Daddies cry, too."

After the program, Sophia motioned for me to bend down. She leaned in and whispered, "I want to meet Kacey." I walked her across the room and introduced her to the newly engaged couple. Sophia gazed up at Kacey and said, "I want to sing for you." In a voice that would have made Sarah Brightman proud, she delivered the opening verse of "Think of Me" from *Phantom of the Opera*.

The celebratory spirit of the evening carried over to the next morning. The colorful deck and meticulous craftsmanship promised a worthy second-year Rose Parade appearance. Although our modest budget and conservative, people-first design precluded award contention, the surge of news stories surrounding the two floats left us feeling like winners where it counted most: media coverage. In fact, thanks to the invisible support of Coalition board member Stu Brower, ABC's Rose Parade telecast included a live curbside interview with the LaRue family as their son's portrait passed by on the Kodak float.

The next morning, as the sun began its rise into an archetypal Southern California blue sky, "Many Families, One Gift" acquired newfound energy as natural light bathed the deck's field of flowers. Our riders' personalities were reflected in their wardrobe choices: the Ruegseggers, Melosios, and Greens wore coordinated winter ensembles, while college gear was the choice for the Floyds (University of North Carolina), Eluskies (University of Michigan), Mocks (University of Oklahoma), and Quintanars (UCLA).

Preparing for the lineup photo, Reg Green looked elegant in a sportcoat. "I bought this tie on the day Nicholas was born," he said. "I've worn it only on very special occasions."

Shortly thereafter, the riders took their positions. As the Green family mounted a swing hanging from the tree, I noticed something that had eluded me during judging: Reg was wedged tightly into the right side. We had informed Phoenix early on that the swing would fit a family of three, but hadn't communicated that all three riders would be adults. Gracious as always, Reg never uttered a word about the inconvenience, but to this day I regret not paying closer attention to that detail.

After seeing our riders off, Laurie and I started making our way to the grandstands. We had walked more than a quarter-mile when I realized my backpack was weighted down by the framed photos I'd prepared for Deborah and Mary. I encouraged Laurie to continue to the stands while I backtracked to deliver the cargo. I had just left our float for a second time when the stealth bomber made its pass, the floats started moving, and the reality sank in: access to the north side of Colorado Boulevard and our grandstands was almost certainly cut off.

Knowing my chances were slim, I continued to the southwest corner of Orange Grove and Colorado and explained my predicament to a security attendant. Pointing to a passageway about sixty feet away between the grandstands opposite media corner, I asked, "Is there any chance I can walk over there to get to the north side of the street?" Absent a grandstand ticket, access was a non-starter. Briefly I resigned myself to disappointment, then a wave of indignation swept me. *I haven't spent the last fifteen months on this campaign only to miss cheering our float from the stands!*

There was only one option. I made a fast track westward along Colorado, then at my first opportunity, I walked down an embankment, trudged through landscaping underneath the Ventura Freeway, and walked up Holly Street. I had made it to the other side of Colorado! I then walked north to Walnut Street, went another mile and a half to the grandstands, and joined my colleagues about ten minutes before Kodak and Donate Life, at number thirty-four and sixty-seven in the lineup, respectively, passed by our grandstands.

At the Castle Green post-parade reception, the husbands of riders Lynn Allred and Tammy Schlesinger recounted their own adventure getting to their grandstand seats at media corner. Walking from the hotel, Sam Allred and Steve Schlesinger somehow ended up on the north side of Colorado Boulevard. Staring across the street at their destination, they waited patiently until the procession stopped to adjust to the pace ahead. Cleared to cross, the men approached the south side of the street. Suddenly, a wave of laughter arose from the towering grandstands just as Sam realized he was now walking alone. He turned around to find Steve—a heavy-set, mustached, no-nonsense native of New Jersey—had been lassoed by one of the equestrian riders. As his captor reeled him in, Steve gamely played the part to the delight of thousands, and in his Donate Life sweatshirt no less.

As the reception drew to a close, I was approached by Steve and Tish Jokela. While Steve's extroverted personality had been unwavering from the moment he walked into the Rose Palace, Tish had come a long way during the week. No longer reliant on sunglasses to shield her emotions, she looked me squarely in the eye and expressed her gratitude with shuddering sincerity. I had always presumed our campaign would have an impact on the public, but this was perhaps my first unadulterated glimpse of what it could make possible for our participants.

2005 DONATE LIFE ROSE PARADE FLOAT
ROSE PARADE THEME: Celebrate Family
FLOAT THEME: Many Families, One Gift
RIDERS: 23
STATES REPRESENTED: 8
PARTICIPATING ORGANIZATIONS: 47
DONATE LIFE GRANDSTAND SEATS: 278
MEDIA STORIES: 97 (30 via Kodak)
ORGAN DONATION CONVERSION RATE, 2004: 56.8 percent[8]

15

SIMPLE IS SMART

*I watched the preparations for the Rose Parade on KTLA.
I was very moved by the people being interviewed about organ
donation. I am forty-six years old and have long been reluctant
to sign an organ donation card, but I did so tonight.*

—**VIEWER** from Toronto, 2005

OVER THE PREVIOUS twelve months, the Donate Life
Rose Parade Float had evolved in a way that we hadn't foreseen. We
originally saw the float primarily as a vehicle for transplant recipients
to thank donors and their families, as well as celebrate the quality of
life that transplantation made possible. That was no surprise: between
the US Transplant Games and various fundraising walks, transplant
recipients had become familiar in the public eye.

In contrast, just as the emotionally devastating event sequence
preceding organ recovery is hidden from public view, historically a
donor family's grief journey was largely limited to the private domain.
Forums for celebrating loved ones' gifts of life were confined to donor
remembrance ceremonies, fundraising walks, or online memorials.

They were rarely featured in the media, the Nicholas Green phenomenon from ten years earlier notwithstanding.

Over the previous two holiday seasons, however, Donate Life's participation in the Rose Parade had given donor families a forum to express themselves publicly. They participated openly and proudly in one of the world's most-watched events, and the media responded with genuine interest. News stories, while acknowledging grief, focused largely on the pride family members felt for their loved ones having saved and healed lives in their passing. Together with the framed portraits held by riders—communicating a corollary message that organ and tissue donors are loved and remembered long after death—millions of people were seeing the faces of donors and donor families for the first time.

Given the prominence of donor families as volunteers and participants, our January 11 debrief focused on ways to improve their experience. Their dedicated decorating shifts were well-received, with families heartened by doing something physical and being able to talk about their loved ones. Touching the float soothed feelings of absence intensified by the holiday season, so we considered ways to create more such opportunities. The media's growing interest in interviewing donor families underscored the need for sensitivity to ensure families did not feel used for publicity.

MILLIONS OF PEOPLE WERE SEEING THE FACES OF DONORS AND DONOR FAMILIES FOR THE FIRST TIME.

We also took inventory of lessons learned in three key areas: volunteers operations, parade week, and public relations. While our volunteer program met our needs, many groups fell short of their share of the seventy slots per shift, leaving us scrambling to fill in the ranks from our waiting list. In addition, although Phoenix Decorating required volunteers to be at least thirteen years old, we turned away younger decorators only if they were clearly not of age. We committed to a policy of strict enforcement to avoid stirring feelings of unfairness.

As for parade week, Phoenix Decorating informed us that the Tournament of Roses had concerns about the behavior of some of our guests at judging. The last thing we wanted was to be restricted from an event that many, including myself, considered the emotional climax of the entire campaign. Communicating expectations in advance would ensure that our guests hewed to protocol.

On the public relations front, once we settled into our groove with Kodak's agency, the results spoke for themselves. Our media coverage spanned a wide spectrum of story subjects: Donate Life's parade participation; the Donate Life-Kodak relationship; our riders and Kodak's honorees; volunteers decorating with purpose; Latino and Asian participants; an op-ed piece by Reg Green, an author and former journalist in his own right. Rivian noted, however, that outside of the greater Los Angeles area, it had proven difficult to get the attention of reporters in large markets.

Nonetheless, the demonstrated potential for medium- and small-sized markets to generate substantial media coverage dovetailed nicely with our strategy to expand the number of rider sponsorship opportunities. Ten rider sponsors had already signed on by late January when the committee took a deep dive into creative development for our third campaign.

At a late January brainstorm session, there was no shortage of ideas as we sought to align our message with the theme of the 2006 Rose Parade, "It's Magical." Selected by Libby Evans Wright, the first-ever female Tournament of Roses President, the theme presented an opportunity to visually convey an emotional experience. To facilitate discussion, the committee was asked to complete the sentence, "Donating life feels magical because _____."

Responses were passionate and varied:

- "It liberates people and allows them to overcome incredible hardship."

- "It takes away the fear and uncertainty of the waiting patient."

- "It honors a loved one and connects a family to the lives of up to fifty other people."

- "It brings hope, faith, and love."

- "It is proof of an individual's capacity to care."

- "It gives people their lives back."

New committee member Kari Barlament, who by then was approaching the second anniversary of her husband Eric's death and subsequent tissue donation, capped the discussion: "Donation has given my life a new purpose. It's transformed my life." With that, we arrived at our thematic focus for the 2006 Rose Parade: *transformation*, a concept that fit perfectly with the parade theme.

How, then, could we convey "transformation" visually? Among the suggestions were an enchanted garden, a magical kingdom, and, more dramatically, a giant heart broken in half, repaired with a bandage. Then came the intriguing idea of the float transforming from one end to the other: dark to light, black-and-white to color, and winter into spring, with stark vegetation transforming into a lush garden.

Following the brainstorm, Reg Green emailed some thoughts that neatly crystallized our creative challenge.

I think the theme of the float should be as simple as we can possibly make it. The concept is not an easy one to absorb, either on television or live, as the float trundles by. Hopefully, [viewers] will feel something like this: "I see. Some of those people are alive because somebody else saved their lives. They look very happy. And the others were the ones who made that decision. They look just like us." I don't think we need anything complicated to say, "This is magical." One unified image alone should be able to carry the whole message. The meaning should be as obvious as we can make it, not something the television announcers ... have to labor to explain.

Reg's advocation of simplicity proved valuable as committee members submitted concepts within a framework of four key questions from the float fact sheet and a preferred length for each:

1. What is the float theme? (Two to four words)

2. Why was the theme chosen? (Two sentences)

3. How does our theme relate to the parade theme? (Two sentences)

4. Float description (75–100 words)

Committee members submitted eleven concepts to stir Dave Pittman's creative thinking. Among the five first-round sketches, three shared the onset of springtime as a general theme, with flowers, birds, caterpillars, butterflies, and trees filling the landscape.

Three weeks later, a clear first choice emerged from the refinement stage: a fallen fifty-foot redwood tree with its roots exposed and new life springing forth from its shelter—a powerfully simple depiction of "Life Transformed."

Meanwhile in early February, Astellas expanded on their volunteer support by sponsoring five float riders chosen through a nominating process involving the nation's two-hundred-plus transplant centers. In May, a first-time $10,000 contribution from UNOS brought us to within ten percent of our $235,000 goal for the year.

The accelerated pace of sponsorship commitments gave us the confidence to add $25,000 to the float budget, allowing Phoenix Decorating to incorporate the kind of floral accents that could make us a legitimate award contender. We were also able to support our guest experience by reserving a block of three dozen hotel rooms at the Sheraton Pasadena.

Most meaningfully, we also invested in developing a new campaign element with the potential to engage constituents nationwide.

16

BUILDING THE BRAND

The transplant has literally given me a completely new life, allowing me to do things that I never had the energy or drive to do before. My family watched as I transformed from a shadow of a person into a healthy and energetic individual.

—ERIKA WELLS,
kidney recipient (2006 rider)

THE IDEA OF A MEMORIAL garden on the float had been germinating since it was originally suggested the previous October. By the time we authorized the final color rendering of "Life Transformed," Laurie and Tenaya had prepared a concept document. The element would feature "dedicated roses" tagged with the name of the honoree. Since the tags would be non-organic with the potential to be visible, Phoenix Decorating requested and received a variance from the Float Entries Committee.

They also adopted "Family Circle" as the program name, appropriating our existing classification for memorial contributions. Since the Donate Life Rose Parade Float campaign was just starting to gain traction, crafting a standalone identity for the garden was somewhat counterintuitive. However, doing so created space to build a donor family-centered program distinct from the float campaign at large.

Laurie and Tenaya envisioned the program's proceeds being directed to especially meaningful campaign components, beginning with the official float website under development. They also saw opportunities to "bring the Rose Parade experience closer to families" by sponsoring riders or enabling families to place their roses on the float in person. With the potential and complexity of the Family Circle program becoming increasingly apparent, the committee commissioned an advisory council to ensure adequate guidance.

Kari Kozuki was asked to survey her donor family services colleagues nationwide regarding the program's pricing structure. The OPOs were comfortable with the proposed $50 entry-level package, understanding that time and materials would be required to fulfill the basic package of a dedicated rose, personalized certificate, and commemorative pins. We also added $100 and $200 packages that added dried flower petals, a Rose Parade souvenir program, framed float photo, and a DVD to the mix.

The announcement of the program was a centerpiece of the float unveiling. Citing her brother Michael as an inspiration, Laurie introduced the "Donate Life Float Family Circle" as an opportunity for families and individuals to "sponsor a flower" to be placed in the "Family Circle Garden," an identifiable area toward the front of the float's camera side that could accommodate for several hundred roses. Tenaya and Laurie also introduced the program to AOPO's Public Relations/Public Education and Donor Family Services councils.

At the unveiling we also announced the opportunity for five transplant recipients to win "The Ride of a Lifetime" courtesy of Astellas. Few transplant centers had the scale or outreach objectives to justify sponsoring a rider, so Astellas' plan to select winners from five different regions promised to engage transplant programs across the country.

Like Astellas, Kodak also sought to build on the success of our partnership to date. We received only positive feedback from volunteers working on their behalf, but Kodak's new float design had no room to integrate our mission. Themed "Magic of the Movies," it featured iconic movie scenes, production equipment, and a colorful film strip evoking the Candyland board game. The concept had none of the emotional resonance or earned media potential that made our 2005 partnership so appealing.

Kodak offered to again feature Donate Life as their cause at the annual Rose Queens Brunch, as well as to publish articles about organ and tissue donation in their company newsletter and website. They planned to outfit volunteers assigned to their float with vests featuring the Kodak logo on the back, which we found acceptable as long as the Donate Life logo was imprinted as well.

The Donate Life/Kodak relationship was one of several branding issues that came to the forefront over the summer. First, we saw an opportunity to appeal to the Latino/Hispanic community, which between 2003 and 2005, accounted for over 40 percent of eligible organ donors in the greater Los Angeles area.[11]

The Tournament of Roses, too, had long counted the Latino community as a key audience, which tuned in to Rose Parade broadcasts on Univision and Telemundo. In addition, Latino families comprised a large and growing share of parade spectators along Colorado Boulevard, mirroring the dramatic increase in Southern California's Latino population since the late twentieth century.

Our June 28 letter to the Tournament of Roses invited them to join us in saluting the Rose Parade's Hispanic audience by allowing us to feature the English and Spanish versions of the Donate Life mark side by side:

> Hispanic spectators and television viewers would appreciate the extra effort that we and the Tournament of Roses are making to send them an inspiring message in their language. Combined with several Hispanic float riders among our twenty-strong contingent, this gesture would be remembered and greatly appreciated by your Hispanic audience.

Within a month, the Tournament's Float Entries Committee approved our request, making Donate Life the first-ever float entry to carry a bilingual logo. A Univision news operations director was thrilled with the development, teeing up Dahiana's media outreach for later in the year.

Branding considerations also extended to the Family Circle. To distinguish the program's unique purpose, Laurie and Tenaya led the development of a program logo: a soft yellow vertical rectangle containing the name of the program, three abstract red roses, and logo-plus-text "Donate Life Rose Parade Float" nomenclature.

Having the Family Circle so formally branded advanced the idea of doing the same for the campaign itself. To date we had employed a composite logo featuring the Donate Life and Rose marks side by side above a nomenclature—"Proud Participant – [Year] Rose Parade®"—to signify our official status. We commissioned the creator of the Family Circle logo, E. Junior Usuraga, to design the campaign's official mark.

Integrating the Donate Life mark, Rose icon, and "Rose Parade Float" text into an elegant logo was a complex assignment. Junior's initial concepts explored two directions. The first group drew heavily on the Family Circle logo's rectangular shape and color palette. The others were much more organic, incorporating rose stems and a banner to unify the elements. The rectangle was the bolder and more practical of the two, but it needed more of a classic "Pasadena" look and feel. Junior graciously accepted our feedback, and with two final touches—filling open corners with filigrees and adding the text "Est. 2004" to acknowledge our heritage and ambition—the Donate Life Rose Parade Float logo was complete.

By the first week of August, twenty-six Family Circle dedications had been mailed in, with one of six options to acknowledge the honoree:

- Deceased Donor to honor a loved one's life and memory.
  Flower tag to read: In memory of [Name]

- Living Donor to honor a gift of life.
  Flower tag to read: In honor of [Name]

- Transplant Recipient to honor a renewed life.
  Flower tag to read: In honor of [Name]

- Transplant Candidate to support those waiting for the gift of life.
  Flower tag to read: In support of [Name]

- Transplant Candidate to honor those who died waiting for the gift of life.
  Flower tag to read: In memory of [Name]

       ▫ Supporter of Organ and Tissue Donation to support donor awareness.

    Flower tag to read: [Name] in support of donating life

While the core offering was straightforward—"a rose with the name of your loved one or honoree in the Family Circle Garden"—the program was decidedly complex. Several administrative components and materials needed to be built from scratch: an accounting and fulfillment database, payment processing, acknowledgement letters, certificates, commemorative items, packing, and shipping. Even the most fundamental component—a "flower tag" that distinguished a dedicated rose from all the others—required research and development, as it had no precedent.

Taking on that project, I started with the last step and worked backward. Ultimately, tagged rose vials would be punched into the foam on the float's deck, so the tag needed to allow for ample room to firmly grip the vial. Since all the components would be continually exposed to water, both the tags and messages (whether handwritten or pre-printed on an adhesive label) would also need to hold up to saturation. The tags would need to accommodate standard address labels, but couldn't be overly visible.

Phoenix gave us a range of vials with barbed anchors at the base to use for prototypes. Starting with an Avery full-sheet label, I cut a 1" x 7.5" strip—double the length of the tag, as it would need to wrap around the vial and stick to itself so that no adhesive was exposed. Since the vials were ever so slightly tapered, defects due to unsightly bubbling or exposed adhesive were a given. Thus, the message labels would need to be applied after the vial was tagged.

For the initial prototype, I used the first rose dedication we received, "In memory of Richard LaRue," the Kodak honoree. When placed in water, the paper tags easily ripped at the stress point where the adhesive joined together after wrapping around the vial. The adhesive was unaffected, however, thus revealing a solution: vinyl tags with standard address labels.

Among the fifty dedications that we received by the end of August, some contributors elaborated on the request for simply a name:

- "In memory of our brother and son Tony"

- "In memory of Christine's heart and liver donor"

- "In honor of Suzanne * Enjoy your second chance at life! Love, Stephen, Heather and Andrea"

- "In honor of Bob—my miracle maker. Thanks for the Gift of Life on 11/19/02—Luv, Suzanne"

Although these non-conventional dedications would require manually adjusting the font size to fit the standard label, we were delighted to honor them. There was no greater affirmation of the value of the float and our dedication garden than having people entrust their most personal sentiments to our stewardship. Most of the submissions came with permission for us to post the dedications to our float website, which was under construction by mid-September.

As we prepared to announce our Class of 2006, the committee considered one more opportunity to increase the visibility of our cause. Throughout float decorating, volunteers relied on two tools: cups for glue, and cardboard: cups for glue and cardboard trays for materials. The artwork on the thirty-two-ounce cups advertised an area casino where they were used to hold coins for slot machines. As for the trays, the beer and food brands revealed their original purpose as shipping cases for canned goods.

Sensing an opportunity to upgrade the decorating environment and save crew chiefs the trouble of scavenging supermarket receiving areas, I proposed offering Donate Life/Done Vida-branded cups and trays to support decorating operations at both the Rose Palace and Rosemont Pavilion. The cups could be sourced from a promotional products supplier, while archival file box lids could be repurposed into trays. The expense was substantial—acceptable price breaks required purchasing a three-year supply of cups—but it would make the Donate Life call to action highly visible at both Phoenix Decorating facilities—the epicenter of media coverage, and our national community, throughout the holiday season.

17

―――――

A LIFE TRANSFORMED

If I could turn back time, I wouldn't change anything.
My transplant has been the most positive event in my life.
It has helped me realize that each day is a gift. Maybe through
it, I can make a difference in the life of someone else.

—KURT WILTCHER,

liver recipient (2006 rider)

THROUGH OUR FIRST TWO parade appearances, our progress was analogous to designing, building, and moving in to a house. In the nine months since, we added a room (the dedication garden), interior design touches (the new float logo), and landscaping (bilingual branding and decorating tools).

With seven weeks until the 2006 Rose Parade, we opened our doors to our remodeled lobby: donatelifefloat.org. Sections devoted to travel resources, volunteer guidelines, the rose dedication program, and a robust media center promised to support our guests, volunteers, partners, and media with newfound convenience and efficiency.

The website launch coincided with the announcement of our Class of 2006, among them committee-sponsored float visionary

Gary Foxen. Hailing from a record twelve states—with first-time representation from Arizona, Indiana, Minnesota, Mississippi, New Mexico, Pennsylvania, and Washington, DC—our contingent's geographic and ethnic diversity augured well for media coverage.

To underscore how our riders' stories embodied the magic of a life transformed by donation, we selected as our anthem a song about hope, courage, and overcoming adversity: "I Can See Clearly Now." It seemed the perfect choice for the four key functions served by music: inspiring the judges, entertaining our guests at the reception, enhancing our presentation in the parade broadcasts, and energizing our riders for their journey. The choice of the cover version by bilingual recording artist Jerry Lopez coincided with the debut of the float's side-by-side Donate Life and Done Vida logos.

In early November, we welcomed a number of our riders to Float Participants Photo Day at the Tournament House, where our guests posed with the Tournament President, Rose Queen, and Court. Meanwhile, media coverage got off to a strong start, with fourteen confirmed and eighteen pending stories by December 1. By comparison, a year earlier only two stories had published by that time.

After backing in to the Rose Palace for our load-in, the first items to come off the truck were 1,500 flat storage box lids. Our volunteers had spent two days placing stickers on all four flaps so that when they were folded up, the Donate Life or Done Vida logo would be visible from all angles. About two-thirds were designated for Rosemont Pavilion, where twelve mostly larger floats were ready for decorating. The remainder were allocated throughout the Rose Palace, with Farmers Insurance receiving over a hundred to support their seventy-footer.

On the first day of decorating, Donate Life's expanded presence in the Rose Palace was immediately apparent. The new Donate Life

Rose Parade Float logo was emblazoned on our volunteer shirts; a full-back Donate Life logo and an Astellas logo on the sleeve rounded out the look. Donate Life/Done Vida glue cups or trays were in the hands of virtually every volunteer, while Kodak's white vests had a three-color Donate Life logo printed on the back below their red wordmark.

By the Tuesday following our first decorating day, we posted the first 175 rose dedications to the Family Circle section of our website. Most followed the name-only guideline, but others offered a window into the hearts of people across the country:

Some honored children who died far too soon:

> *In memory of Aaron, 06/14/77 – 10/10/02, Love Mom*

> *In memory of Becky, 2/14/81 to 6/4/05*

Others expressed their pride in their loved ones' gifts of life:

> *In memory of my son—Hal 04/24/01 (saved three lives)*

> *In memory of Angela, Dec. 30, 1978 – Sept. 9, 2000. We love Angie and we're very proud to honor you with this.*

Several messages communicated the heartache of grieving parents:

> *In memory of Maegan—we miss you and will love you always. – Mommy and Daddy*

> *In memory of Gregg—we miss you terribly. – Mom*

Dedications to transplant recipients communicated gratitude:

> *In honor of Ricky, with each breath we give thanks to the donor family for their gift of life.*

That sentiment was echoed by one of our riders, Kathy Hasan, who two decades prior was diagnosed with an autoimmune disease that affects the bile ducts. Her first-person account on our website was an exemplar of our theme:

For fifteen years, my body functioned fine. My specialist was able to treat me with medications, but he told me that one day I would need a transplant. [Eventually] he referred me to the UCLA transplant center, and, after days of testing, placed my name on the national transplant waiting list. Over the years my husband, brothers, and sisters watched as my physical appearance deteriorated as I waited for a transplant.

In December of 2000, after being on the waiting list for three years, I received a call from my transplant coordinator alerting me that a liver had become available for me. I went to the hospital immediately and began to prepare for surgery. However, after a few hours, the doctor came in and told me that they had to give the liver to someone who needed it more than I did. I wasn't sad. I knew that it must not have been my time.

Unfortunately, a couple of weeks later I began to feel more fatigued and one night I began to feel very ill. I went to the bathroom to try and ease the pain, and suddenly blood started pouring from my body. I went to the hospital immediately, and once admitted I improved for a short time, and then I took a turn for the worse. I went into full body failure, then into a coma, and was placed on life support and dialysis due to acute kidney failure. The doctors told my family that I had between twenty-four to forty-eight hours to live if I did not receive a liver transplant.

I am grateful that soon a liver did become available, and on January 15, 2001—Martin Luther King Day—I received my liver transplant. At the time the doctors were leery of performing surgery on me because they thought I might not survive the procedure. With God at the forefront and with the skilled hands of all the physicians and nurses, the surgery was a success and my road to recovery began. After the surgery and with the aid of physical therapy, I learned to walk again.

My instruction after receiving the transplant was not to do anything but rest for the first three months, but I didn't have that luxury to relax. Two months after my receiving my transplant, my husband died from liver cancer. My heart still aches knowing that he was not able to see the extent of my recovery.

Receiving a liver transplant was not only life-saving, but it was life-changing. None of it would have been possible if a family had not decided to say yes to donation. Their decision gave me the gift of life, and my family and I have since been blessed with more time to enjoy our lives together. Words cannot express the gratitude I felt toward them for making that decision.

Over the last two years, Kathy expressed her gratitude through volunteer service and her full-time position at Huntington Hospital in Pasadena. A stranger would have no idea of the medical challenges she faced. She exuded health, radiated beauty inside and out, and her calm sincerity belied, and was borne of, years of extreme hardship. After all she had been through, she once said, "I don't sweat the small stuff."

As I escorted Kathy into the barn, her eyes surveyed the length of the structure, from the exposed roots to the wildlife and colored foam that would soon house thousands of blooms. "That was me," she said. "I was that tree." Since then, hers had been a life transformed. Through my experience in the field, I was beginning to sense that mine was, too.

18

I CAN SEE CLEARLY NOW

This past year, our son Stephen was part of the Rose Parade float through a dear friend in Colorado. As the float was presented I touched the TV screen ... another step was taken with my journey of grief.

—DONOR MOTHER FROM VIRGINIA, 2005

IN SOUTHERN CALIFORNIA, ten-day forecasts were often dismissed due to their frequent inaccuracy. With so much at stake, we took them seriously. As of December 26, indications for January 1 were positive. That was no comfort, however, as convention dictated that the 2006 Rose Parade would not be held on New Year's Day.

The unofficial "Never on Sunday" tradition first came into effect in 1893, when New Year's Day fell on a Sunday for the first time since the Tournament of Roses was founded. To avoid scaring the horses tethered outside Pasadena's churches and interfering with worship services therein, officials decided to move the events to Monday. The tradition held, and there was no shortage of tournament insiders that half-jokingly cited it as the reason the Rose Parade had been rain-free for a remarkable fifty-one years. Alas, the forecast for January 2 left no doubt that the streak was in jeopardy.

We put aside concerns about the weather to focus on our individual roles and common purpose. OneLegacy's family services team of Jeff Fleming, Kari Kozuki, Luz Diaz, and Sonia Navarro welcomed their constituents to Donor Family Decorating Day. Our media specialists, including OneLegacy's new Hispanic communications specialist, Elena de la Cruz, ensured our volunteers were interviewed with utmost sensitivity.

We were stunned by the overwhelming response from Los Angeles media: reporters and photographers from two English, two Spanish, and two Chinese newspapers; crews from all five major television stations and Telemundo, as well as Chinese and Korean stations; and correspondents from the top two talk radio stations. We were on track to shatter the previous year's total of nearly one hundred stories.

Decorating went like clockwork throughout the week, with groups including donor families, Tzu Chi Buddhist Foundation volunteers, and Sav-On Drugs employees commemorating their shifts by taking photos at the front of the float. While scores of Donate Life volunteers faithfully executed Kodak's "Magic of the Movies" under the guidance of Mike and Mimi Thompson, our green jackets—Karen and crew chiefs Misty Harlan and Yona Richman—transitioned to floral decorating after weeks of applying tree bark to Donate Life's centerpiece element. As our volunteers applied flowers by the thousands, one area was left untouched: the Family Circle Garden.

To prepare for placing three hundred dedicated roses from thirty-six states, Laurie and Tenaya selected and trained a team of volunteers to wrap tags around each of the vials—a time-consuming task requiring considerable manual dexterity. The tagged vial was elegant, with the Donate Life and Family Circle logos arrayed from the cylinder outward on both sides. Labels reading "Life Transformed—2006" were applied to the back side of the tags.

The second stage involved placing the hundreds of dedications onto the tags. Messages entered into an Excel spreadsheet were merged into a Word document and printed onto address labels. Once printed and cut to two inches wide, the labels were applied to the front side of the tags. With the labels in place, the vials were ready to be filled with water and a freshly cut bloom hand-picked by Laurie.

The same attention to detail governed our hospitality and events team's preparations for our guests' arrival and packed five-day schedule. Housing our riders and sponsors at the Sheraton solved transportation issues and allowed more quality time for our riders from the December 29 rider orientation onward. The following night at Castle Green, the traditional appearance by the Rose Queen and Royal Court was followed by remarks from UNOS executive director Walter Graham, whose presence affirmed our campaign's importance to the nation's transplant community. Underscoring our aspirations for the Donate Life float to become a longstanding tradition in its own right, Gary Foxen inaugurated a namesake Inspiration Award by acknowledging Laurie's service as a volunteer and Family Circle coordinator.

The following morning, Laurie and Tenaya led preparations for a new event, Rose Placement. They staged the vialed roses alphabetically by the honoree's first name while Karen cleared a path for donor families, recipients, and sponsor representatives to place their roses in the designated area. Laurie and Tenaya had the privilege of placing the first two roses, followed by Kari and Erica Barlament. Over the course of the day, three hundred roses formed a multicolored garden, their dedications a treasure hidden underneath the petals.

On December 31, the decision to enlist sponsor representatives to apply their type-A energy to the final push paid off. Flowers flooded onto the decks of both floats, creating fields of blue orchids, pink carnations, yellow and orange gerber daisies, and pink, orange, and yellow roses. Many volunteers returned the next morning to prepare for judging.

I had come to appreciate judging not just for its emotional jolt, but for a first look at each rider's parade-day attire. Jackie Colleran, Miryam Correa-Sherman, Edith Gonzalez, and Kathy Hasan chose elegant winter wear accented by scarves and hats. Reflecting their allegiance (or a gentle nudge from their benefactor), several riders wore apparel identifying their sponsors: Robin Barrett (Lifebanc), Sahra Torres-Rivera (Washington Regional Transplant Community), Christine Galán (Cedars-Sinai), Ilene Feder (TRIO), and the Astellas contest winners: Leyda Kroening, America Leyva, Avery Livingston, Nicole Brook Stoe, and Kurt Wiltcher.

The Astellas sweatshirts were quite handsome, with a beautiful logo embroidered into thick, cream-colored fabric. However, they were accessorized with sailor hats straight out of *Gilligan's Island* (save for the logo). The sponsor meant well, as protection from the sun was vital for immunocompromised transplant recipients susceptible to skin cancer. Seeing the deflated expressions on the riders' faces eased my executive decision to have the riders drop the hats in favor of sunblock. Soon thereafter, Bill Lofthouse's trademark voice over the PA system declared the third Donate Life float complete, sparking a thunderous ovation for Misty, Yona, and Karen for their leadership of the monthlong decorating effort.

Once judging concluded, all attention was redirected to the dire weather forecast. The mission: to procure as many ponchos as possible. Many nearby stores were sold out, so we drove to surrounding areas to buy enough for our contingent, plus a few extra for good measure. The next morning, the overnight rain stopped for a moment, giving us some hope that we might be spared a deluge.

Pre-parade media appearances at the makeshift studios on the Tournament House lawn proceeded as scheduled. Kathy and Sahra were interviewed by KTLA, while Sahra, Edith, Miryam, and America appeared on Telemundo. Coincidentally, America enjoyed meeting Bill Richardson, the governor of her home state of New Mexico, whose interview immediately preceded ours.

By the time our riders gathered for the traditional lineup photo, the weather had taken a turn for the worse, with a steady rain that made photography difficult. Rumors circulated that the parade organizers were discussing cancellation—an automatic decision if lightning came within six miles of the parade route—but the countdown proceeded without interruption. As the riders pulled back their hoods amid a break in the rain, I was happy to see them smiling amid the uncertainty. Surely the current circumstances paled in comparison to the hardships they had overcome. Hopefully they shared Kathy's mantra: *I don't sweat the small stuff.*

The hoods went back in place as the storm's intensity gradually accelerated. Between media corner and our grandstands, the worst of what was forecast—torrential rain with winds gusting up to forty-five miles per hour—came to be. After giving our passing riders the greatest ovation we could muster, the two-thirds of our guests who had braved the elements to this point hastily evacuated the stands as "Life Transformed" proceeded eastward.

Guiding the bus driver to the pick-up area, I was riddled with anxiety. On any given day, immunosuppression left transplant recipients susceptible to the common cold; what would be the effect of two hours in a gusty deluge? As the riders boarded, I studied their faces, checking for signs of distress. Jackie Colleran shivered uncontrollably, her teeth audibly clacking. One by one, I saw only steely resolve. Once all were seated, I stood at the front of the bus: "Does anyone need medical attention? I'm not kidding." Erika Wells replied on behalf of the contingent: "We just want to get warm." I turned to the bus driver. "Let's go."

Upon our return to Castle Green, our riders were hailed as heroes who had conquered the elements, and within half an hour, the combination of a wardrobe change, hot beverages, a large fireplace, and fellowship had done their magic.

While the 2006 Rose Parade was remembered for the rain, our dramatic float entry was somewhat forgotten for having not been seen in the sunlight. In hope of photographing our float as it was meant to be seen, the day after the parade I made my way to the post-parade viewing area. The floats were in surprisingly good condition given what they had been through. Ours was missing only the sesame seeds and brown paint that had washed off the tree roots, leaving a white base that left the impression the tree had only recently fallen.

As the sun peeked through fluffy clouds, the purple flowers near the front exploded with vibrancy. The natural light also brought to the forefront the float's new life in its many forms: birds, butterflies, a caterpillar and bee, mushrooms, new branches sprouting leaves, and the thousands of blossoms draping from the bark and spilling onto the landscape.

Later that day, I received an email from Jackie Colleran:

Before all the memories are fading I want to thank you for the wondrous experience that is the Rose Parade, rain or shine. No one can explain to a rider beforehand what it all means. I was very focused on honoring my donor family and had not given much thought to the experience that awaited me.

The soaked, yet enthusiastic, spectators continually made eye contact with us, first looking puzzled ... as I touched the picture of Wade and then pointed to my heart (liver would be too hard to pantomime). Then they looked at our logo and this look of wonder came across their faces and they would give a thumb's up.

Having a great tune with lyrics that everyone knew was helpful as we all happily sang along and all the singing spectators were laughing and pointing to the sky.

As it turned out, the song we had chosen to inspire the masses helped to lighten the gloom:

> *I can see clearly now, the rain is gone,*
> *I can see all obstacles in my way*
> *Gone are the dark clouds that had me blind*
> *It's gonna be a bright, bright*
> *Sun-shiny day.*

For our lifesaving mission, it most certainly was.

2006 DONATE LIFE ROSE PARADE FLOAT

ROSE PARADE THEME: It's Magical

FLOAT THEME: Life Transformed

RIDERS: 23

STATES REPRESENTED: 14

PARTICIPATING ORGANIZATIONS: 45

DEDICATED ROSES: 306

DONATE LIFE GRANDSTAND SEATS: 299

MEDIA STORIES: 127

ORGAN DONATION CONVERSION RATE, 2005: 58.9 percent[8]

19

OUR GOOD NATURE

I was very thankful that someone cared enough to donate blood so that it would be there when my godson needed it. Now, I was that person for someone else.

—DAN SANDOVAL,
blood donor (2007 rider)

IN THE WEEKS that followed, riders and sponsors emailed me to share their reflections, affirming that we were making steady progress toward our goal to reposition organ, eye, and tissue donation as a solidly life-affirming cause. More importantly, it instilled a belief that we were contributing to the rise in organ donation rates over the last two years.

New committee member Ginny McBride, who had returned for a second year to volunteer in the Rose Palace, was a leader of the Organ Donation Breakthrough Collaborative, a federal initiative launched in October 2003 to elevate organ donation authorization rates by spurring process improvement at hospitals, "where donation happens." Utilizing a performance improvement process developed by the Institute for Healthcare Improvement (IHI), the Collaborative brought together hospital and OPO professionals to replicate best practices identified at leading institutions nationwide.

Since the launch of the Collaborative in October 2003, the organ donation conversion rate—the percentage of eligible organ donation opportunities resulting in authorization—increased from about 52 percent to over 60 percent.[2] Formal recognition by the US Department of Health and Human Services was a major incentive for hospitals to strive toward the national goal of 75 percent.

Ginny saw the emotional appeal of the rose dedication program as an inroad to engage hospital administrators, physicians, and nurses. If hospitals were inspired to dedicate roses to the donor families they served, she wondered, would they take even more ownership of their essential role in supporting the donation process? Ginny's invitation for Laurie to present at February's national Collaborative meeting spurred us to set a goal of one thousand dedications for the year.

On the partnership front, we noted two encouraging trends: since our first campaign, sponsorship support had increased 44 percent to $231,000, and for the upcoming year, only two float rider positions remained to be claimed. However, our partnership base was not growing, with only nineteen of the nation's fifty-eight OPOs sponsoring our third campaign—seven less than in our inaugural year. The implications of two-thirds of OPOs sitting on the sidelines were much more than financial, as they were in a unique position to secure news coverage beyond national Rose Parade broadcasts.

To bring more partners into the fold, adding the American Association of Tissue Banks (AATB) and NATCO—an organization of administrative and clinical transplant professionals—to our exhibiting schedule seemed like a natural step, which was reportedly the general direction for the 2007 Rose Parade theme.

That turn of phrase rang familiar, as OneLegacy board chairman Robert Mendez had once shared his vision of organ donation one day being "as natural as giving blood." While the percentage of people who regularly donate blood has always been in the single digits, blood donation was supported by almost everyone. In order to inspire people to see donation as the natural thing to do, our immediate inclination was to consider having our rider contingent be limited to donor family members and living donors.

Reprising the process that had been so efficient the previous year, the committee prepared five detailed, widely varying concepts illustrating how giving life was a penultimate example of "Our Good Nature," which was confirmed as the parade theme. Despite the prominence of a frog on the official poster, we had no qualms about pivoting to a humanistic interpretation of the phrase, which elicited our most robust creative brainstorm to date.

One potential direction, "A Celebration of Giving," was media-friendly, but invited a central question: would donor families use the term "celebration" to describe their experience? We concluded it would be more respectful to turn the phrase into a call to action: "Celebrate Giving."

A second concept, "The Essence of Life," was received positively but lost points for being disconnected from the parade theme. In addition, not only was its wildlife-heavy visual concept overly close to our most recent entry, but it lacked a point of view—a "so what"—that can excite an audience.

To gauge the committee's interest in tying in to the Coalition on Donation's national campaign slogan, I submitted "You Have the Power," dramatized by three superheroes. The visual concept wasn't meant to be taken seriously; rather, I sought to incite a departure from the organic designs that marked the tentative approach of our first three years. Although the clarity of the theme was appreciated, we moved on.

Thomas Asfeldt's "From the Heart," on the other hand, hit a nerve, with Tenaya weighing in right away. "I love this, but I don't know why," she said with her trademark combination of assertiveness, sensitivity, and curiosity.

"It's very simple, and it speaks equally for all kinds of donors," I concurred.

The theme invited exploration. Rivian and Tenaya suggested prepending the proposed verbiage with "Gifts" or "Giving," spurring me to consider how the theme might be expressed visually.

"What if the Family Circle Garden was in the shape of a heart?" I suggested.

As caretakers of the Family Circle program, Tenaya and Laurie expressed a valid concern that it might look cheesy if it was not well integrated into the overall float design.

In a subsequent email, Thomas explained his inspiration for the concept, which drew upon his experience as a transplant coordinator:

I really tried to think of this as a donor float and the opportunity to focus all the attention on them. As I thought about the many donor families I have worked with, and the living donors I know, or even myself when I donate blood every few months, the parade theme really resonated with me: it is only those with A Good Nature that donate. Some people who you wouldn't think were good natured, had you met them in a different setting, choose to donate. Underneath it all, what they choose to give comes from the heart, the core of their being.

As an outcome, our design brief freed Dave Pittman to run with the ball. We simply informed him of the theme semifinalists—"From the Heart" (in any iteration) and "Celebrate Giving"—and two parameters: an element that could contain 1,000 to 1,500 dedicated roses, and our strong desire to shift away from trees and fauna. We not only sensed the Rose Parade audience's readiness to see us in a more colorful posture, but after three years of using organic materials to create organic materials, Karen, Kevin, Esther-Marie, and our decorating crew were ready for a new challenge.

20

ALMOST NATIONAL

While I was on vacation, a woman sitting next to me said
she watched the Rose Parade on television. She saw our float,
listened to the announcer, cried, and told her husband that
she wanted to be a donor if something happened to her!

—CATHY OLMO

(2005 rider)

THE CREATIVE DEVELOPMENT process was representative of the highly collaborative nature of our committee work. Decorating and volunteer operations, media outreach, and special events all required leadership from subject matter experts and support from a dedicated team. When it came to our finances, however, I felt a deep sense of personal responsibility to balance our budget. Over time I had come to rely on Thomas's financial acumen to scrutinize our expenses and budget projections, but the other side of the ledger—sponsorship revenue—was squarely in my court.

We'd made considerable strides since our bare-bones first year. A federal grant and volunteer support from Astellas was key to balancing our second-year budget. While the third campaign benefited from more rider sponsorships and the Family Circle program, expenses outpaced revenue by nearly $15,000, largely owing to investments in documentary video production.

Each of the first three years, we had presumed promotional videos would prove critical to engaging new partners. For our most recent campaign, we took the extra step of hiring an acclaimed photographer to shoot photo essay-quality images that could be used for exhibiting purposes. However, in the end, the $50,000 invested over the first three years proved to hold only sentimental and historical value. While the first-year video produced by Laurie and Neil Van Harte was a beloved account of our Rose Parade debut, in retrospect I would have traded these commissioned projects for solid financial footing.

The forecast for the coming year didn't look reassuring. As current partners increased their investments and new partners signed on, I felt pressure to enhance our guest experience, lodge our operations team during the final week, and raise the bar on media outreach. We also needed to reduce our reliance on OneLegacy's provision of cash, staff, office space, and media consulting services. In the first three years, OneLegacy's $75,000 annual contribution represented 46, 36, and 33 percent of overall pledges respectively, so at least we were making progress toward a more reasonable 25 percent share.

Our spring fundraising push concluded with an encouraging reversal of OPO attrition over the last two years. Four OPOs came forward to sponsor riders for the first time: Center for Donation and Transplant (northeastern New York and western Vermont), Donor Alliance (Colorado and Wyoming), Donor Network of Arizona, and Trillium Gift of Life Network (Ontario, Canada). Three more OPOs—Louisiana Organ Procurement Agency, Iowa Donor Network, and Sierra Donor Services (Sacramento)—joined as contributing partners, further expanding the campaign's national footprint.

I appreciated when partners committed prior to the June unveiling, entrusting that our design would exceed their expectations. Once again, Dave Pittman did not disappoint as he combined the symbolic, emotional, and literal power of "Giving from the Heart": eight colorful gift boxes (one for each of the lives that can be saved by a single organ donor), fifty floral bouquets signifying how many people can be saved or healed by a single tissue donor, and an interwoven red ribbon with three loops representing the lives that can be touched through a single blood donation. In addition, gift tags on the boxes with to/from messages in multiple languages acknowledged the Rose Parade's multicultural audience.

The design could not have been a more welcome departure from our first three entries. Gift boxes in all manner of shapes (cube, flat, round), colors (orange, pink, green, purple, gold) and patterns (solids, stripes, florals, and French wallpaper) were arranged from front to back, led by a giant heart-shaped box in the front to house more than a thousand dedicated red roses.

Our goal to more than triple the pilot's three hundred rose dedications was supported by the Family Circle's bifurcation. The program for individuals and families closely mirrored the pilot, with a dedicated rose, online posting, and acknowledgement card being the common denominator among four tiered packages starting at $25. Contributors were invited to write a message of up to twenty-five words to appear on the tag and (with permission) website.

The second program offered hospitals, transplant centers, and organizations the opportunity to honor five or more donor families or patients they served. We also offered two items—a personalized certificate and a replica of the tagged rose vial—to be presented to each honoree, potentially at a ceremonial gathering.

Laurie's February presentation at the Collaborative meeting caught the imagination of attendee Candy Smith, MD. The New Orleans physician, Ohio State alumnus, and liver transplant recipient offered a generous grant to Lifeline of Ohio, whose family services staff were poised to extend the opportunity to parents of pediatric donors from the Buckeye State.

Following the June unveilings at the annual meeting of Donate Life America (the rechristened Coalition on Donation) and AOPO, RTI became the Family Circle's first "Rose Sponsor" by accepting Kari Barlament's request for a matching contribution to honor twenty-eight RTI donor families. In early August, Ginny announced the first participating hospital—William Beaumont Hospital of Royal Oak, Michigan—to the Collaborative's eleven thousand listserv subscribers.

Summer settled into a relative lull as we onboarded and announced the Class of 2007. The second edition of the Astellas "Ride of a Lifetime" contest introduced us to five living donors, four of whom hailed from areas served by non-participating OPOs, extending the campaign to new frontiers:

- Norman Biondi (Ellicott City, MD), who gave a kidney to his daughter Emily

- Robert Bonner, Jr. (Philadelphia, PA), who donated 60 percent of his liver to his sister Lisa

- Rachel Lentz (Gates Mills, OH), who left college for a quarter during her sophomore year to give a kidney to her mother Elizabeth

- Shannon Payne (Damascus, AR), a "miracle baby" conceived despite his mother Kathy's longtime battle with lupus, who then came to her rescue by giving his kidney when hers failed

- Tyson Wood (Placerville, CA), who donated a kidney to his seventeen-year-old sister, Lacey, a heart transplant recipient since infancy

Our contingent also featured three pioneers: the first Native American participant, Camille Nighthorse (Cave Creek, AZ), riding in honor of her brother, organ donor Wabeyuma; our first Filipino rider, Reverend Fr. Elly Tavarro (Orange, CA), who became a chaplain at St. Joseph Hospital three months after donating a kidney to his sister Richa at the same hospital; and Dan Sandoval (Ontario, CA), our first rider sponsored by a blood bank.

In early November, I traveled to Sacramento for a formal announcement of a rider whose participation warrants insight into one of the most important pillars of organ, eye, and tissue donation in the US: state motor vehicle agencies.

After Uniform Anatomical Gift Act of 1968 laid the groundwork for the nation's voluntary organ donation system, states began issuing donor cards along with driver licenses and ID cards. A signed donor card legally authorized the donation of all or specified organs, tissues, and corneas if circumstances upon death allowed for their recovery.

Throughout the 1980s, routine distribution of donor cards sparked countless household conversations about organ donation, and many Americans prided themselves on documenting their legally binding decision by signing their card or license. There was one problem: medical professionals rarely saw them. Once the identity of a trauma patient was confirmed, the hospital locked up the patient's personal belongings. (I once asked an audience of hospital nurses to raise their hand if they had ever seen a patient's signed donor card. Out of nearly one thousand attendees, only four hands went up.)

Computerized donor registries solved this problem. Pioneered by Illinois Secretary of State Jesse White in 1993, thirty-five state donor registries were already in operation by the time Donate Life California (DLC) launched their website in April 2005. Its effectiveness was supercharged after California's governor signed SB 689 (2005), which authorized the California Department of Motor Vehicles (DMV) to register donors at the time residents applied for or renewed their driver license or ID card.

In November 2005, the DLC board trekked to DMV headquarters to plan the integration. From the outset of the meeting, it was clear the DMV team—approximately fifteen managers whose tenure probably averaged twenty years—felt overworked and underappreciated. Midway through a session dominated by hesitant and rote responses to our questions, I sensed an opportunity to express not just in words but in action our genuine appreciation their partnership. In other words, this was a perfect time to make a bold offer.

After explaining the importance of the Donate Life Rose Parade Float campaign to our outreach to the public, I pledged that beginning with the 2007 Rose Parade, as an acknowledgement of the agency's life-saving contributions, DLC would sponsor a DMV employee to participate. Immediately, one of the DMV team's thirty-year veterans, whose participation had been particularly animatronic up to this point, turned toward me and asked, "What would be the process for selecting this person?" From that point forward, the meeting, and our relationship, acquired a decidedly more collegial tone.

Now, a year later, I stood before scores of DMV employees assembled to congratulate the rider chosen to represent them in the Rose Parade: Brenda O'Donnell, one of the managers on the DMV-DLC implementation team. In 2002, she donated her father's organs and tissues, bringing a special pride to her role in a partnership that accelerated donor designations by a factor of six to nearly 25,000 Californians per week.[3]

Both donor designation and organ donation conversion rates stood to increase with expanded media coverage. We accelerated efforts to secure news stories by activating our PR working groups earlier than ever before, commissioning GOAL Productions to produce B-roll tapes for local TV news, and adding a Done Vida version of the float logo to all Spanish-language media resources.

By the end of November, news stories had been published in seven states and Canada, the pace of rose dedications picked up dramatically, and for the first time we felt like an award contender. After five years of dedicated work—our own kind of giving from the heart—we were poised to leap forward.

21

GIVING FROM THE HEART

My brother, from the Hualapai and Hopi Tribes of Arizona, became our hero. His death did have a purpose in giving life to others.

—CAMILLE NIGHTHORSE,
donor sister (2007 rider)

BY THE END OF NOVEMBER, the number of organizations sponsoring roses had grown to sixteen, including eight hospitals and two transplant centers. A generous $5,000 grant from the Heart-to-Heart Foundation—founded by parents Jayne and Peter Stanyon in memory of their daughters Kirsty and six-organ donor Hollie—honored fifty pediatric donors. Coupled with an equivalent grant from Tenet Healthcare Foundation, the total number of roses sponsored by organizations surpassed four hundred.

The rose dedication program's fulfillment operation at OneLegacy's Placentia office had been running at full-speed for weeks. Between preparing vials, printing certificates, and packing and shipping packages, the program was highly labor intensive, relying heavily on a cadre of elder Donate Life Ambassador volunteers affectionately known as the Golden Girls: Norma Hostert, Cora Johnson,

Shirley Douthit, Cheryl Thorpe, Sharon Miller, and Fidelma Brach. The first week of December, individual dedications surged to ten per day—they would crest at twenty-five per day later in the month—filling the space with boxes, tissue paper, padded mailers, and hundreds of rose vials.

Meanwhile, we inaugurated our 2007 Rose Parade decorating season by welcoming DMV employees to the Rose Palace. Selected through an agency-wide lottery, the winners came from up to 350 miles away, testifying to the pride they felt in supporting the cause.

While we always welcomed first-time decorators, veterans played an increasingly critical role, as they required no training and had valuable experience applying materials. For the last three years, our volunteers had learned the nuances of sponges and brushes, gooey and white glue, various surfaces, and covering large areas with powdered rice, coconut, corn husks, tree bark, and onion seed. The wildlife and mushrooms on "Life Transformed" introduced detailed bean work, preparing us for more intricate decorating challenges.

Material specifications—known as "call-outs"—on the two large boxes immediately behind the heart required thousands of kidney and lima beans to define the intricate gift-wrapping patterns. Placing them one by one required skill and patience, especially on vertical faces constantly opposed by gravity. Two identical striped boxes used lima beans to define straight lines between white rice and purple statice. Two other boxes were covered in crushed green peas and orange lentils, both of which were challenging to apply consistently.

In a break from decorating mode, we teamed up with Huntington Hospital on the first-ever Rose Dedication Ceremony. Although I'd participated in over a dozen OneLegacy donor remembrance ceremonies, this was new territory. It was five days before Christmas, and some of the seventeen invited families were experiencing their first holiday season without a parent, sibling, or child. They were also returning to the place where their loved ones had died, so every part of the experience—parking, entering the hospital doors, walking through the lobby, seeing the nurse who had cared for them—had the potential to trigger painful memories.

In preparation for the event, Marcia Penido and her Huntington Hospital colleagues created an elegant and welcoming environment, with linens and decor befitting such a meaningful gathering. As I introduced myself to some the guests, I gauged the "emotional temperature" to which I could calibrate my remarks. Recognizing the wide spectrum—from sadness and bitterness to hope and pride—I kept things simple, focusing on how our Rose Parade participation would represent them and their loved ones. After Laurie introduced the symbolism of the dedicated roses, Tom Mone and the hospital's CEO presented each of the families with a replica of the red rose and vial to be placed in the float's red heart.

After the ceremony, I locked eyes with a man in his mid-fifties, shook his hand, and thanked him for coming. He looked me straight in the eye and said, "It's nice meeting you, and after today I never want to see you again." Though I didn't take his comment personally, coming face-to-face with such an honest expression of grief shook me to the core. It gave me a new understanding

I FELT THE MAGNITUDE OF WHAT WE HAD CREATED: A DONOR MEMORIAL FOR ALL THE WORLD TO SEE.

of what each single rose meant to a donor family. Seeing the dozens of dedications that were now arriving daily, I felt the magnitude of what we had created: a donor memorial for all the world to see.

The day after Christmas, twenty media outlets descended on the Rose Palace to interview donor family decorators. Throughout the week, Spanish-language media covered our three Latino riders as well as decorators from OneLegacy's cadre of Latino volunteers, *Embajadores de Done Vida.* The *Los Angeles Times* and *Orange County Register* followed Father Elly as he toured St. Joseph Hospital's dialysis clinic, passing out roses and having patients sign the jacket he would wear on New Year's Day.

Reporters and volunteers alike responded favorably to our multicultural touches, especially the gift tags in Spanish—*Para: Un papá, De: Una hija*—and Chinese. For the latter, my colleague Sabrina Ho left me a voicemail so I could surprise our volunteers from Buddhist Tzu Chi Foundation. During our orientation, I pointed to the Chinese characters and did my best to channel Sabrina's cadence: *ee WAY, CHONG sen duh NEE-yer, eek KUH, bah-bah d'AYE sheen.* The volunteers' smiles and applause were genuine, as was my appreciation for a language that could say so much with just a handful of characters: "The gift of life to my beloved daughter. Love from your father."

That sentiment would have been the fondest wish of float rider Emile Therien, whose daughter Sarah Beth made organ donation history in Canada. Only seven months prior, Sarah Beth had suffered a sudden heart attack, which left her with an extremely low level of brain activity. She did not progress to brain death, which at the time was a required precursor to organ donation in America's northern neighbor.

Determined to honor their daughter's wish to donate, Emile and his wife Beth insisted that Trillium Gift of Life Network, Ontario's organ and tissue recovery agency, pursue donation after cardiac death (DCD), a protocol whereby organs can be recovered and transplanted if the heart stops beating within one hour after removal of life support. DCD was increasingly common in the US, where one of the Collaborative goals was to increase their frequency to 10 percent of all organ donation cases.

Emile and Beth's initiative and Sarah Beth's gift of life opened the door to DCD in Canada; stories in the *CTV National News, Ottawa Sun, Ottawa Citizen*, and *Toronto Globe and Mail* broadened public understanding of what it made possible. (In the ten years following her death, 1,067 organs were transplanted from DCD donors in Ontario—a truly remarkable, and ongoing, legacy.)

Emile's high profile in Canada made it a *fait accompli* that he would occupy a highly visible position on our float. Each year there was no shortage of participants anxious to know whether they would be on the camera side, facing the sun. From the outset, I made rider placement my decision, and mine alone, as I knew any disappointment on the part of riders or sponsors would be tempered by their confidence that I had taken all considerations into account.

Assigning positions started with an overhead diagram built in PowerPoint or Illustrator, with squares and circles denoting sitting and standing positions, respectively. This gave me a clear picture of how the riders were grouped and which positions required agility. Physical limitations required some riders to be seated for the duration of the parade, with some needing a seat as close to the street as possible so as not to have to climb backward into their position.

After the initial grouping, the second round of sorting factored in the rider's familiarity, which may have been built up over years or a final-week surge in media stories. The need to present a diverse rider contingent, especially on the camera side, was a factor, as was the goal of having each rider sponsor represented on the camera side in alternating years. From that point, I tried to pair riders whose personalities or life experiences seemed to be a good match. On the rare occasion that a rider's position was isolated, I sought out someone who would enjoy giving and receiving energy from the spectators lining the street.

Each float's unique combination of structural design and participants required a tailored approach to rider placement. Our first year, the many riders facing forward on an open bridge eased the process. "Many Families, One Gift" was even simpler with eleven pairings and only two standing positions. "Life Transformed" had no complicating factors, as the riders were all seated.

The topography of our 2007 Donate Life float, however, required careful consideration. Given the largely memorial nature of the dedication garden, it made sense to have donor family members occupy the four positions standing vigil over the heart. Positioned about ten feet behind them were seven standing positions arranged in a steep arch, requiring three agile riders to ascend the stairs to the summit. Rounding off the landscape were ten seated positions, six of them on-camera.

Final decisions would wait until after the Float Rider Orientation, which offered the first opportunity to gauge each participant's personality and true agility. As the riders briefly shared their stories, the tone was decidedly different than in years past. Marvin Reznick, a funeral director who received a liver transplant soon after his son, Michael, became an organ donor, was our contingent's lone recipient. In the absence of the deep gratitude, *joie de vive*, and occasional quirkiness that recipients brought to their participation, a purity of spirit enveloped the room. We were in a sacred place, encapsulated by Marvin's summation of Michael's gift of life:

> *His heart is still beating, his lungs are still breathing, his eyes are still seeing, and the last thing he did on Earth was godly.*

22

WHEREVER YOU WILL GO

One lady with tears in her eyes tried talking with the person
next to her, but she couldn't get any words out. She just sat
there grabbing the other person's arm. This played out over
and again to varying degrees all the way down the street.

—**KEVIN MONROE,**
living kidney donor (2007 rider)

THE SPIRIT OF KINDNESS and remembrance
united our Class of 2007, and made our first full-scale presentation of dedicated roses that much more meaningful. By the end of
November, the four hundred roses dedicated by organizations vastly
outnumbered the 150 contributed by individuals and families. We
expected contributions to surge over the final thirty days, but we
hardly anticipated the number of individual dedications would
quadruple in that time.

The last-month rush severely tested our operation in Placentia.
The Golden Girls and other volunteers worked feverishly to keep
pace while our team made plans for Rose Placement, which coincided
with float rider decorating. Among the one hundred roses placed by

appointment on December 30, rider Tammy Mitchell had the honor of placing all nineteen roses dedicated from the state of New York.

After the official reception—and proudly wearing a Canada baseball cap presented to me onstage by Emile Therien—I returned to the Rose Palace to see Donor Alliance employee contest winners Frank Garcia and Myrna Panza placing dedicated roses one by one, reading passage after passage with reverence:

In memory of Allison—She gave me a second chance at life the day I almost died. She is a daughter, sister, and friend. She is also my hero.

In support of my sister Lacey—I feel honored to be the one who was able to give you this gift. It's been a long road you have traveled with courage and I'm proud of you! Love, Tyson.

In honor of my donor family—Somewhere out there is a wonderful family who gave me the most precious gift of a new heart. Thank you.

As our riders arrived for judging the next morning, the completed Family Circle Garden was the crown jewel of "Giving from the Heart." Laurie had taken great care to ensure even spacing and consistent height among the sea of red roses framed by white zinnias. The white dedication tags were plainly visible, revealing their special nature for at least one more day until the expanding blooms filled most of the space between.

Riders honoring loved ones carried photos in identical frames, lending some uniformity to their otherwise personal choices of attire. Three donor mothers joined Emile directly behind the heart: Erica Rangel-Báez (Arleta, CA), whose nine-year-old son, Frankie Hernandez, saved the lives of five children after suffering a fatal brain aneurysm; Kelli Jantz (Centennial, CO), a transplant coordinator whose fourteen-year-old son, Jake, collapsed during a high school football game; and Charity Guergo-Ramos (Miami, FL), mother of four-year-old Alejandro, who donated six organs less than two years prior.

After the bell rang to signal the official start of judging, the camouflaged speakers came alive with "Wherever You Will Go," the 2001 song by The Calling about following someone to the ends of the earth. When I originally nominated the song, it resounded as one a donor, living or deceased, would dedicate to their recipient. But standing along the perimeter of the Rose Palace, I was drawn to the tears streaming down Charity's face as she clutched the framed portrait of her son. Then it struck me: *This is a song from a donor to the family they left behind.*

> *So lately, been wondering*
> *Who will be there to take my place*
> *When I'm gone you'll need love to light the shadows on*
> *your face*
> *If a great wave shall fall and fall upon us all*
> *Then between the sand and stone, could you make it on*
> *your own*
>
> *If I could, then I would,*
> *I'll go wherever you will go*
> *Way up high or down low, I'll go wherever you will go*
>
> *And maybe, I'll find out*
> *A way to make it back someday*
> *To watch you, to guide you through the darkest of your days*
> *If a great wave shall fall and fall upon us all*
> *Then I hope there's someone out there who can bring me back*
> *to you*
>
> *I know now, just quite how*

My life and love might still go on
In your heart, in your mind, I'll stay with you for all of time

As the judges circled below, Bob Bonner, standing atop the arch, turned to Dan Sandoval and said, "Those damn Donate Life people, they are either laughing or crying. There is no in-between." The living donor's levity was welcomed amidst the good tears.

Following judging, 150 attendees boarded buses to Universal Studios CityWalk as Stephanie Jansky, a first-year committee member from Lifebanc, helped me break down the scores of chairs we had set up in the Rose Palace to accommodate our growing numbers. About halfway through the task, I broke down, overcome by the intensity, authenticity, and beauty of the past two weeks. Stephanie boarded the last bus, and I was alone.

Alas, my opportunity to decompress in quiet reflection was interrupted by a call from our seating provider. Earlier that morning, I had left a voicemail informing my contact, Debbie, that a dozen guests had left their tickets behind. I presumed there would be no issue, as our block of three hundred seats took up an entire grandstand, complete with its own entrance, and I had a chart of assigned seats.

Despite these assurances, Debbie, took a hard line. "They must have their tickets in hand," she said. "No exceptions." There was no possible way we could comply with her mandate. My increasingly desperate pleas were met with intransigence, then silence. As Debbie muffled her phone to talk to a colleague, in the background I heard a sound that was unmistakable: someone walking up grandstands.

Ten minutes later, Debbie was shocked to see me. "What are you doing here?" she asked, offering no deference to the purchaser of half her inventory. Brushing off the insult, I told her we needed to come to an arrangement. She accepted my offer to have someone with a checklist stationed at the point of entry starting at six o'clock the morning of the parade, an assignment graciously accepted by Stephanie Jansky and Sandra Madera, OneLegacy's first-year communications assistant who had come into our orbit as one of the Kodak donor families.

The morning of the parade was the inverse of the previous year: a glorious blue-sky day. In the natural light, the giant red heart was iconic: a blanket of red roses with scattered flecks of white offering a hint of the sentiments contained therein. The expressions on the faces of our riders—most memorably Erica, for whom the experience was particularly wrenching—reflected the spectrum of human emotion: joy and sorrow, pride and loss.

After the riders dismounted, a woman approached Dan Sandoval at the post-parade exit gate. "She had dedicated a rose for her son who had lost his life earlier this year," he recalled. "She asked if we could give her any part of the float to have as a memento, even if it was only a single rose petal. I ran as fast as I could in the direction I saw the float go. I gave her a flower that I had picked. She said with tears in her eyes, 'Thank you so much. You don't know how much this means to me!' She gave me a strong hug and I said to her, 'Yes I do.' As I boarded the bus, she smiled."

2007 DONATE LIFE ROSE PARADE FLOAT

ROSE PARADE THEME: Our Good Nature

FLOAT THEME: Giving From the Heart

RIDERS: 23

STATES REPRESENTED: 12

PARTICIPATING ORGANIZATIONS: 81

DEDICATED ROSES: 1,052

DONATE LIFE GRANDSTAND SEATS: 330

MEDIA STORIES: 212

ORGAN DONATION CONVERSION RATE, 2006: 64.2 percent[8]

DESIGNATED DONORS, US: 63,222,077[6]

April 17, 2001

Robert Mendez, M.D., President
"One Legacy" Organization
2200 W. Third Street, 4th Floor
Los Angeles, CA 90057

Dear Dr. Mendez:

Yesterday, I saw you kick off "National Organ Donor Awareness Week" with a television interview on NBC Channel 4. I thought you articulated the facts surrounding this important issue very well and am hopeful that your message will encourage more people to choose organ donation as a life saving option at the time of their demise.

I am one of those whose life was saved by receiving a new lung at UCLA in 1999. It truly has made me a new person and I will be forever indebted to the family that made me the object of their generosity. I have been trying to find a way to repay society for this wonderful gift and I believe I have a good idea on how to do that.

The thought I have is for the entry of a [...] organ recipients and their loved ones, o[...] families who have shown their unselfish [...] and "color" commentary that would acc[...] million people and would focus substant[...] appeals for organ and tissue donations. [...] this somewhat abstract subject and com[...] generate a feeling of accomplishment fo[...]

I have contacted the Tournament of Ros[...] person with whom I spoke, Wendy Mat[...] said that a float entry of this sort must b[...] business. Further, the sponsor would h[...] the Tournament's "Float Entries Comm[...] enclosed information packet to acquaint [...]

With that somewhat lengthy backgroun[...] sponsor a float of the type I have descri[...] That is a substantial amount of money, [...] project like this might generate interest [...] companies and transplant centers as wel[...] touched by these medical miracles. I re[...] assessing this aspect of the proposal.

Robert Mendez, M.D.
4/17/01
Page 2

If you are willing to do this, I will do everything I can to work with you to make this happen. It is likely too late to enter a float this year but I have no doubt that we could have an entry ready for the January 2003 parade. I am not a professional float building organizer but I have some contacts that might be able to assist with information on how to manage the process as well as helping to recruit float decoration volunteers. I would be willing to write letters to generate support and contributions for the project and to enlist volunteers. I would also be willing to study the float construction process to determine what the needs are at that level and to lend my knowledge and physical support to the effort.

Can I count on your support? If so, please call so we can discuss what the next step should be. Thanks for your help.

Sincerely,

Gary Foxen

In April 2001, Gary Foxen, supported by his wife Lois, wrote a heartfelt letter to OneLegacy suggesting the entry of an organ donation-themed float in the Rose Parade.

Scott Weersing

2004 | A SYMPHONY OF LIFE

On January 1, 2004, tens of millions of Rose Parade spectators and viewers welcomed the Donate Life community to "America's New Year Celebration."

Pasadena Tournament of Roses

Hundreds of float riders have followed the footsteps of the pioneering "Class of 2004."

Scott Weersing

Chris Klug, Olympic snowboarding bronze medalist, and Sharon Maupin, both liver recipients, wave to the grandstands.

Scott Weersing

Ten rider pairs and a trio illustrated how organ, eye, and tissue donation saves lives and strengthens familes.

Scott Weersing

Kay LaRue decorates a portrait of her son Richard, one of eight organ, eye, and tissue donors featured on Kodak's "Memory Lane."

Bryan Stewart

The family of Nicholas Green—Reg, Eleanor and Maggie—wave to the grand-stands alongside Cathy Olmo and her daughter Kelly, a liver recipient.

Scott Weersing

The deeply metaphorical "Life Transformed" withstood the storms of the 2006 Rose Parade, the first affected by rain in more than 50 years.

Scott Weersing

The Family Circle program piloted Donate Life's dedication garden with over 300 messages of love, hope, and remembrance.

Bryan Stewart

An iconic red heart filled with 1,052 dedicated roses was shepherded by 23 donor family members and living donors.

Scott Weersing

Donor families and recipients personally placed roses in the dedication garden, an ongoing tradition.

Scott Weersing

OneLegacy's Family Services team instituted donor family decorating shifts for the first time, offering a healing experience for the holiday season.

Bryan Stewart

The parents of Erin Choe and wife of Johnathan Sim created their loved ones' floragraphs at Rosemont Pavilion in Pasadena.

Bryan Stewart

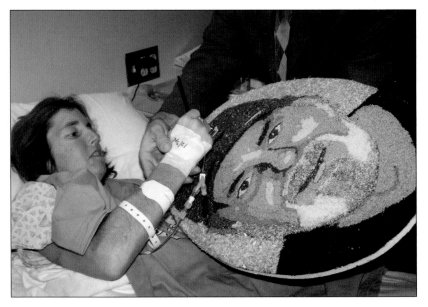

Raymond Costlow's daughter Lori completed her father's portrait from her hospice bed.

Kathleen Hostert

Donate Life introduced floragraphs and walkers to their first over-height entry, an ingeniously engineered hot air balloon festival.

Pasadena Tournament of Roses

Float Committee members attending the 2008 Rose Parade celebrated Donate Life's first award, the Judges' Special Trophy for showmanship and dramatic impact.

Unknown

Decorating and volunteer operations were led by green-jacketed Phoenix Decorating crew chiefs and blue-jacketed OneLegacy staff and volunteers.

Luis Ramirez

A quarter-century after her liver transplant, Lily Allen, with husband Brian, decorated her donor Matthew's floragraph with his parents, Milt and Janet Bemis.

Luis Ramirez

Designed by Dave Pittman, "Stars of Life" was the first abstract float design in Rose Parade history.

Pasadena Tournament of Roses

The late Bill Lofthouse of Phoenix Decorating was among 14 "Walk of Fame" honorees.

Scott Weersing

Thanks to its revolutionary design, the lush floral canopy appeared to be floating above the deck.

Scott Weersing

A fiery phoenix with 77 floragraphs woven into its tail soared above 24 float riders.

Scott Weersing

Floragraph finishing events brought the beauty of the Rose Parade to markets across the country well before the New Year.

Intermountain Donor Services

The float design featured elements inspired by the UNOS National Donor Memorial's Wall of Tears and Wall of Names.

Scott Weersing

Donor mom Jody Dossler and living kidney donor Ann Lopez were among four walkers leading an elegantly interwoven menagerie of kites.

Scott Weersing

Ribbons trailing the delta kites presented sixty floragraph honorees.

Scott Weersing

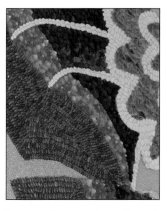

Intricate bean and petal work brought the butterfly kite to life.

Scott Weersing

John Green placed the floragraph of his daughter Christina-Taylor, a cornea donor, completing the 2012 entry for judging.

Scott Weersing

As the eagerly awaited time for judging approached, Donate Life's "pilgrims to Pasadena" linked hands to encircle the float.

Scott Weersing

As in prior years, committee chairman Bryan Stewart welcomed and oriented volunteers at each decorating shift.

Scott Weersing

The 2012 Donate Life float imagined "... One More Day" to live or be reunited with loved ones.

Pasadena Tournament of Roses

Seventy-two floragraphs occupied the hour positions on six 10-foot-tall floral clocks.

Scott Weersing

The dedication garden featured a memorial to the victims of the Sandy Hook tragedy.

Pasadena Tournament of Roses

After the conclusion of judging, Decorating Committee leaders celebrated a month of tireless work.

OneLegacy Foundation

Donate Life's floragraph and float decorating operations filled an open bay at Rosemont Pavilion.

Chris Chavira

Over the years, float judging evolved into an emotional climax for hundreds of participants, sponsors and guests traveling to Pasadena.

Scott Weersing

Twelve living kidney donors walked alongside a lantern festival carrying 30 recipients, 81 floragraphs, and over 7,000 dedicated roses.

Pasadena Tournament of Roses

The dedication garden included personal messages of hope to all 1,842 pediatric candidates on the organ transplant waiting list.

Chris Chavira

PART THREE

THE GREAT LEAP FORWARD

23

AIMING HIGH

As we rode down the street you could feel that the people knew just what the float was about. We had people cheering, clapping, saying we love you. Some were even crying. The Donate Life float has done its job.

—TAMMY MITCHELL,
donor mother (2007 rider)

OUR FOURTH ANNUAL CAMPAIGN generated more than two hundred news stories nationwide, including thirty-seven Spanish-language and twenty-three Asian media stories. The 50 percent jump, despite no change in the number of riders or states represented from the prior year, assured us that the media's appetite for life-affirming stories was stronger than ever. In addition, with the success of the Family Circle program, our aspiration to be a truly national campaign seemed closer than ever.

While Rose Parade broadcasts reached tens of millions of US households, a "national campaign" implied a breadth of active participation that to date had been restricted in terms of time (mainly the last three weeks of December) and place (our riders' home states, which had peaked at fourteen). Rose dedications were bounded by neither, so for our fifth campaign we set an ambitious goal of three thousand dedications from all fifty states and the District of Columbia, plus ten countries.

Our interest in international dedications was motivated by the 2008 Rose Parade theme, "Passport to the World's Celebrations." Upon receiving early guidance in October, the word "celebrations," plus the donor-focused entry approaching its final stretch, suggested the possibility of a contingent composed entirely of transplant recipients. Over the last two months of the year, our committee gradually introduced other ingredients that would eventually make our fifth Rose Parade float entry a true milestone.

First and foremost was our desire to win an award. For years, I had countered, and even preempted, dashed hopes for a trophy banner by affirming our status as the most inspiring float in the Rose Parade's long history. The attendant news and broadcast coverage of our entries touched the hearts of millions year after year. Most meaningfully, our campaign's expansion coincided with the gradual rise in organ donation conversion rates, which had risen to 64 percent. We felt like we were doing our part where it counted most.

Nevertheless, formal recognition by the Tournament of Roses had its benefits. Award winners often received extra attention from parade broadcasters and post-parade news roundups. In addition, a banner preceding our float would validate the years-long efforts of our volunteers, sponsors, and national community.

Legitimate questions were raised, however, as to whether winning an award was compatible with our current model. Our substantial rider contingent—by far the largest for a fifty-five-foot entry our size—was the main driver of fundraising, sponsor participation, and news coverage. Tenaya posed an important question: *Would it even be possible for a "people-mover" to win an award?*

I consulted Bill Lofthouse to get his perspective on the formula for an award-winner. He had a ready answer: a stockpile of fully developed sketches that his lifetime of experience predicted would be strong contenders. One by one, he stacked the black-and-white renderings in front of me, punctuating each with his trademark voice. A cherub: "This would win an award." Birds: "This would win an award." After the fourth sketch, I stopped him. "Bill, these are beautiful, but they aren't us," I said. "How does a Donate Life float win an award?" Understanding where I was coming from, Bill paved the way for me to meet with someone who had seen judging deliberations first-hand.

Arriving at the Tournament House, I felt like an emissary as I introduced myself to Bob Miller, Chairman of the Float Entries Committee. Bob conveyed the Tournament's appreciation for our float participation. I countered with anecdotes dramatizing how the Rose Parade had become so meaningful to our community. Then came my straightforward question: "Bob, our float committee wants to win an award, and we want to earn it. What do we need to do?"

Bob's reply was as concise as it was illuminating. "Keep in mind that there are around fifty floats," he said. "The judges see them all in a matter of two days, and then they gather to discuss their merits. A winning float needs to be memorable, with a strong central visual concept that is easily recalled." While our first float had that quality, the last three did not. I left the meeting with newfound clarity: simplify our storytelling approach and design a float that not only inspires, but is memorable in its own right.

In late November, I shared Bob's guidance with the committee. As a precursor to brainstorming creative concepts, we made the decision to feature an all-recipient rider contingent. Despite our enthusiasm for the direction, concerns were raised about losing the donor perspective. "What about the floragraphs?" one member suggested, using a newly streamlined term to recall the portraits that Kodak featured in their penultimate parade entry. Reprising them seemed like a natural progression, but we had to carefully consider what they would adorn.

Cued by the parade theme, we brainstormed "celebrations" that were both highly visual and appropriately reverent backdrops for floragraphs. Hand-held balloons were suggested but seen as both overly celebratory and not of preferable scale, prompting Lisa Rhodes, a transplant financial coordinator at Cedars-Sinai, to chime in. "What about hot air balloons?" The idea made perfect sense. A hot air balloon festival would fit neatly into the parade theme, was more beautiful than celebratory, would elevate the portraits, and could be described in a single word: *balloons*.

Sharing an idea raised by one of our Ambassadors, Gary suggested we: "broaden the landscape" of our presentation by introducing walkers. The Tournament allowed "outwalkers" (the official term), but they had to be integrated into the visual story. Hot air balloons provided a completely natural role for walkers: they could hold tether lines.

The appeal of the creative concept had two caveats. First, the scale of hot air balloons would require the structure to be much taller than the standard eighteen feet, and going over-height would require more money. Second, we wouldn't get past the starting line without securing the concept through the Theme Draft.

Each February, Rose Parade float builders gather to select themes in a manner similar to the process by which professional sports teams choose players. The draft ensures variety in the lineup, with popular themes such as dragons, castles, lions, dogs, trains, and rain forests picked in the early rounds. Our first four float entries were so distinctive that protecting them from competition was a non-issue. Hot air balloons, however, would surely be one of the coveted world celebrations.

Phoenix secured our theme, but we faced an early May deadline to approve a final sketch or risk another float builder claiming the theme for their client. Only when our sketch was finalized would we know how many riders, walkers, and floragraphs would be available for sponsorship—and how much higher we could soar.

Our float presentations to date had been decidedly earthbound. Introducing ourselves to the Rose Parade's global audience required us to carefully calibrate our message. Upon our debut, the subject of organ donation was uncomfortable, if not something to be feared outright. To counter negative perceptions, we gently invited people to explore the value of the decision to donate: how it bridged life and death with symphonic beauty, brought families together, transformed lives, and was a gift from the heart.

Our initial instinct was to continue with the softer approach, eschewing modern balloon silhouettes in favor of the ornate Victorian-era variety. In addition to allowing more creative art direction and call-outs, their open-air baskets and carriages lent themselves to carrying riders aloft.

Dave Pittman guided us through four Victorian sketches incorporating one to four balloons, ranging from spherical to blimp-shaped. Several fused a steampunk aesthetic, flying ships, and other historical design references. To our surprise, Dave also prepared two sketches utilizing contemporary hot air balloons, with the baskets employed to carry flowers instead of people.

We selected one from each genre for color studies. Dave valued the Victorian concept depicting a single balloon and launch platform for its "large presence, nice small touches, and lots of floral opportunities." The committee raved over its clean arrangement of the riders, depiction of a balloon lifting off, and elegant integration of the dedication garden. A clear downside, however, was its historical setting; to work, the riders would need to wear period costumes.

The second featured three contemporary balloons rising to a high apex at the midpoint. Dave noted "the composition is great with movement of color going up," while the committee was impressed with the height and integration of walkers. The incomplete sketch focused on the composition of the balloons, so we were looking forward to seeing his ideas for the deck.

The richness of both directions was reflected in our refinement brief, which included thirty-seven potential themes employing various conjugations and combinations of the words *celebrate, launch, soar, hope, flight, up,* and, of course, *life.* We also affirmed our intention to go over-height, introduce floragraphs and walkers, and accommodate up to three thousand dedicated roses. Either direction allowed ample space to distribute twenty-four riders, thus meeting the challenge of making a "people-mover" a legitimate award contender.

Donate Life Rose Parade Float's evolution had reached a turning point. Once we made the decision to go bigger, there would be no turning back. Construction expenses would rise, floragraphs would invite new partners and operational complexity, and decorating operations would move to the roomier Rosemont Pavilion.

More profoundly, the committee's immediate acceptance of the modern balloons as an option was startling. The concern we had raised only months ago—being too celebratory—had become a nonissue. On the spectrum between reverence and celebration, our shift toward the latter emanated from a convergence of factors.

First, within the Rose Parade's sphere of influence, the admiration of our Rose Palace neighbors, an ever-warmer reception by parade spectators, glowing commentary by broadcasters, and expanding news coverage of our participation indicated that perceptions of our cause were shifting toward the positive end of the spectrum.

Second, donor families had demonstrated great willingness to share their stories. Welcoming volunteers, interacting with riders and the Kodak families, and reading hundreds of rose dedications exposed us to the pride that accompanied their grief.

We were also encouraged by Organ Donation Breakthrough Collaborative data showing that donation rates nationwide had increased dramatically since October 2003.

These three factors primed us to embrace Dave's vision that modern balloons could serve as a reverent celebration of organ, eye, and tissue donation. When asked which direction had the most potential to be an award contender, Dave replied, "Originally I would have said Victorian, but with changes, the modern direction would have even odds."

While the Victorian direction had merit, the committee's decision to go with contemporary balloons was cemented by a concise penetrating comment from Jacki Harris of Astellas: "Organ donation is of this era." While some refinement remained, one outcome was certain: the 2008 Donate Life Rose Parade Float would be called "Life Takes Flight." We had six weeks to approve a final sketch that would live up to that celebratory, uplifting theme. Otherwise, we would need to start from scratch.

24

LIFE TAKES FLIGHT

As a donor family, you may lose them in body but never in spirit. Somewhere in this world their heart still beats, their eyes still see, and they still live on.

—JOSIE FLORES,

donor daughter (2008 walker)

BY THE END OF MARCH, Dave sent a refined sketch with four balloons in a row: the first was half-inflated, the second two gradually more so, and the rear one rose high above the deck. It was on the right track, but balloons that were less than fully inflated diminished the celebratory spirit. Tenaya shared my concern that we had only five weeks remaining before we would cede our right to the balloon theme. Within an hour, she sketched a "Festival of Life" with three rising balloons and baskets overflowing with flowers. I sent the sketch to Dave with hope for a breakthrough.

Three weeks later, Dave's nineteenth sketch nailed it. Oval floragraphs were distributed around the circumferences of four fully inflated balloons. The balloons on each end were aloft—the rear one majestically so, its entire weight supported by only a tangential connection to the third one. From the highest balloon, eight tether lines descended from floragraphs to the base of the envelope before extending downward. The lines were held by eight individuals who would literally be walking with their loved ones. With a week to spare, the color rendering was complete.

While the final number of portraits would not be finalized until construction was well underway, the committee agreed that, like riders, the thirty-plus floragraphs would be sponsored by organizations only. Not only would the policy establish that a floragraph was not a commodity that could be purchased, but only organizations had the resources to engage local media.

My concerns about getting such a late start securing walker and floragraph sponsors were alleviated somewhat when Washington Regional Transplant Consortium and Louisiana Organ Procurement Agency, followed by Donor Alliance and Life Alliance, pledged to send walkers. With OneLegacy and the float committee each inheriting one, all but two of the eight walkers were sponsored by June 1. In addition, eight floragraphs were designated to OneLegacy to ensure a substantial number of families would be able to decorate their loved ones' portraits, which was both meaningful to the families and highly appealing to media.

As floragraph sponsorship opportunities crystallized, the Family Circle program continued to evolve. When the program was originally conceived, it was envisioned that contributions would come largely from donor families. However, organizations were now driving a large share of dedications, and of the individual contributions, about 30 percent were "in honor of" or "in support of" individuals other than donors.

The diversification of the Family Circle begged a fundamental question: should the program be treated as its own entity or a subset of the float campaign? Dedicated roses had little value without the float upon which they were placed. Only through years of foundational work had we developed the reach and operational capacity to launch and maintain the program. With only several weeks until the unveiling, the potentially divisive question was tabled.

As expected, our colleagues at the Donate Life America and AOPO meetings were captivated by the sight of "Life Takes Flight." Between riders, walkers, and floragraphs, the number of opportunities for organizations to join our campaign nearly tripled, once again begging the question: *Will they come?*

Our fourth campaign was supported by more than eighty organizations, including OPOs, tissue banks, associations, transplant centers, for-profits, and nonprofits. While twenty-two OPOs joined OneLegacy in supporting the 2007 campaign, for the second straight year only seven of them sponsored riders. Floragraphs created an newfound opportunity to activate dozens of OPOs and their media relations teams to dramatically expand our geographic reach.

To spur commitments, floragraph sponsorships were capped at $2,500. In several cases, suppliers to the field collaborated with OPOs to introduce the campaign into new markets: Inetz Media Group with Donate Life South Carolina, Sallop Insurance Agency with LifeGift in Houston, and the Mendez National Institute of Transplantation with Kentucky Organ Donor Affiliates. A steady stream of commitments between Memorial Day and Labor Day left only eight floragraphs remaining to be claimed by the end of August. By then, Phoenix Decorating had made significant progress on construction, though the complete lack of paint as of T2 testified to the time needed to build such a complex structure. Our first over-height float required three of the balloons to retract to under eighteen feet while fully loaded and in motion. Solving the engineering challenge would be up to operations manager Sean McMinimy, the calm commander of a dozen mechanical wizards and welding artisans.

Collapsing the foremost balloon was straightforward, as its standalone position allowed a simple hinge mechanism to bow forward. The two rearmost balloons were a decidedly more challenging proposition. The base of the fourth balloon was connected at a single point of contact near the top of the third balloon, which itself was about twenty-two feet tall. Having the conjoined balloons simply lean backward was not an option, as the fourth balloon would still be over-height. Sean's solution was genius: break the third balloon into three pieces so the top half could fold down, retracting the fourth balloon with it.

Efforts to fill the balloons' baskets with dedicated roses took a poignant turn when the University of Michigan Transplant Center honored the six transplant surgeons, perfusionists, and pilots who died in a June plane crash while transporting recovered lungs. Soon thereafter, I was invited by Pamela Shute, the hospital services director at Midwest Transplant Network, to introduce the Donate Life Rose Parade Float campaign and rose dedication program at a regional hospital conference.

The summer months offered an opportunity to fine-tune our operations. Stephanie Schmitz reduced the risk of volunteer attrition by having each decorating shift filled by three groups of twenty, which had the added benefit of bringing new decorating groups into the fold. In addition, after two years of outfitting our volunteers in olive green, Kari Kozuki suggested introducing a new color. One of the Donate Life colors, light blue, was suggested as a starting point for her research into options.

On the media front, after reassessing our approach to providing video footage, we chose to ship B-roll tapes to our partners, who in turn would hand-deliver them to TV stations for a more personal and flexible approach. We also moved up the launch of our National and Regional PR Working Groups by over a month, hoping that orienting our colleagues prior to the September 17 float rider announcement would spur early pitching and story placements.

By mid-September, building web pages for each of our seventy-three float participants and honorees was a top priority. The twenty-four riders hailed from thirteen states, ranged in age from fifteen to sixty-three, and had collectively received kidneys, hearts, lungs, livers, corneas, bone, ligaments, and blood.

Notable riders included Tom Berryhill (Modesto, CA), the only heart transplant recipient elected to office in the US. Joining him was California DMV manager Jan Barney (Elk Grove, CA), who as the first cornea recipient to ride would have a special appreciation for the parade's explosion of color.

Dale Wade Davis (North Hollywood, CA) was diagnosed with a hereditary kidney disease in 2006. After more than thirty friends volunteered for testing as potential donors, the best match turned out to be Dale's good friend Phillip Palmer, the morning news anchor for ABC7 in Los Angeles.

Another rider, Nikki Cortez of Greeley, Colorado, had experienced a lifetime of medical setbacks in her twenty-one years. Acute lymphocytic leukemia had forced her to undergo extensive chemotherapy and corticosteroid treatments, which in turn severely weakened her bones. A series of bone grafts and an elbow transplant enabled by her sponsor, AlloSource, allowed her to thrive. I was looking forward to meeting Nikki and learning from her courage in the face of adversity. I would never have that opportunity.

The morning of our rider announcement, I received the news that Nikki had been murdered by her estranged husband, an Iraq

War veteran. In a fit of jealousy, he had entered their home with a shotgun, and as she sought escape he shot her twice in the back. I was utterly devastated knowing that after all she had been through, her life had come to such a sudden, tragic end.

Working in the organ and tissue donation field, death was an everyday presence. Each day, emails broadcast to all OneLegacy staff notified us of a donation case. Abbreviations and acronyms communicated the who, how, and where: 48 M H, ICB, LLUMC. *48-year-old male Hispanic, death due to intracranial bleeding at Loma Linda University Medical Center.* A moment of reflection would follow. *A family lost their husband, son, or father today. My colleagues are supporting them through their emotional turmoil. Hopefully they can find some hope and meaning through his gifts to others.*

But Nikki's death was different. There was no donation story to offer a silver lining. Nikki's courageous journey had ended with terror, the explosion of gunfire, and silence.

25

FLORAGRAPHS
AND FAMILY

*I saw how they fought to save Hernán's life, but it wasn't
meant to be. Donation was a way for him to keep living.*

—EVA PEREZ,

donor mother (2008 walker)

NIKKI'S DEATH DEEPENED my sense of gravity as we
prepared to introduce floragraphs into our campaign. Our first four
parade entries featured thirty-three donor family members as float
riders, who—as front-facing representatives of our cause—were often
selected because of their volunteer activity and media experience.

So-called "floragraph families," on the other hand, didn't neces-
sarily have extensive experience in the public realm. Honorees were
typically selected with guidance from OPO family services professionals, who were familiar enough with the families to feel assured
they could handle such a high-profile opportunity. Some donors
were chosen because of the well-publicized circumstances of their

passing, while others had family members for whom the pilgrimage to Pasadena would be a healing part of their grief journey.

First in line were the donor family walkers for whom the tether lines represented a profound connection to their loved ones. Most prominent among them were a pair of young women joined by fate. Missy Tipton (Waleska, GA) was the seventeen-year-old sister of Ransom Tipton, who was only sixteen when he died in a car crash three months after his family's home was destroyed in a fire. Their family was featured on ABC's highly rated *Extreme Makeover: Home Edition* in March, and the episode's focus on Ransom's donation of life-saving organs sparked a nationwide surge of donor designations. Lifeline of Ohio added even greater meaning to Missy's participation by sponsoring Ransom's heart recipient, Rachel Ball (Lancaster, OH), to walk by her side.

Another walker distinguished by special circumstances was Mike Moore, whose tether line would connect to two floragraphs. Between June 2006 and March 2007, Mike lost his seventeen-year-old daughter, Katie, to a car accident and his wife, Melanie, to a ruptured brain aneurysm. Together they saved six lives as organ donors, and their gifts of corneas and tissues restored sight to the blind, treated victims of trauma and debilitating disease, and aided various research projects.

Also chosen as floragraph escorts were Jeannie McGuire and Eva Perez, who shared the heartache of losing their children, five-year-old James and six-year-old Hernán, respectively; Josie Flores, honoring her mother, Ana Maria; Terry Murray, participating in memory of her husband, Allan; Laurie Wolowic, walking in honor of her brother, Michael; and Arthur Stone, who would undertake his five-mile walk on a prosthetic leg in memory of his son Nicholas.

Weeks later, the float website revealed the faces of our forty floragraph honorees. We placed a high priority on securing the best possible images to use as the basis for the 18" x 24" oval artworks. Official portraits taken for school, work, or military service worked best, as a close-up, focused, and well-lit image of the face and hair detailed features that would allow for the most photorealistic portraits. High-resolution birthday or vacation photos worked as well, with some revealing wonderful personality traits.

One of the most memorable photos of that or any year depicted Terry Lee Snow of Riverside, California. An active nineteen-year-old who enjoyed his motorcycle, Terry was in a fatal accident while riding in Arizona in March 1998. His mother Kathy submitted a photo of Terry at a black-tie event with his studded tongue hanging out of his wide-open mouth—the very essence of his personality. Kathy looked forward to sharing the experience with Terry's liver recipient, Tracy Copeland of Sparks, Nevada, one of Astellas's five sponsored riders.

Other floragraphs were memorable for what the honoree's donation made possible. Julie De Rossi of Houston, Texas, a free-spirited forty-four-year-old mother whose careers included race car driving, interior design, and managing musicians, was killed by a drunk driver in 2004. Among the thirty-five people she helped as an organ and tissue donor was Carson Palmer, a veteran NFL quarterback whose severely injured knee was repaired, and career restored, with an allograft crafted from Julie's Achilles tendon.

Given the addition of floragraphs to our campaign, it was ironic that our most reverential float entry to date promised to also be the most uplifting. Aiming for a song that captured the spirit of our float design and theme, we zeroed in on "Breaking Free," the "soaring" and "flying" track from the 2006 pop culture phenomenon *High School Musical*.

The parade theme "Passport to the World's Celebrations" not only influenced our inspiriting thrust, it also dramatically expanded our multicultural posture. We imprinted volunteer T-shirts with Spanish and Chinese versions of the Donate Life logo on the back. We also supplemented Spanish and Chinese float renderings with versions for each country represented in the dedication garden. Laurie's attendance at the ISODP conference in Philadelphia and ETCO conference in Prague helped to secure dedications from Belgium, Brazil, Canada, Denmark, Germany, Italy, Malaysia, South Korea, Spain, Taiwan, Turkey, and Vietnam.

On the domestic front, the combination of forty floragraphs and twenty-four riders more than doubled the previous year's representation to twenty-six states. Moving up the launch of our PR Working Groups paid early dividends with nineteen stories in eight media markets published by Thanksgiving. The range of subjects testified to the multitude of story angles: rider D.J. Lampert's lifelong transplant journey ("Life's a Kick for Teen Ambassador of Organ Donation," from the *St. Louis Post-Dispatch*); rider Ozzie Herrera's gratitude ("Transplant is Priceless Gift on Thanksgiving" from the front page of the *Orange County Register*); Kelly Sim's plans to decorate her husband Johnathan's floragraph ("Widow Makes Sure Husband's Legacy Lives On," from KOMO-4 Seattle); and rider Daniel Ronco's first-time meeting with the family of his donor, floragraph honoree Johnny Lopez ("Recipient of Kidney Finally Finds, Thanks Family of the Young Donor," from the *Ventura County (CA) Star*).

In addition, the *Arizona Republic* covered the rose dedication ceremony at St. Joseph's Hospital and Medical Center ("Organ Donors Honored at Phoenix Hospital"), one of several such events that replicated the previous year's successful pilots. In early December, the *Joplin Globe* reported on a remarkable joint rose ceremony honoring

110 donors and families served by Freeman Hospital West and host St. John's Regional Medical Center. An outcome of the regional Collaborative conference hosted by Midwest Transplant Network, the cooperation between two southwestern Missouri hospitals reflected the capacity for organ donation and the Rose Parade to unite competing organizations in common cause.

Through its ongoing evolution, the Family Circle program realized Laurie's vision of "families helping families. Twelve OPOs honored one hundred families of pediatric donors thanks to a gift from the Stanyon family's Heart-to-Heart Foundation, while the Jason Boozer family enabled OneLegacy to offer complimentary rose dedications to forty-one donor families for whom the cost was prohibitive. Kari Kozuki later recounted how the families felt honored for having been personally chosen by their OneLegacy liaisons, who in turn valued the opportunity to reconnect with their constituents.

Over the past two years, the Donate Life Rose Parade Float had become a catalyst for donor families to remember their loved ones, support one another, and inspire the public. The introduction of floragraph decorating promised to elevate these qualities—and our operational complexity—to a new level.

26

AIR DROP

I met Jesus, the recipient of Jemil's heart, and what a blessing it truly was. He allowed me to hear my son's heart beat with tears in his eyes and mine.

—DENISE ARMSTRONG,

donor mother (2008 floragraph)

ON THE EVE of the first decorating day, I departed from OneLegacy's Placentia office behind the wheel of a twenty-six-foot box truck filled to the rafters with supplies. My first stop was the Rose Palace, where Phoenix operations staff unloaded five hundred Donate Life-branded box lid trays to support the eleven floats stationed at our former home. As I prepared to depart for our new decorating home, Bill Lofthouse suggested I take a back way that would ease entry into the Rosemont Pavilion parking lot.

I found myself driving north on a beautiful scenic road overlooking the Arroyo Seco watershed. As I drove underneath the historic Colorado Street Bridge, it didn't dawn on me that the road wasn't suitable for large cargo trucks. Navigating a slight curve, I heard a loud noise as the top of the truck clipped a thick tree branch. Since I had only a mile to go, I brushed it off and hoped for the best.

As I got out of the truck at Rosemont, Stephanie Schmitz, who had been tailing me, had a look on her face. The upper right side of the cargo area had been ripped open as if by a can opener almost the entire length of the vehicle. Damage to the roll-up door's horizontal track forced our team to unload the entire contents of the truck through a narrow two-foot opening. (Later, I was appropriately roasted by my staff, who insisted on a group photo with a four-foot section of the cargo area's wood frame.)

Decorating supplies were carried into the 250-by-125-foot warehouse, which was divided into twenty-by-sixty-foot bays. Twelve floats faced each other across a center aisle running the length of the building, with narrow six-foot-wide corridors separating adjacent floats. The entire west side of the building was equipped with massive overlapping sliding doors separating the interior from a concrete-paved plaza known as the "apron."

"Life Takes Flight" was backed into the fourth bay from the entrance just inside a sliding door. We had about ten feet of space between the center aisle and the chassis, plus an adjacent shared bay, to situate decorating supplies, tables, and chairs.

Supplies to support volunteer operations were placed on the apron directly opposite our float. After years of being confined to a ten-by-ten tent on a sidewalk, quadrupling our space was a godsend. Two tents and six tables fronted a mountain of boxes dominated by more than a thousand light-blue T-shirts to outfit the expanded volunteer force needed to support a larger float and floragraph decorating.

With the unloading complete, I reacquainted myself with our new crew chiefs, Mike and Mimi Thompson, who had retired from

Phoenix Decorating upon Kodak's final appearance in the Rose Parade. After taking a year off, they accepted Bill Lofthouse's request to return, but only if they were assigned to Donate Life. We couldn't have been more fortunate, as the Thompsons brought three assets that elevated our decorating operations beginning on day one.

First, their extensive experience gave them a keen understanding of the time it would take to complete various components, allowing them to set up a solid game plan. Second, they brought a welcome spirit of partnership. Mike eagerly communicated challenges and progress so our team could anticipate volunteer needs accordingly, while Mimi's focused energy, encyclopedic knowledge of materials, and experience as an educator made her an ideal trainer of our supervisors and volunteers alike.

Mike and Mimi had also cultivated a loyal cadre of decorators with deep expertise in key skill areas. Bob Bruno brought an engineer's mind to tasks involving patterns made of corn husk, silver leaf, and anything with wood. Gee Wong provided incredible attention to detail, and Cheryl Kimmel's skill with photorealism made her especially valuable as we took on not just a handful of floragraphs, but forty of them.

Floragraphs essentially required a second decorating operation, with the portraits completed in two stages: primary decorating before Christmas, then touching up between December 26 and 28 before they were mounted into position. Local donor families were scheduled to complete their portraits from start to finish. Only six family members at a time could be seated at the 3' x 6' tables, so larger parties split the shift or rotated into float decorating.

Out-of-area families who were unable to travel to Pasadena before Christmas relied on our volunteers to decorate on their behalf—an enormous responsibility for which we had some difficulty recruiting.

Those volunteering and selected for the deeply meaningful assignment required not only some measure of artistic skill, but the ability to handle the pressure of decorating on a family's behalf.

Only three of the thirteen floragraphs slated for decorating on the first day were assigned to volunteers. The remainder were decorated by forty donor family members, including three journeying from Kansas City (the mother of David Starr), San Diego (the mother of Brian Rand Wos), and Seattle (the wife and children of Johnathan Sim). Among the local families were the mother and relatives of Jamil Jamison, who invited his heart recipient, Jesus Nava, to join them.

We asked our floragraph decorators to arrive at noon to bypass the hustle and bustle of orienting and training seventy volunteers. One by one the families were welcomed, outfitted with T-shirts, and formally presented with the floragraph canvas. As family members gazed upon the honoree's face, we gave them the time they needed to process and share their love, pride, and heartache before escorting them into the barn.

Each canvas was prepared with great care by the Phoenix Decorating president Chris Lofthouse. The filtered image was printed onto heavy paper and glued to a wood oval, which in turn had two four-inch posts affixed to the back for mounting the finished piece to the balloon. Chris had the foresight to drill holes into the plastic tabletops so the canvases could lie flat, which promised to shave hours off the time required to decorate each portrait.

In addition to farina, cinnamon, and ground coffee for skin, a host of other materials were used for hair, eyes, and clothing: chili powder, paprika, flax seed, onion seed, poppy seed, powdered rice, ground parsley, pampas grass, statice, and strawflower. Ground freeze-dried strawberry was reserved for the lips and blush. Light-purple statice had to suffice for blue eyes; in future years, Esther-

Marie cultivated a supply of blue hydrangea as a much-improved substitute.

Achieving a photorealistic appearance required one cardinal rule above all: follow the artwork. Not only was the enlarged image extremely low resolution, but the materials allowed for only so much detail. The face was particularly challenging. With only four skin tones at the most, the patchwork of light-to-dark areas had the potential to be confusing up close; like impressionist paintings, floragraphs were best viewed from a distance. Carefully applying each color in order, from light to dark, and blending the borders between them, achieved stunning results.

Kelly Sim surprised us by completing not only her husband's floragraph but Ransom Tipton's as well, all within the space of four hours. Kathy Snow brought both spirit and skill to her memorable portrait of her son Terry Lee, which required a hefty supply of freeze-dried strawberry to cover his exposed tongue.

Some families veered from the artwork, enlarging the eyes or adding shadow to define the nose. While these creative flourishes had the potential to distort the image or reduce consistency from one floragraph to another, we welcomed variation as evidence that they had been created in the most meaningful way possible: by the families themselves.

WE WELCOMED VARIATION AS EVIDENCE THAT THEY HAD BEEN CREATED IN THE MOST MEANINGFUL WAY POSSIBLE: BY THE FAMILIES THEMSELVES.

To our pleasant surprise, all the floragraphs were completed within the allotted five hours, save one. Raymond Costlow, a donor of corneas and tissue upon his passing earlier in the year, had for years participated in the Donate Life Run/Walk in support of his brother-in-law Ted, a lung recipient of six years. As Raymond's family of ten decorated his floragraph, his widow Karen expressed to Kathleen Hostert her sadness that their daughter Lori could not come to Pasadena. Following a long-running battle with breast cancer, Lori was in hospice care.

Laurie Wolowic had an answer. "The floragraphs are mobile," she said. *Yes! We can take it to her!* Kathleen, Laurie and I made our way to their table and noticed the portrait's standout feature: a red baseball cap with a white-outline Chevrolet logo, honoring Raymond's lifetime love of classic cars. "Lori can decorate the logo," I said.

Three days later, Kathleen and I joined Raymond's family in Lori's room at Coastal Communities Hospital. Though weak and in pain, Lori was alert and eager. Standing at the foot of her bed, I revealed Raymond's floragraph. The purest expression of love and longing enveloped Lori's face as she gazed upon her father's portrait.

I stepped to her bedside and positioned the floragraph upside down and at an angle so she could reach it without effort. Holding her delicate wrist and mindful of the IV bandaged to her hand, I guided her artist's paintbrush into a small cup of Elmer's glue, then dabbed it onto the designated area. After several applications, she took a pinch of powdered rice between her thumb and index finger. I positioned the canvas, then gave her the cue to release the material: "Air drop." Lori remained focused and resolute as we repeated the exercise through to completion.

Prior to leaving I held up a mounted rendering of the float and pointed to a floragraph on the first hot air balloon. "When you watch the Rose Parade, this is where he will be." With four weeks to go, she might not live to see it, but one way or another, on New Year's Day she would see her father again.

27

YOU GET WHAT
YOU PLAN FOR

I wouldn't be walking if it weren't for someone's generous gift.

—DAWN GEISE,

bone tissue recipient (2008 rider)

THE COSTLOW FAMILY graciously allowed us to share
their story with CBS2 in Los Angeles, one of more than seventy
media outlets nationwide to publish and air stories before Christmas.
B-roll tapes shipped to sponsors' offices and agencies seeded thirty
markets for post-holiday coverage, with one hundred stories running
the first three days alone.

We benefited greatly from having five distinct and compelling
story angles: float participants, floragraph honorees, volunteer decorators, rose dedication ceremonies, and our meaningful Rose Parade
participation. In addition, Spanish- and Asian-language media
outlets continued to gravitate to participants with ties to the communities they served.

Floragraphs proved by far to be the primary media draw, accounting for close to half of all news coverage. While the concept and visual of families decorating the portraits of their loved ones was utterly compelling, the degree to which they impacted our operations cannot be understated. Preparing canvases, setting up infrastructure, and hosting families required extraordinary planning, conscientiousness, and execution.

Careful consideration was also required when positioning the floragraphs on the balloons. The three portraits linked to riders were placed so the donor and recipient could be visible in a single photo. At the request of Bill Lofthouse, the floragraph of his late wife Gretchen, a cornea donor, was placed in a tight spot between two balloons where it could be seen only with deliberation. The other floragraphs were placed in positions that would be visible to the honorees' families seated in the stands.

We had long since decided to move our reserved seating across the street and three blocks east to 300 East Colorado, where the view of our towering float would not be obstructed by trees. The move also enabled us to expand our seating block to four hundred seats to accommodate the influx of floragraph families.

The surge of guests led us to expand Rose Placement to a full seven hours, as well as allowing us to split our December 30 morning decorating shift into two four-hour blocks to double the number of volunteers. The Welcome Reception was modified as well, with a video feed doing our best to unify the experience for attendees split into adjoining Sheraton ballrooms.

Continuing our tradition of enlisting the emcee from the prior year's rider contingent, Dan Sandoval brought his trademark humility and sincerity to the task. The event kicked off in style with the award-winning Powerhouse show choir from Burbank John

Burroughs High School performing an *acapella* medley of our songs from the first four years. Remarks by float participants and the traditional appearance by the Rose Queen and Royal Court preceded Powerhouse's rendition of "Breaking Free."

Following the presentation of the Gary P. Foxen Inspiration Award to Tenaya Wallace—Karen Libs had been honored the previous year—I announced plans by NBC's *TODAY* show to have Al Roker report the weather live from Rosemont Pavilion the next morning. To add visual interest, they requested two dozen Donate Life volunteers to stand in as float decorators. It was no small ask: we would have to arrive at the very cold barn by four o'clock in the morning, a half-hour before the first cut-in.

Our guests leapt at the opportunity, with those from the Eastern and Central time zones eager to make use of their non-acclimated sleep schedule. Despite the early call time, our guests were thrilled to be part of such a high-profile media opportunity and took in stride the long delays between live stand-ups. Alas, none of them got the opportunity to meet the painfully shy Roker, who hardly noticed the people around him as he waited for his cue. Once it came, he turned on the charm, adding to the illusion that the brightly lit but mostly empty barn was buzzing with activity.

Later that day, judging took on a whole new flavor with the emergence of our float onto the apron—the first time we had seen a Donate Life float in the natural light prior to the parade. The bright colors and vivid blooms exploded in the sunlight as floragraph families circled the towering structure to photograph their loved ones. As judging got underway, the two-hundred-plus guests ringing "Life Takes Flight" dwarfed the audience for any other float by a factor of at least five.

The *TODAY* segments were the first of an astounding forty stories that aired and were published on New Year's Day, completing a three-day run of eighty that took us well beyond the prior year's total. The wave continued into New Year's Day, when our position in the "first third" of the parade line-up allowed KTLA to schedule a 7:20 a.m. live interview alongside our float. Slated to be interviewed with me was nineteen-year-old Indra Michaca, who two years prior had suffered sudden liver failure. Within a week she awoke from a coma with a transplant, fortunate that liver allocation favored patients most urgently in need.

As usual, I encouraged our participants to get some breakfast at the Sheraton restaurant while our float contingent gathered for the 5:30 a.m. departure. We were joined by *Orange County Register* reporter Keith Sharon, who was trailing St. Joseph Hospital rider Ozzie Herrera for the day to follow up the paper's Thanksgiving story. It was a bittersweet day for Ozzie, as his sixteen-year-old daughter's battle with leukemia relegated her to watching from her bed at the Children's Hospital of Orange County. Ozzie planned to blow her a kiss in front of the cameras to bridge the distance.

After the coach dropped us off on California Boulevard, a quarter-mile walk north on Orange Grove led us to "Life Takes Flight," illuminated in the pre-dawn darkness by forty-foot kleig lights, which lined the street as far as the eye could see.

Shortly before 6:30 a.m., Laurie returned from the Tournament House, where officials publicly announced the award winners to the media. She delivered the eagerly anticipated news that we had received the Judges' Special Trophy for most spectacular in showmanship and dramatic impact. After our collective jubilation subsided, one of the walkers approached me and asked, "Are we going to have something to eat?" I came to a full stop.

"You didn't eat at the Sheraton?" I replied. Several walkers shook their heads while others leaned in. I scanned their faces; blank looks and more head shaking said it all.

A wave of anxiety and visions of disaster swept through my mind. *Nine walkers on empty with five miles ahead of them. How long will they last? By mile four, will tether lines be dragging on the street, abandoned by their handlers?* The implications were too terrible to complicate. *It's 6:35 a.m. We're live on KTLA in forty-five minutes.* There was only one option. With a promise to my charges—"I'll be right back!"—I took off.

Weighted down by thirty-five cloisonné Rose Parade pins adorning my blue jacket, I headed east on Del Mar, running past marching bands patiently awaiting their cues to fold into the procession. After five hundred meters, I veered south onto Pasadena Avenue and repeated the distance to my destination: Vons supermarket.

I took a cart and made four passes through the aisles, grabbing whatever could be eaten quickly and without utensils: bagels, donuts, hard-boiled eggs, granola bars, bottled water. I counted the seconds as two customers preceded me at the register. Receipt in hand, I headed out the door and took off—with the cart.

The first four hundred yards along California Boulevard were uneventful, but once I turned north onto Orange Grove, I found myself in the thick of traffic. Migrating hordes were compressed into narrow lanes between the floats and the curb. A steady stream of warnings—"Excuse me! Coming through!"—and an imposingly full shopping cart cleared the way for the final quarter-mile. Upon my arrival, a cheerful greeting quickly transitioned to claims on the bounty.

Fifteen minutes later I was live on KTLA, with a radiant Indra Michaca joining me in a lavender knit hat and a matching scarf that partly obscured a full-front embroidery of Eeyore on her purple pullover. If the classic character had opined about the morning's drama, he likely would have taken it in stride, remarking, "We haven't had an earthquake lately."

The food emergency reminded me of an interaction I had several years before with Ken Moritsugu when he was invited to host a OneLegacy donor remembrance ceremony at Loma Linda University. Protocol required the onstage display of three flags: the Stars and Stripes, US Department of Health and Human Services, and US Public Health Service.

"I have good news and bad news," I said upon his arrival at the venue. "The good news is that we received the flags, and they are beautiful. The bad news: we don't have flagpoles." Our attempts to secure them at the last minute had been rebuffed by the skeletal Saturday staff at the Seventh Day Adventist institution. Ken paused to consider his words carefully, then replied, "You get what you plan for."

Our close call was a classic demonstration of his axiom. By the time we completed the KTLA interview, I had resolved to add breakfast at Vons as a pit stop en route to the formation area. Mike and Mimi stopped by to celebrate with us while our participants fueled up for the five-mile journey ahead.

As the riders boarded, their tone was set by Isabel Stenzel Byrnes (Redwood City, CA), who with her twin sister, Anabel, had written a book, *The Power of Two: A Twin Triumph over Cystic Fibrosis,* documenting their lives before and after receiving lung transplants. The spirit that led Isabel to run relays, climb mountains, and hike the Grand Canyon lifted everyone as she contagiously exclaimed, "I am so excited!"

Toward the rear, our walkers took their positions and grasped the gold, strawflower-covered ropes leading up to the portraits of their loved ones. Arthur Stone, whose titanium-blue prosthetic leg made such a memorable impression, spoke for all the walkers when he remarked that the experience "was like walking with my son again."

2008 DONATE LIFE ROSE PARADE FLOAT

ROSE PARADE THEME: Passport to the World's Celebrations	
FLOAT THEME: Life Takes Flight	
FLOAT AWARD: Judge's Special Trophy	
RIDERS AND WALKERS: 33	
FLORAGRAPH HONOREES: 40	
STATES REPRESENTED: 26	
PARTICIPATING ORGANIZATIONS: 75	
DEDICATED ROSES: 1,222	
DONATE LIFE GRANDSTAND SEATS: 396	
MEDIA STORIES: 335	
ORGAN DONATION CONVERSION RATE, 2007: 67.1 percent[8]	
DESIGNATED DONORS, US: 69,368,476[6]	

28

IN THE STARS

What an overwhelming feeling, seeing the float, seeing the faces of others who have journeyed with us—a journey of heartbreak and life.

—RECIPIENT FAMILY, 2008

"LIFE TAKES FLIGHT" was a metaphor not only for our cause, but the Donate Life Rose Parade Float campaign itself. Floragraphs propelled a 57 percent increase in media stories nationwide. In addition to saturation coverage in the greater Los Angeles area and an article in the fourteen million-circulation *AARP Bulletin*, our partners achieved remarkable success placing stories in twenty-seven major daily newspapers.

Furthermore, in its second full year, the Family Circle program cemented its role as a way for individuals (729 dedications) and organizations (522 dedications from thirty entities) to participate from afar, with representation from all fifty states, the District of Columbia, twenty-one countries and all seven continents.

These two elements—dedicated roses and now floragraphs—had dramatically expanded the reach of our campaign, but they were costly to execute. Volunteer-related expenses increased 40 percent, while costs related to promoting and coordinating the Family Circle program almost tripled to nearly $60,000. Ensuring a quality experience for ever more guests also contributed to a $15,000 operating deficit that was generously subsidized by OneLegacy.

After six years of constant invention and evolution, I felt optimistic that the coming year would bring us into the black. Except for the prospect of expanding our opening reception into a full-fledged gala, the structure and elements of our 2009 Rose Parade campaign were projected to remain largely constant. The committee met in early February to lay the groundwork for the year ahead, with three central questions focusing discussion on our greatest stress points.

First, how could we increase partner contributions and maximize value without giving the store away? Achieving a balanced budget was the top priority, beginning with reining in unnecessary expenses. However, travel and lodging for core operations staff as well as guest transportation were expected to grow. On the revenue side, we were confident that our rider sponsors would accept a 20 percent increase to $6,000. Floragraphs had proven their value, but with less than a quarter of OPOs participating, any increase in sponsorship fees would need to be carefully vetted.

Second, how would we deliver a quality experience to all guests as the number of visitors continued to increase? We only had so much capacity to accommodate our guests' desire to touch the float. Instituting four-hour decorating shifts relieved some pressure, but our growing numbers demanded a broader solution. We saw the opportunity to position judging as an alternative to decorating, though doing so would require Phoenix Decorating's approval and an ironclad crowd-control plan for the all-important day.

Third, how would we meet the staffing and operational demands of the campaign without burning out? Weeks prior, I needed a

Christmas Day visit to the ER and a steroid shot in the neck to get through the New Year. Our Rosemont, guest services, and special events teams had gone above and beyond for years. We resolved to lessen our reliance on OneLegacy staff during the critical last week of December.

We embarked on our sixth campaign with clarity of purpose and operational priorities. If only our creative vision had been so clear. Thanks to unusually early guidance, for the last six months we had been ruminating on how to work with a parade theme centered around "entertainment." As the leader of the national Donate Life Hollywood initiative, Tenaya was at the forefront of efforts to engage the entertainment industry into more accurately depicting donation and transplantation in scripted films and television. She saw the potential to involve celebrities with a personal connection to our cause. This possibility inspired me to suggest "Stars" as a direction, with Dave's pre-existing sketch of a theater offering a jumping-off point for creative exploration.

Throughout the fall, Gary championed the idea of expanding our contingent to include transplant surgeons, who were very much "stars" in our field. After careful consideration, we decided to uphold our tradition of limiting float participants to donor families, living donors, and recipients. However, the idea of spotlighting professionals spawned the notion of acknowledging transplant pioneers with stars modelled after the Hollywood Walk of Fame.

Entering the New Year with only the vague concept of "stars" as a creative direction, Dave presented variations on theater concepts. One featured visually arresting flourishes invoking classic Broadway: art deco styling, balcony seats, and floragraphs in the form of headshots. But the design was overly complex and potential themes did not work, with "You Can Be a Star" overly trite and "Theater of Life" simply puzzling.

For the next round, I suggested revisiting the abstract design Dave prepared during our first year, but with stars as the building blocks. It was a risky move, however, as sketches would be judged on how effectively they communicated a message that had already elicited broad committee support: *Donors and recipients of organs, eyes, tissue, and blood are true "Stars of Life."*

Given the subjectivity involved, for the next round of development, it made sense to apply Supreme Court Justice Potter Stewart's threshold test for obscenity in *Jacobellis v. Ohio*: "I know it when I see it." Chris Lofthouse expressed concern about moving forward with such an unmoored concept, as after fourteen sketches we were still a long way off from a final rendering. I assured him that there was promise in the energy and beauty of the stars floating above the deck, if only they could be arranged in such a way as to capture the essence of "Stars of Life."

In mid-March, Bill invited me to the Rose Palace, where sketches reflecting two weeks of intense development lay scattered across the floor of his upstairs office. It was clear that Bill had immersed himself in the process, and not just to make a client happy or keep things moving along. In the twilight of his career, Bill saw the potential to create something truly pioneering: the first abstract design in the 120-year history of the Rose Parade. There it was, in Sketch 24: a shower of five-pointed stars, sweeping from front to back in arched bands before sharply ascending to an over-height, comet-like finish.

My hopes were dashed, however, when two color studies—color stars on white flowers and white stars on color flowers—received lukewarm grades from the committee, with the infrastructure drawing comparisons to snakes, lizards, and a cornucopia. I assured the committee that "a 2D rendering just doesn't do it justice" and promised a refined sketch "from a slightly lower vantage point to better capture its dynamic features."

As Dave went back to the drawing board, we received reports that the floragraphs from "Life Takes Flight" were starting to arrive at their final destinations. As the balloons were being dismantled, Phoenix Decorating recovered and removed the metal backing from all forty portraits so they could be returned to the honorees' families in a meaningful way. Thanks to the Tournament-approved polyurethane treatment prior to mounting, the portraits stayed in remarkably good condition even after extensive handling.

One of the special reunions of floragraph and family involved the portrait of Jacob Smith. During a first-time meeting between his mother Cindy and the recipient of her son's liver, the mayor of her hometown of Millington, Tennessee, presented the framed artwork to her as the *Commercial Appeal* and local ABC and NBC affiliates covered the priceless moment.

The proven ability of floragraphs to yield media coverage months into the year made them that much more appealing as a sponsorship opportunity. Glenn Abercrombie, general manager of a funeral home in San Bernardino, California, noticed how our Rose Parade participation was shifting organ donation to a life-affirming posture. He saw the potential for Dignity Memorial—the consumer brand of SCI, the nation's largest operator of funeral homes—to achieve a similar transformation by aligning with our campaign. As a bridge-builder between SCI's corporate office and their affiliates, he saw the potential to grow quickly from a pilot test to honoring multiple families each year.

By mid-April, six weeks of refinements, color studies, and two committee votes concluded what Thomas described as "one of the more painful years" of creative development. As Dave confronted the twin challenges of preparing a blueprint "with not a single straight line" and engineering a hidden support structure for the massive floral canopy, we took pride in a ground-breaking design featuring thirty-four floragraph-laden gold stars; dozens of white stars representing those touched by donation; transparent stars symbolizing people in need; and five large multicolored stars at the front reserved for dedicated roses.

I stopped by the Rose Palace before and immediately after our national meeting to see how construction was proceeding. I had never seen one of our floats at such an early stage. It was fortuitous that I did, as several issues came to the fore. On my first visit, one of the five large stars had points of at least 45 degrees, evoking Lucky Charms rather than classic five-pointed stars. After bringing the issue to Chris's attention, he assured me that all the stars would have standard 36-degree points.

Once most of the stars were mounted, the number designated for floragraphs stood at twenty-six—well short of the thirty-two and thirty-four that had been confirmed and announced, respectively. We solved the problem by extending the floragraphs onto and up the tail. Seeing the float at the skeletal stage made the ingenious support structure easy to discern, revealing that the entire weight of the canopy would be held up by only seven points of contact: four in the front, two in the back, and a beam extending from the back into the interior. It also resuscitated an idea that had been germinating for months.

In early April, Stephanie Schmitz reintroduced the notion of applying names to some of the stars. While our committee readily embraced the idea of a "Walk of Fame," we didn't want to interfere with the integrity of the design. The early construction phase revealed an ideal location: along the interior beam, where their integration into the support infrastructure would mirror the roles performed by our honorees in their service to the cause. While we hoped to closely emulate the iconic stars lining the sidewalks of Hollywood, the pink terrazzo with brass letters and border would be a challenge to replicate with organic materials.

Soon thereafter we formally announced our intent to "honor fourteen luminaries in the field of donation and transplantation" on the 2009 Donate Life Rose Parade Float. The nominating criteria drafted by Rivian were straightforward: "A positive, lasting impact on organ, eye, and tissue donation and transplantation through contributions to medicine, the community, or public policy."

Alas, one of the individuals who would surely be honored would not live to see his star.

29

WALK OF FAME

Our purpose in life is to help one another and leave this world a little kinder, gentler, and more joyful. I can only hope to be half as successful with this as Amber was in the short time she was with us.

—**ROSE DEDICATION** from Indiana, 2008

AS "STARS OF LIFE" was taking shape as both a sculpture and a campaign, we received the wrenching news that Bill Lofthouse had died. His impact on us over the years was profound as he shepherded our application, offered parade theme guidance, facilitated our relationship with Kodak, and welcomed our ever-growing presence at the decorating places. His obituary stated that Bill was "widely regarded as the 'Granddaddy of Rose Parade float builders.'" To us, he was family.

Days later, the pall was lifted by an email distributed through Phil's List. Ray Gabel, my colleague at Midwest Transplant Network and a heart recipient in his own right, was on a quest. "Does anyone know what happened to this girl?" Below the message were pre- and post-transplant photos of an infant girl, whom I immediately recognized. It was Lily, who remained a staple of OneLegacy's community and professional presentations. Knowing her story was influencing people halfway across the country warmed my heart.

Two hours later, Stephanie Lochmiller of Nebraska Organ Recovery responded with the news that Milton and Janet Bemis, the parents of Lily's donor Matthew, were longtime volunteers in their state. There was more: "In three weeks, they are traveling to New York for her wedding." *Lily is getting married!* The question healthcare professionals and the public had been asking for years—*How is Lily doing?*—had finally been answered. I immediately made a promise to myself: "She will ride this year."

By mid-July, all the rider sponsors had selected and notified their honorees, save one: Loma Linda University Medical Center, which over the years had been represented by two heart recipients, a kidney recipient, a liver recipient, and the daughter of a donor to one of their liver patients. After spotlighting their transplant programs for four years, I thought they would perhaps consider acknowledging the work of their ER and ICU staff on the donation side by sponsoring a floragraph instead of a rider. My contact at Loma Linda's Transplantation Institute, Julie Humeston, loved the idea, creating an opportunity to honor a donor family—and opening a rider position for Lily.

With OneLegacy's commitment to sponsor Lily's ridership, I was utterly delighted to extend the invitation to her. After briefly introducing myself on the phone, my excitement got the best of me.

"Do you have any idea how many people know who you are?" I asked.

"No," she replied, "but I'm starting to feel like Harry Potter." Indeed, to our community her story was magical.

Lily's transplant center, UCLA Health, had long since committed to sponsor a floragraph. Upon informing them of Lily's participation, they readily accepted the opportunity to honor her donor. Once we brought the Bemis family into the picture, we finally learned Lily's complete story.

Lily Mandel was diagnosed with hemangioendothelioma, an extremely rare tumor, in November 1983 when she was only six months old. At the time, there were only thirteen cases of the disease published worldwide. Nothing stopped the growth of the benign tumors in her liver; as they grew, they took up the space needed by her other organs. Just one spoonful of food would take up too much room for her lungs to expand. She was slowly starving to death, and each breath became more labored.

When she stopped breathing on her own, she was put on a respirator. Lily was too sick to be accepted into the transplant program, but with nothing to lose, UCLA decided to attempt a rare infant liver transplant. Shortly thereafter, the parents of Matthew Bemis donated their son's organs and tissue after he drowned in a Nebraska lake. Lily's transplant during the Los Angeles Olympic Games and dramatic recovery thereafter made her a nationally recognized case study.

Lily met her donor family at ages two and five, but she was too young at the time to remember. Her fiancé was with her when she met the Bemises for the first time in memory in 2004.

"I was so incredibly nervous to meet the parents of the child whose liver had been keeping me alive all these years," she recalled. "As soon as Mr. Bemis's arms enveloped me, I knew everything was just the way it was supposed to be."

When Lily and her husband Brian Allen married on August 8—the twenty-fourth anniversary of her life-saving transplant—Milton and Janet participated as family members. They attended the rehearsal dinner, sat in front during the ceremony, and stood in the receiving line.

As it turned out, Lily was not the last rider to come aboard. In mid-July, Chris Lofthouse made a personal appeal for us to accommodate a rider from San Antonio-based nonprofit Transplants for Children. His request—which included a floragraph as well—coincided with AATB's expressed interest in elevating their participation to our top-tier Benefactor level, including sponsorship of a rider, floragraph, and our gala.

AATB valued our campaign's success at placing media stories about tissue donors, whose contributions to more than one million bone, skin, and other tissue transplants per year (compared to twenty-eight thousand organ transplants) warranted greater public attention. Nominations from AATB member organizations resulted in Eric Miller riding in memory of his sixteen-month-old son, Micah, a donor of heart valves. Five years earlier, Eric had been carrying Micah on a back-mounted carrier when a van struck them, turning a quiet neighborhood walk into sudden tragedy.

AATB and Astellas performed a valuable service by offering float participation opportunities to organizations that lacked the funding to sponsor on their own, but they created the potential for geographic overlap. The family of Micah Miller lived only three hours from the LifeCenter Northwest-sponsored family of BJ Miller, with their shared surnames further compounding matters when it came to pitching media in their native Washington State.

Likewise, the Denver market was complicated by Astellas's selection of kidney recipient Mandy Trolinger, who lived only ten miles from Donor Alliance float rider and donor mother Melody Connett. Although the two participants were distinguished by their experiences, we offered a floragraph to Donor Alliance to further differentiate them. With the likelihood that Dignity Memorial would extend their participation to multiple markets, mitigating the potential for conflicts emerged as a priority for our next annual planning meeting.

In the Los Angeles area, we had grown accustomed to combining multiple participants to craft a breakthrough story. At the August 2006 press conference announcing the partnership between the California Department of Motor Vehicles and Donate Life California, DMV employee Hooshang Torabi shared about his wife's struggle with kidney disease and their daughter's donation of a kidney to her once she turned eighteen. Also speaking was Chris Gonzalez, who spoke of her husband Gaston's two-year wait for a kidney transplant and its impact on his DMV career. After the press conference, Hooshang approached Chris and said, "I'll give your husband a kidney." One year later, he did just that.

The cross-cultural living donor transplant between an Iranian-born Muslim donor and Cuban-born Catholic recipient powerfully supported our commitment to present an appropriately diverse rider contingent each year. Floragraphs, however, presented new challenges in this regard, as OPOs from more homogeneous markets leaned toward selecting younger, Caucasian donors whose parents actively volunteered for their organizations. The committee offered two of our three remaining portraits to non-participating OPOs in Oklahoma and Hawaii under the conditions they honor non-white donors over fifty years old.

The committee directed the final floragraph to honor the inspiration for Wisconsin's Kelly Nachreiner Bill, the nation's first bill to require all driver education programs include instruction on organ donation. The bill was signed by three-term Wisconsin governor Tommy G. Thompson, whose passion for organ donation led to the emergence of the Organ Donation Breakthrough Collaborative, Workplace Partnership for Life, and National Donate Life Month during his tenure as Secretary of the US Department of Health and Human Services from 2001 to 2005.

Secretary Thompson was among sixty-five individuals nominated for our Walk of Fame. After narrowing the list to twenty-seven finalists, the committee selected Gary Foxen and the late Bill Lofthouse for their seminal contributions to the Donate Life Rose Parade Float campaign. The committee named me as an honoree as well. I accepted the gesture reluctantly, since I felt my contributions to the field did not compare to the truly pioneering achievements of the luminaries selected to round out the cluster of fourteen stars:

- Clive O. Callender, MD, FACS, a senior African American transplant surgeon, founder of the National Minority Organ/Tissue Transplant Education Program (MOTTEP), and expert on the relationship between minorities and organ and tissue donation and transplantation.

- Reg Green, founder of the Nicholas Green Foundation, author and global ambassador for donation who, with his wife, Maggie, is internationally recognized as the "first family of donation" after the death of their young son Nicholas in Italy in 1994.

- Richard J. Kagan, MD, FACS, a world-renowned burn care surgeon and prominent proponent of using human allogeneic skin grafts as the gold standard for burn care.

- Robert and Rafael Mendez, MD, FACS, kidney transplant surgeons and founders of OneLegacy and the Mendez National Institute of Transplantation.

- Kenneth Moritsugu, MD, PhD, donor father and husband, former acting surgeon general of the United

States, and one of the nation's most respected ambassadors of donation and transplantation.

- Joseph E. Murray, MD (1919–2012), recipient of the 1990 Nobel Prize in medicine who conducted the world's first kidney transplant, allograft transplant, and transplant of a kidney from a deceased donor.

- Barbara Schulman, RN, CPTC, co-founder and first president of the North American Transplant Coordinators Organization (now NATCO).

- Thomas E. Starzl, MD, PhD (1926-2017), groundbreaking surgeon who performed the world's first successful liver transplant in 1967 and won the 2004 National Medal of Science for his innovation in transplantation medicine.

- Tommy G. Thompson, former Governor of Wisconsin and former Secretary of the US Department of Health and Human Services.

- Jesse White, Illinois Secretary of State, whose Illinois Organ/ Tissue Donor Registry—the nation's first computerized database allowing individuals to document their donor designations—was a model for the nation.

- James S. Wolf, MD (1935-2007), pioneering transplant surgeon whose vision of the value and need for public education and collaboration among organ, eye, and tissue recovery organizations led to the founding of the Coalition on Donation (now Donate Life America).

Memorably, I approached Thomas Starzl at the 2008 US Transplant Games in Pittsburgh to inform him of the likelihood that he would be honored on our float in the Rose Parade. He smiled and said simply, "Fantastic."

30

A FATHER'S ANGUISH
... AND HOPE

Hi, just want all to know I am waiting for a new heart
with the love and support of others. I hope God gives me
more time to be with my children and family!

—**ROSE DEDICATION** from Kentucky, 2012

THE SELECTION OF OUR Walk of Fame honorees
ushered our transition to full implementation mode. Stephanie
Schmitz moved our volunteer signups to RegOnline, which promised
to save hours of time, albeit at a cost of $4 per registration. Each
decorating group lead was given their own password, giving them
complete control over their allocated slots. The system automatically
tracked numbers, created a waiting list, and emailed confirmations
as standbys were elevated to active. The Family Circle committee
also invested in technology, developing a back-end database with
one-click email confirmation and automated posting to the float
website.

Our optimism was tainted, however, by circulation of an updated budget showing a shortfall of more than $15,000 despite a 13 percent increase in sponsorship revenue. Upgrading from a reception to a full-scale gala dinner was proving to be a decidedly expensive proposition. In addition, the Family Circle continued to carry considerable overhead amid doubts about growth, resurrecting questions regarding the program's status as a quasi-independent entity.

We had hopes that float merchandise could evolve into a fundraising engine, and to that end I applied some energy to formalizing a program with Health Promotions Now. To date we had sold only one commemorative item: a lapel pin supplied by the Tournament's exclusive pin licensee, Milestone Products. For the past five years, their artists graciously allowed input into the pin design, with results that were acceptable for a pin, but nothing larger.

Fueled by my improved skill with Adobe Illustrator and lifelong fascination with type and logos, I took ownership of the pin design with the goal of creating a multi-purpose "Stars of Life" mark that could be used for an expanded line of merchandise as well as print and digital applications.

The inspiration for the pin design—a gold star and four white stars trailed by technicolor streaks—was unmistakable as I joined Mike, Mimi, and Phoenix floral director Lyn Lofthouse at Rosemont Pavilion to review call-outs. Normally clients were not afforded such a behind-the-scenes look at the creative process, but Mike and Mimi saw it as an educational opportunity. As we reviewed each of the elements, they pointed out specific materials or structural nuances that might impact volunteers or the decorating game plan.

The sheer number of blooms called out for the canopy made it virtually a second deck, practically doubling the number of flowers that would need to be placed and likely pushing completion right up to judging. As for dry decorating, the stars were so numerous that our volunteers would be kept busy applying rice powder, finely blended everlasting, and yellow strawflower to cover their considerable surface area.

The confluence of operational intensity and the sheer number of participants limited our editing capacity, resulting in regrettably abbreviated web pages for our floragraph honorees. It was preferable to have sixty-word capsules and three-to-five hundred-word narratives for each of them just as we had for our float riders, but with limited time we were relegated to posting one-to-two hundred-word passages for each floragraph.

Two of our 2009 floragraph honorees made national headlines. On February 22, 2008, Senior Corporal Victor Lozada, 49, died in a motorcycle accident while on duty protecting presidential candidate Senator Hillary Clinton during a campaign stop in Dallas. His wife Theresa and their children discussed donation and decided that it was the right thing to do. "We saw it as a way for him to live on, and we wanted to give someone else a second chance," she said. Theresa and Victor, who first met during their elementary school years, would be reunited during her ride aboard "Stars of Life" on New Year's Day.

Jason Ray was enjoying life as a twenty-one-year-old honor student and basketball team mascot at the University of North Carolina at Chapel Hill when on March 23, 2007, a car struck him while he was walking along the shoulder of a busy highway. He was committed to helping others, having registered as a donor with his first driver's license application, and made missionary trips to Haiti and Honduras. News of his death was featured in news reports nationwide. After ESPN aired a special show about him, donor registrations increased markedly across the country.

One honoree, Quentin Dachis, left an especially deep impression on me. It could have been for any number of reasons: his age—only sixteen months—or the tragic circumstances of his death due to drowning while his Minnesota family was vacationing in Palm Springs during Christmas 2003, or his stunning photo, taken by a professional as he was playing on a hammock.

But what seared into my heart was a journal penned by Quentin's father, Louis, as the tragedy unfolded, offering a window into the emotional whirlwind felt by families facing the suddenness and blurring speed of events that often precede opportunities to donate:

12/24/03, 3:00 a.m.: *I just woke from a happy dream to the sounds of one of the life support alarms you are hooked up to. You are now no more than a breath and a heartbeat. Your body is perfect—lying there like nothing is wrong. But I'm hopeful that no matter how comforting it is to know you may hear us, that you left two days ago when you fell in the pool.*

I woke that day to some commotion outside and not thinking much of it, I slowly got out of bed. As the screams came inside, I could tell something was very wrong and I ran to see you being carried into the living room. Your arms were outstretched—you were blue and lifeless. Your eyes were bloodshot. I did CPR and mouth to mouth to the best of my ability. Paramedics were there in probably five minutes, and it looked like they were doing the same thing as me. It wasn't working for them either.

They took you via helicopter to Loma Linda Children's Hospital and stabilized you. I knew right away this was not going to be okay, and tonight the neurologist confirmed it. You are not going to pull through.

Now I see you there with Cookie Monster lying on your chest and I just want you to go. To be at peace. But we are waiting until Friday. I've ordered a DNR and we are meeting with the organ donation people tomorrow. Hopefully, we can look past the horror to allow you to help some other kids.

12/24/03, 8:00 a.m.: *We just came back from breakfast and they gave you another bath—I wish I could have done this. The organ donation people come in an hour—I'm not sure if your mom will be able to do this. I need to detach a bit and focus on the kids you would help. Lots of questions.*

12/24/03, 3:30 p.m.: *It's coming to an end now. Morgan is on her way and you are breathing only on the respirator. Everyone has said goodbye and told you how much we love you. I hope this is quick.*

12/24/03, 8:45 p.m.: *We are now just waiting for you to be pronounced brain dead. I never thought I'd say this, but you need to stop breathing, Q. You need to let go and drift off. It's not even you, I know. Your body just has to stop doing this.*

There are going to be so many hard times without you. You gave us such incredible joy.

12/24/03, 9:45 p.m.: *You are riding the vent and I lifted you and put you on a heating pad. If you continue like this for thirty minutes, the doctor will come in and do the first of the final exams to pronounce you brain dead.*

12/25/03, 3:25 a.m.: *Your eyelid is cracked open and you are breathing above the vent a little. Go to sleep, Quentin. Everyone* *is at peace and you need to help some sick kids now.*

12/25/03, 2:40 p.m.: *They brought you back from the CT scan and we are waiting for the results. They put you back in your bed with your blankets folded nicely over you and Cookie by your head. Waiting for the word.*

12/25/03, 3:53 p.m.: *Still waiting—everyone is in the room— it's silent. I brushed your hair and cleaned out your boogies.*

12/25/03, 5:00 p.m.: *They declared you brain dead a half hour ago.*

12/26/03, 1:45 a.m.: *We were awoken a few minutes ago with the call. They are almost ready to take you now. Your mamma is holding you in the chair in her arms. One last time to say goodbye. We met with the organ donation people last night, and out of all this horror the fact that some families got Christmas Day calls gives me some strange sort of happiness ... peace ... I'm not sure what it is ... it's good.*

I don't think there is anything else to say. I'm out of words, out of tears, and thankfully, out of time for this part. We all understand there will be many hard days in the future, but we are relying on the rich memories that you leave us with and the good you have done for those kids in your death to keep us going in life. While your time was short, the time you had was crammed with love and experience. You touched so many lives and you touched us so profoundly. You were and will always remain a part of our core.

We love you with all our hearts.
Be at peace, bucko.

You have done so much good with your life.

12/26/03, 3:20 a.m.: *We left you just now with the organ donation people. As we left the hospital, a chopper was landing on the roof as it did with you. It was almost poetic in a tragic sort of way. Ours was just one beat of an unending rhythm. Some with a positive outcome, some negative. Right now the Hispanic girl from the Ronald McDonald House is on an operating table and you are about to save her life. Her mother is crying tears of joy and hopefully her story will end well.*

Nearly five years after the final entry, her story was indeed going well as the two families reunited on the first day of decorating to create Quentin's portrait together.

31

STARS OF LIFE

I was an example to other patients that it is possible to
get through it, and that you must not give up.

—SERGIO GOMEZ,
kidney recipient (2009 rider)

QUENTIN'S SIX-YEAR-OLD liver recipient Maria traveled with her family from Mexico City, attracting reporters from Spanish-language outlets *Hoy Newspaper*, Mega-TV, KMEX-34 (UNI), and Univision Network. The same Saturday, floragraph honoree Ernest Goh and several Asian volunteers caught the attention of *Singtao Daily News*, Phoenix TV, Skylink TV, *Chinese Daily News*, China Press, *Taiwan Daily*, and *Cultural News*.

Media activity extended to Monday morning, when the two-hour Univision morning show aired six live interviews with Quentin and Maria's parents, float rider Sergio Gomez, and the family of BJ Miller, who had traveled from Washington to decorate his floragraph.

Special care was taken to accommodate reporters and cameras at Rosemont. High-profile portraits were decorated close to the bay doors to minimize the impact on float decorating, and Phoenix Decorating media liaison Larry Palmer ensured reporters had easy access to the facility.

Managing floragraph decorating operations was the more fundamental concern, so Esther-Marie was assigned to the role as our fourth "green jacket." She had actually earned her green jacket during the final week the previous December, but she wore it for only one day before slipping off a ladder and breaking her wrist. Her misfortune became a cautionary tale, told with humor and affection, as Mike and I oriented volunteers about safety on the decorating floor.

While Esther-Marie's relegation to ground-level work was a practical consideration, she was the perfect choice for the responsibility. Her background in microbiology and quality assurance brought a methodical approach to the specialized materials and production steps required to ensure the dozens of portraits progressed in an organized fashion.

To support the process, Dan Sandoval fabricated two seven-foot towers to house the thirty-eight floragraphs throughout the month as they progressed through preparation, decorating, touching up, edging, coating, and mounting. Enlisting volunteers with the skill and confidence to decorate floragraphs was also essential, so they were identified ahead of time.

For the float itself, Karen and Kevin onboarded experienced volunteers quickly to work on the stars, which were proving to be a serious challenge despite 80 percent of the float being floral. Their positioning along the outside of the canopy made them very hard to reach, gravity played havoc with the various angles, and with each having a front, back, and edges, the surface area added up.

While we held down the fort in Pasadena, around the country, partners creatively extended their rider and floragraph sponsorships into the community. Donate Life Indiana planned three meet-and-greets with their float rider, heart recipient Dave Murphy, to allow donor families and transplant recipients to contribute stories or photos to a scrapbook that Dave planned to carry with him on his five-mile New Year's Day journey.

More ambitiously, Melody Connett wanted to decorate her daughter Jill's floragraph but was unable to travel to Pasadena prior to Christmas. Donor Alliance communications director Jenn Moe asked if Melody could apply the finishing touches in the presence of media—in Colorado.

Weighing our options, it was worth a test; if the portrait was damaged during shipment, we would still have time to replace it. Studying Jill's thirteen-inch round canvas—designed to fit the center of a star—we zeroed in on the eyebrows. They required only one kind of material, and if decorated upside-down her face would be in full view of the audience and cameras throughout the process.

After the first-stage of decorating was completed on Saturday, we allowed a day for the canvas to dry. On Monday, we packed the bubble-wrapped canvas, a small cup of coffee grounds, two small paintbrushes, and a miniature bottle of Elmer's glue into a box, then trusted FedEx to do their part.

The overnight shipment arrived in time for an early-morning student assembly at the elementary school where Jill was a special education teacher. Carol, the recipient of Jill's liver, and Melody took turns applying glue and material in front of four TV news crews. Three days later, the completed floragraph arrived back in Pasadena in perfect condition. The floragraph finishing event was born.

Decorating went so smoothly that we were able to devote considerable time to brainstorming among each other and with Dave Pittman about our 2010 float design. Rose Placement also went off without a hitch as 135 families were joined by dozens of community partners, including Los Angeles Police Department Chief William Bratton and Los Angeles County Sheriff Lee Baca.

The next night, our Gala Committee welcomed more than four hundred guests to the Historic Ticket Area at Union Station in Downtown Los Angeles. The art deco landmark was a perfect match for our entertainment-inspired theme and easily accessible via the Metro Gold Line. However, with no services on site, it took considerable planning to bring in food and beverages, audio/visual, and a stage. Under Stephanie Jansky's leadership and support from Rivian, Sandra and OneLegacy's Christina Courtney, Kari Williams, and Margaret Wylie, the Stars of Life Gala was remarkable.

Our second annual New Year's Eve engagement with Al Roker and the *TODAY* show preceded the final hours of a three-day sprint to apply two decks' worth of florals. Three hours before the judges' afternoon arrival, Fox11 News sent a helicopter to capture an overhead view of the Donate Life float emerging from the barn.

The beauty and significance of our unconventional design wasn't lost on the Rose Parade broadcasters. ABC's coverage noted that Donate Life's floats are "as inspirational as they are beautiful," concluding with a lingering aerial shot from the Goodyear blimp as the commentator said, "Absolutely remarkable." NBC noted that "Stars of Life" was the "first abstract float design in the modern era," adding that Donate Life is always "such an emotional float." KTLA called it "one of the most touching floats ever" before recounting Hooshang and Gaston's living donation story.

The broadcasts also cited our second consecutive award, the prestigious Queen's Trophy for best use of roses. The shower of stars made for an extraordinary sight in the January 12 issue of *PR Week*, capping another impressive run of earned media stories outside the Los Angeles area, including fourteen focusing on our Walk of Fame honorees. Regional TV news outlets aired seventy-nine segments while print stories appeared in twenty major dailies.

While we were experiencing success on the operational and media front, Thomas led off our last two committee meetings of the year with in-depth discussions of our finances. His thoughtful analysis made it clear that six years of constant expansion and investment, combined with an accounting process that relied heavily on Excel and my fragmented attention, had left us in a vulnerable position.

While overall revenue increased about ten percent over the prior year, expenses increased by more than twice that rate—"not a good thing for an event in its sixth year," Thomas reported. Floragraphs, media resources, and ongoing increases in the float budget expanded our campaign's reach, and the Family Circle and gala dinner had fundraising potential—but all had a cost. As Thomas noted, "We need to take a close look at expenses versus the value."

From his perspective in South Dakota—removed from the day-to-day management of sponsors, participants, operations, and events—Thomas saw our strategic imperative with utter clarity. "We need to decide when we have reached our apex of what we need to do with the float, and focus on revenue and PR." Meeting that challenge required much more than our standard mid-January debriefing. Charting the campaign's future required a full-day of planning—and the first-ever face-to-face meeting of the Donate Life Rose Parade Float Committee.

2009 DONATE LIFE ROSE PARADE FLOAT

ROSE PARADE THEME: Hats Off to Entertainment

FLOAT THEME: Stars of Life

FLOAT AWARD: Queen's Trophy

RIDERS: 26

FLORAGRAPH HONOREES: 38

STATES REPRESENTED: 33

PARTICIPATING ORGANIZATIONS: 68

DEDICATED ROSES: 1,318

DONATE LIFE GRANDSTAND SEATS: 427

FLORAGRAPH FINISHING EVENTS: 1

MEDIA STORIES: 288

ORGAN DONATION CONVERSION RATE, 2003: 66.4 percent[8]

DESIGNATED DONORS, US: 79,742,797[6]

32

RESET

This Saturday the Sears repair man was at our house and asked me what I do. Then said he saw the float with all those pictures and told his wife he would want to be a donor if anything happened to him! Neat, huh?

—TRANSPLANT PROFESSIONAL, 2009

FOR THE PAST SIX YEARS, all top-level committee meetings had been conducted via conference call. Most of the debrief, creative brainstorming, and standing monthly meetings fit within the scheduled hour—adequate for creative development, operational updates, and adjustments, but not the deep assessment primed by Thomas's in-depth analysis.

On February 20, all but four committee members joined in person or by phone. Of our twenty-four committee members, eighteen had served for four years or longer, ensuring a high level of informed discussion and participation. To kick off the meeting, Thomas posed two overarching questions: "Going forward, we need to ask: what are we, and what do we want to become? What is the value?"

Tom Mone offered his perspective as CEO of the float's primary benefactor. "OneLegacy has always recognized that the float plays first and foremost in Southern California, so we are quite content with our investment to this time," he affirmed. "Many peer OPOs have donor memorials such as gardens and parks. Ultimately, the float is our rolling donor memorial, and our job is to bring it to the public. It has also served as an element to define OneLegacy as the hub of transplantation activity in our area, where we have thirteen transplant centers and two hundred hospitals. The float brings everyone together."

While Tom's support had been unwavering since day one, his reaffirmation that OneLegacy's board saw the float as a valuable investment was reassuring. Getting our finances in line would go a long way toward maintaining their crucial support

On the revenue side, the committee agreed to increase floragraph sponsorship by $500. The lowest-hanging fruit on the expense side involved the gala, which would benefit from its relocation to the new Pasadena Convention Center Ballroom. We also had to factor in the addition of a Floragraph Family Orientation and the alternating-year $25,000 increase in our Phoenix Decorating contract, bringing the float's total cost to $200,000.

Rivian launched into our discussion of PR with an observation that the Internet was starting to affect media coverage. "There are staff cutbacks and fewer outlets," she noted. "If we're facing that, we need to look at blogs and other Internet channels." Hers was a keen observation, but with social media in its infancy and Internet metrics lacking actionable data, the way forward was unclear.

The Family Circle program had built a solid track record of engaging distant hospitals in our campaign, but as a whole the program was basically breaking even. Two years of heavy investment in promotion and fulfillment had yielded only a 20 percent increase in dedications, with a slight drop-off in the most recent year. Some changes were in order, but restructuring the program was more than a simple business decision.

The rose dedication program was founded with the noblest of intentions: honoring donors and allowing their families to participate from afar. Translating heartfelt expressions of love, hope, and remembrance into experiences that were both personal and tangible required extraordinary diligence and effort. Laurie's guiding and promotional role over the last three years, initially as a volunteer and then in a consulting capacity, was greatly supported by OneLegacy staff and the Golden Girls, ensuring a positive experience at every touchpoint.

With so many contributing to the Family Circle, the committee was skeptical about Laurie and Tenaya's assertion that the rose dedication program was separate from the float housing its namesake garden. They acknowledged the need to reduce expenses and rebrand the program as the "Donate Life Family Circle," both of which signaled a desire to hew closer to the campaign's core. However, a proposal to cap the program's fundraising contribution to the float at $10,000—calculated as a percentage of the float's "real estate" occupied by the roses—was denied in favor of consolidating all revenues and expenses associated with any component of the float into one financial statement.

Tom Mone underscored the overall direction going forward. "We have now moved into the 'integration' phase of the float campaign whereby all components are part of one whole," he said. Encouraged by the sense that we were all in it together, the committee agreed on a goal of two thousand rose dedications for the year—an increase of more than 50 percent.

Two years under Mike and Mimi's leadership had made for a deep and formidable decorating committee anchored by assistant crew chiefs Karen and Esther-Marie, supervisors Kevin, Ginny, and Dan, and donor sister Tina Vanderhorst, our "barista" in charge of basic materials, supplies, and equipment. Karen recalled the value of meeting ahead of time ("we were very prepared"), while Ginny noted our speed at getting families and volunteers up to speed on floragraphs and flowers. "With our experience," she affirmed, "there's nothing we can't handle." Their top priority going forward: cultivating talent to improve our collective skills and spread the workload.

On the volunteer front, we saw an opportunity to amplify our impact at the two-day Post-Parade float showcase. On January 2, I had ventured to Victory Park to get close-up photos of our Walk of Fame stars. Tournament volunteers posted inside the float's taped-off perimeter gave me permission to climb aboard. As I took photos, I overheard them answering questions from passersby. Responding to an inquiry about the floragraphs, one of them explained, "Those are people who received transplants."

Seeing an opportunity to train the White Suiters, I offered to answer questions for a few minutes. Soon a dozen people at a time were flocking around me, listening intently as I introduced them to our purpose, the float's symbolism, and floragraph honorees. More than a few walked away moved by the experience. Having attended many community events where people shied away from engaging with our volunteers, I thought of how meaningful it would be for our Ambassadors to serve as "Post-Parade Storytellers."

The rise of social networking spurred our Fundraising Committee to consider ways to activate our "alumni." We also launched two new committees: Special Events, consisting of leaders for our four major gatherings—float rider dinner, floragraph family brunch, the gala dinner, and post-parade reception—and a Floragraph Committee, which gave chair Kathleen Hostert a wide berth to cultivate emotional experiences and develop efficient systems just as she had through her eight-year leadership of the Donate Life Run/Walk.

Our day-long immersion accomplished what we had intended. We came away with a better understanding of who we were after six parade appearances, what years of invention, expansion and lessons learned predicted for the future, and how each of us could contribute to getting there.

Things were looking up for our 2010 Rose Parade campaign, and in more ways than one.

33

ABOVE THE REST

*After ten years of dialysis, a transplant just
wasn't to be. We miss you, Sis.*

—**ROSE DEDICATION** from California, 2009

THE SPEED WITH WHICH our seventh float design
evolved was a welcome departure from years past. Upon informing
our committee in mid-November that the 2010 Rose Parade theme
included the phrase "a cut above," black humorous suggestions of
medical procedures quickly gave way to an exploration of the phrase's
utterly relatable last word.

We began with a thesaurus-driven flurry—higher, highest,
elevate, tall, pinnacle, peak, top, superior, surmounting, overcoming, summit, lift, ascend—which led to above-and-beyond transplant breakthroughs, such as domino transplants (now referred to
as kidney chains) and increasing donation rates, which had risen to
almost 70 percent.[4]

By mid-December we had made no progress on a visual concept,
but a suggested theme, "Soaring with New Life," sparked informal
brainstorming during the final week at Rosemont. By the time I

corralled Dave Pittman for a sidebar conversation, the idea of a bird soaring "above" had evolved into a dramatic metaphor for donation and transplantation: a phoenix rising from flames. As I shared the concept with committee members on the decorating floor, discussion rapidly advanced from the idea's merit to what form the mythical creature would take. After six years of creative explorations ranging from arduous to excruciating, our concordance at such an early stage was a revelation.

A phoenix was featured prominently in *Harry Potter and the Chamber of Secrets*, but the filmmakers' depiction of Fawkes—red, yellow, and a hint of orange feathers—contrasted sharply with Dave's vision of a completely white bird emerging from a bed of brilliantly colored flames, its anatomical features distinguished by a range of textures.

By mid-January, Dave presented two sketches. The first, a reworking of a concept prepared for another client, was far too revealing of its origin as an American eagle. The second sketch, however, was right on target: a phoenix rising almost straight upward, with dozens of floragraphs embedded in a tail originating from a flame-filled deck. By our strategic planning meeting, the next round of five sketches explored variations on birds, launch trajectories, and the distribution of flames and riders.

To help us consider the various composition and color options, I invited the incoming Float Entries Committee Chair, Pam McNeely, to join us. The daughter and granddaughter of two past tournament presidents, Pam had impressed me with her media presentation at the 2007 Sponsor Summit. In addition to her background in advertising and marketing, her thirty-one-year-old stepson had received a liver transplant at age two. (As was uncommonly the case with long-term liver recipients, his organ had regenerated to the point that his body no longer recognized it as a foreign object, allowing him to cease his regimen of anti-rejection medications.) Pam's unique background was ideally suited to help us extend our run of standout, award-winning entries.

Right off the bat, Pam helped us settle the lingering issue of the bird's color. "To me, a phoenix is always white," she said. "Color moves from the flames into the bird, with a transition through different shades of white, to a bright white head." The point and pace of the color transition could be settled later.

Dave's firebird silhouettes evoked common species. A "hawk" rising straight up with wings thrust forward was overly aggressive, while a "pheasant" with short wings and an elaborate headdress seemed too soft. The third sketch—a "crow" with swept-back, dissipating wings, rising with a softer arc—was met with instant acclaim. "It's strong and invincible," said Betty McNamara of MTF. "The upturned head and puffed out breast look heroic," a colleague chimed in.

Pam shifted the discussion to enhancements. Go as high as you can afford, and camber the wings so it cheats toward TV," she recommended, knowing well the value of height and movement. Beyond that, our guidance for refinement was minimal: add flames in front to accommodate dedicated roses, and seat the riders more organically and less theater-style. We also affirmed our plan for twenty-six float riders, forty floragraphs, and no walkers.

Four weeks later, we reviewed a refined sketch presented with three color options. More than ever, I was thankful that Dave welcomed our feedback, because with the benefit of time—April had not yet arrived—we didn't hold back. I appreciated Dave advocating for his vision of a white bird, but we insisted that the white be concentrated on the head and front of the wings before transitioning quickly to increasingly yellow, orange, and red, with full saturation from the tail on down.

Tom then recognized a critical issue: our riders were seated within the flames. *Of course! How could we have not seen that before?* Not only did we need to move the riders out from the interior, but it made sense to physically protect them from the floral inferno. I suggested "a brick perimeter like a fire pit, perhaps with the incorporation of names on the bricks like the National Donor Memorial," which prompted Tom to suggest a tie-in with UNOS, whose Richmond headquarters housed the monument

We had come a long way—the bird, floragraphs, flames, and color palette were in place—but integrating the riders, wall, and rose dedication garden had major design and structural implications that would take time to resolve. Suddenly we didn't seem to have so much time after all. I teamed up with Dave, complementing his thumbnail sketches with research on the National Donor Memorial.

Dedicated in April 2003 and funded entirely by private contributions, the ten-thousand-square-foot memorial garden symbolizing "the emotional journey experienced by donor families during the donation process" inspired a new possibility: incorporating virtual replicas of the National Donor Memorial's most distinctive features:

- The Wall of Tears: At the memorial entrance, water flowing over the words, "friend, wife, son, daughter, mother, sister, husband, brother, father," symbolizes tears shed by donor families.

- The Wall of Names: The central room of the garden contains names of donors, representing the diversity of America's donors. Without them, organ transplantation would not be possible.[5]

The symbolism and aesthetics of the two elements fit our needs perfectly. A long simulated-woodgrain slatwall and inset shelves made the Wall of Names an ideal perimeter wall against which riders could be situated. The stacked stones and protruding engraved bricks denoting interpersonal relationships made the Wall of Tears a natural complement to the dedication garden. I contacted UNOS for specifications that could be applied to the sketch and, eventually, blueprints.

Within two weeks Dave provided two detailed color sketches with variations on the wall (oval versus rectangular), dedication garden (stone planters versus unstructured), and deck (extension of the wall versus floral accents). I spent the next day using Photoshop to compare various combinations of elements and colors. By the end of April, our work was complete, validating a collaborative creative process that once again led to possibilities unforeseen at the outset.

Dave's most elegant and sophisticated composition to date—a majestic phoenix, organically embedded floragraphs, dramatic flames, detailed and purposeful structures, and evenly distributed riders, all seamlessly integrated into a whole—invited a theme that was neither a call to action nor a straightforward description, but rather an elevated summation of our three-dimensional canvas. With a publication-ready rendering in hand by the end of April—a full month ahead of our usual schedule—I was eager to preview our seventh Donate Life Rose Parade Float to my OneLegacy colleagues.

My presentation at the quarterly all-staff meeting began with images of our first six float entries, the theme of the 2010 Rose Parade, our focus on "soaring above," and the rendering. But far from the *oohs* and *aahs* of past unveilings at our national meetings, scattered applause was accompanied by expressions ranging from curiosity to puzzlement to concern. For the audience of two hundred mainly clinical and operations staff, our jump from a shower of stars to a rising phoenix was simply too abrupt. In addition, they seemed to focus not on the majesty of the bird, but the violence of the flames.

Once I explained the many features of the design, approving nods assured me that our concept was sound. The point was made nonetheless: the official unveiling demanded a carefully constructed narrative leading up to the reveal, delivered via PowerPoint:

[SLIDE: Graphic of Rose Parade theme, "2010: A Cut Above the Rest"]

[SLIDE: Series of float renderings from 2004 to 2009]
Since our first year in the Rose Parade, Donate Life's float designs have evolved, becoming increasingly confident and bold. The combination of memorial and spectacle is not an easy balance to reach. As the committee searched for a design that would truly be "a cut above the rest," we focused on the ultimate symbol of death transformed into life:

[SLIDE: Bird standing on flaming twigs, the first of six images to appear]
The PHOENIX. Commonly called the "firebird," the phoenix is a mythical creature that, at the end of its life-cycle, builds a nest of twigs that it then ignites; both nest and bird burn fiercely and are reduced to ashes, from which a new, reborn phoenix arises.

[CLICK: Abstract phoenix from medieval parchment]
Egyptian and Greek mythology and cultures over the ages have embedded the phoenix as an archetypal symbol of death and rebirth,

230

[CLICK: Bird in kaleidoscope of colors]
astounding in both its beauty

[CLICK: Fire-hot phoenix rising from the surface of the sun]
and immortal power.

[CLICK: Fawkes]
The phoenix is even found in popular culture, with Harry Potter rescued by the creature's powerful wings, sharp beak, and healing tears.

[CLICK: Bird with glowing, celestial quality]
This soaring icon of death transformed into life will truly be "a cut above the rest" as on New Year's Day 2010 . . .

[NEW SLIDE: float rendering]
. . . NEW LIFE RISES.

34

FLOOD OF FLORAGRAPHS

Kate's organ donation restored a sense of order in my world
after it had been violently and abruptly turned upside down.
We may not be in control of our lives, but we can always make
meaningful choices that affirm life, love, and humanity.

—LUCY REINHART,
donor mother (2010 floragraph)

THE MYTHOLOGY of the phoenix—explained in a slideshow on our website—was hardly the only complexity introduced by our 2010 Rose Parade float entry. A month before the unveiling, I stopped by the Rose Palace to photograph the float in its earliest stages of construction. As I circled the skeleton, I noticed several poster-size pages mounted to foamboard, the likes of which I had never seen before. Gazing upon them, I felt the rush of discovering a priceless artifact: the blueprints for "New Life Rises," hand-drawn by Dave Pittman himself.

Adapting the float rendering to our pin artwork had left me deeply familiar with the nuances of our float, but seeing it in its most elemental form gave me a profound appreciation not only for the beauty of the design, but also the skill required to build it from the ground up.

Even as a line drawing with an overlaid grid of one-foot demarcations, "New Life Rises" looked mesmerizing in a side view, front view, and two top views—one for the base and the other detailing the "flame feathers" and "bird position." Another board detailed side and below views of the phoenix and its feathers. Turning back to the side view, it was apparent we had created something spectacular. But then I noticed something: the bird's tail had more—many more—than the forty floragraphs we had originally requested.

It was too early to know the exact number—the blueprint had its limitations—but we were looking at a potential doubling of floragraphs year-over-year. As Thomas put it, it was "a big leap" with massive implications. How many more floragraph sponsors would come forward? In the likelihood that we needed to offer discounted or even complimentary portraits to fill the space, how would full-paying sponsors react?

Further, each portrait would need to be supported by a web page with a full-length narrative. Skilled supervisors and volunteers would be essential for both decorating and touch-up. The prospect of dozens of floragraph finishing events loomed, adding a new layer to the decorating plan. Each honoree's family would require the degree of care and emotional support upon which we prided ourselves. Welcoming another 150 "pilgrims to Pasadena" would dramatically expand our hotel, seating, events, and transportation requirements. The ramifications were truly daunting.

At the unveiling, we kept the stresses hidden from our Donate Life America colleagues; our promise of "dozens" of floragraphs was the only outward indicator of uncertainty. In the ninety days since the first wave of sponsorship proposals were distributed, twenty-two riders and thirty-nine floragraphs had already been claimed. However, with at least another thirty-five floragraphs still available, attracting more partners was a top priority.

To spur interest, I enlisted my Memphis-based counterpart at Mid-South Transplant Foundation, Randa Lipman, to complement in the unveiling by sharing her secrets to successfully placing nineteen TV, eight radio, and six newspaper stories about her floragraph honorees, Jacob Smith and Rachel Escue, over the last two years. True to form, Randa framed her disciplined approach in the charming colloquialisms of her native Tennessee: "grab it like a dog with a bone" (pitch every outlet); "run with the bone" (engage workplace partners, volunteers and government agencies); treat it like "it's my bone" (take ownership and pitch with tenacity); and "lap up your success" (celebrate the results). Not at all lost in translation was her overarching message: at every PR touchpoint, treat floragraph sponsorship as the special opportunity it is.

During the session we also took the opportunity to highlight Donate Life Louisiana's partnership with the Louisiana Office of Motor Vehicles. The state employees' dedication of forty-three roses demonstrated how the rose ceremonies pioneered by Los Angeles, Missouri, and Ohio hospitals could be extended to the places where donor designation decisions are made and often influenced by the clerk's disposition when asking the donation question.

Efforts to grow hospital participation received a huge boost from Dr. Candy Smith's endowment of a matching grant for hospitals and transplant centers. Named in honor of the donor of her transplanted liver, the Michael Creighton Grant halved the $250 contribution required for hospitals to dedicate their first five roses. Surely the grant's genesis as a transplant recipient's expression of gratitude—and from an MD, no less—would inspire broader participation in the program, which was undergoing substantial changes as an outcome of our strategic planning meeting.

Rebranded as the Donate Life Family Circle, a new horizontal logo inspired by the now-iconic vial tags included the nomenclature "Rose Dedication Program" to clarify the evocative name. The committee approved Laurie's proposal to invest $7,500 in back-end technology that promised to improve productivity during the critical months of November and December, when more than 75 percent of dedications would come in.

Throughout the summer, Sandra worked closely with Laurie and the developer to incorporate one-click credit-card processing, online entry of both hospital and individual dedications, automated web posting, and web-based back-end access. Meanwhile, OneLegacy special events coordinator Christina Courtney stepped in to organize four local rose ceremonies as well as make the events more turnkey for out-of-state partners.

With OneLegacy staff in place to manage and administer the rose dedication program, Tenaya rolled off the committee to focus on leading the Donate Life Hollywood initiative, which had evolved into a full-time undertaking complete with a film festival and awards ceremony. Knowing I would still be able to draw upon the wisdom of my most experienced and passionate colleague was reassuring as I shifted to securing and activating sponsors.

As predicted, Dignity Memorial's successful pilot led to an expansion to four floragraphs, each a complicated undertaking in its own right. Identifying a qualifying family was a complex endeavor, as funeral homes did not have records of who organ and tissue donors. Only OPOs possessed the information—decedent's name, funeral home, donation outcome, and family dynamics—required to select an honoree whose kin would be ready to undertake such a public, emotional, and transformative experience. OPOs also had the expertise to vault the funeral home's gesture into the media. Through their symbiotic teamwork, funeral homes came to better understand the donation process, while OPOs gained a valuable community partner.

For the last two years, I had seen partnerships like these thrive as sponsoring suppliers were matched with current or prospective OPO customers. As CryoLife, LifeCell (tissue developers), Mendez National Institute of Transplantation (a testing lab), and Sallop Insurance reenlisted as floragraph sponsors, I paired them with LifeLink of Georgia, New England Organ Bank (now Donor Services), Pacific Northwest Transplant Bank (Oregon), and LifePoint (South Carolina), respectively.

The partnership between LifeCell and New England Donor Services brought a new kind of transplant story to the fore. Joseph Helfgot was a colorful professor at Boston University before launching a revolutionary motion picture market research company in Los Angeles. Unfortunately, Joseph suffered from congestive heart disease most of his adult life and died from complications shortly after receiving a long-awaited heart transplant at the age sixty on April 7, 2009. His family honored his commitment to donate with the gift of facial tissue, making possible the nation's second face transplant. Notably, the heart that had been directed to Joseph was re-transplanted to save another person's life.

AlloSource introduced a remarkable story of their own. In 2003, Manuel Salazar was working on a construction site when a crane hit a power line, sending two 115,000-volt jolts of electricity through his body. His life-threatening burns required his arms and legs to be amputated, but the twenty-nine-year-old was now thriving and able to ski, swim, drive, and own an auto body shop. A bone allograft prepared by AlloSource helped to reconstruct a shoulder, anchoring a prosthetic arm that enabled him to feed himself and brush his teeth.

Positive feedback from their members regarding our campaign's equitable presentation of tissue and organ donation led AATB to schedule a twenty-minute plenary presentation at the association's annual meeting, with the 2010 Donate Life Rose Parade Float unveiling and introduction of their sponsored participants preceded by the return of Micah Miller's floragraph to his father Eric. It was the final portrait from "Stars of Life" to be returned to the honoree's family, and among many that were presented in ceremonial fashion.

Our campaign's seminal role in raising the public profile of donor families came full-circle when I was approached by Anna Squire, who had established a robust charitable foundation in Allen, Texas, in memory of her son. Six-year-old Spencer Patton Squire's organs were transplanted after the sudden rupture of an asymptomatic stage IV brain tumor. Her 501(c)3 organization, Spencer Squire All-Star Foundation, was approved to honor Spencer with a floragraph on the condition that they sponsor another donor family the following year. With their commitment, the first "donor family foundation" came aboard.

As participant activation forms started flooding in from our sponsors, construction and art direction had advanced to the point that we determined a total of seventy-six floragraphs would adorn the tail of our rising phoenix. With a respectable total of forty-seven sponsored floragraphs, we considered appropriate ways to have the final thirty adopted. Sixteen were bonused to current Float Rider Sponsors in appreciation for their support. Another eight were allocated to the Kodak donor families, whose pioneering participation was not associated with the Donate Life float per se. We held out the final six for the committee to allocate as media opportunities arose.

In addition, we had one final rider position open. After considering a number of options, including selecting a wait-listed patient, the committee decided to add more poignancy to the participation of the rider sponsored by the Donate Life Run/Walk Committee. As a sixteen-year-old, Tyla Newbold's doctors gave her two weeks to live due to an extremely rare condition that had been ravaging her liver for more than four years. Her spirits were brightened when her favorite music group, Grammy Award-winning R&B and pop group All-4-One—mainstay performers at the Run/Walk—visited her in the hospital.

Days later, Tyla received a new liver from a local woman who was thirty-six weeks pregnant with her first child when she and her husband were involved in a tragic car accident. When the baby's heart rate became too elevated, an emergency C-section delivered the child safely. Carter James Bryant was born on August 1, 1997; his mother died the next day.

After the transplant, the Bryant family met Tyla, who gave Carter a quilt in honor of his mother. On New Year's Day 2010, Tyla and Carter—and the quilt he still slept with every night—would ride the Donate Life float underneath a floragraph portrait of Caroline Elizabeth (Ball) Bryant, the twenty-one-year-old woman who gave new life to Tyla the day after her son was born.

35

IN THE DETAILS

*My family and friends, teachers, doctors and nurses, and even
people that I didn't know, were there for me. These people made
sure that I did make it through the day and never gave up.*

—**NIKKI MCKENNA,**
kidney recipient (2010 rider)

THE VISION OF ONE HUNDRED float riders and
floragraph honorees against such a dramatic backdrop inspired me
to consider instrumental music accompaniment for the first time
since our inaugural year. The committee favored the idea, but by
our first round of balloting, we had identified only two such candidates, including my personal favorite, the largely instrumental
"Hoppípolla" ("Hopping into Puddles") by Icelandic group Sigur
Rós. The song's prominence in the trailers for the films *Slumdog Mil-
lionaire* and *Children of Men* pointed to its potential as an emotional
centerpiece.

With the instrumental choices seen as too esoteric, three pop
songs emerged from the field of contenders, with a small plurality
favoring R. Kelly's "I Believe I Can Fly." *That cannot be*, I thought. It

wasn't just my aversion to the singer's well-publicized controversies; it just didn't feel right. The drama of our rising phoenix demanded not just a song but a score, as if we were watching the climax of a movie.

Since the three pop songs had basically split the vote—with the top choice receiving the fewest first-place votes at that—I sensed an opening. I reminded the committee of our original preference for an instrumental, then offered to edit a strictly instrumental version of "Hoppípolla." Ultimately the committee assented to my impassioned lobbying effort, if perhaps only out of fatigue. I was confident that the track's soaring crescendo during judging would redeem the process—that is, if we made it through decorating with our spirits intact.

THE DRAMA OF OUR RISING PHOENIX DEMANDED NOT JUST A SONG BUT A SCORE.

Our Decorating Committee foresaw early on that "New Life Rises" would be by far our most complex assignment to date. Walking through the floral call-outs with Lyn Lofthouse, Mike and Mimi pointed out to Esther-Marie that strawflower and everlasting would be cut into fine, medium, and large pieces. New species of tropical plants entered our vocabulary, and roses were slated to be tightly packed into the bird's descending tail. As for our tribute to the National Donor Memorial, coming as close as possible to replicating the Wall of Names and Wall of Tears required a high degree of pre-production and onsite experimentation.

The Wall of Names was in the form of a 35' x 9'8" racetrack oval, with a continuous 56" tall, 86-linear-foot face featuring narrow horizontal grooves placed 11 inches apart. One of the major challenges—applying material evenly across over 250 square feet of vertical facing—was complicated by the lettering that gave the wall its moniker. Simulating engraved letters required a degree of precision that required decorating on a tabletop surface. My job was to determine the appearance, number, and choice of first names, then print them onto card stock. It fell on Karen to figure how to apply materials to the paper, adhere the finished strips to the wall, and obscure any seams that might betray the appearance of an engraved wall.

Determining the number of names that would appear along the top three rows of the wall involved identifying the replica font (Poppl-Laudatio Regular), then calculating the number of spaced-apart, six-character names that would fit into nearly 250 feet of linear space. The final list of over one hundred names included the fifty most common ones, plus a list of names that were of identifiably Hispanic/Latino, African American, Asian, Middle Eastern, and other ethnic origins in accordance with their popularity and proportion of US population. ("Baby Girl" and "Baby Boy" were added as well.)

The Wall of Tears on the front and rear of the float was a different challenge altogether. Consisting of three fused semicircular planters in the shape of a clover, each stood two feet tall with about thirty-eight linear feet of stacked stone. The simulated stones, grout, and protruding engraved stones required trial and error to determine the right mix of color and texture.

To meet the challenges of more than doubling our floragraph output as well as the structural elements, Karen and Esther-Marie deputized six supervisors to monitor the portraits and prep tables, while Kathleen enlisted a "floragraph specialist" for every two portraits so that donor families and volunteers would have adequate training, support, and supervision. Fortunately, after two years of floragraph decorating experience, we had developed enough experienced volunteers to staff thirteen specialists each of the first three weekends, and Kathleen made sure they felt empowered by attiring them in embroidered green aprons. Kathleen also tapped her substantial base of Donate Life Run/Walk committee members to bring new floragraph volunteers into our ranks.

Those historically involved with floragraphs were deeply committed to a level of quality that would please the honorees' families, but our pressure to perform was heightened by the explosion of floragraph finishing events. Encouraged by Donor Alliance's successful pilot the previous year, sponsors of thirty-nine floragraphs made plans to stage finishing events at a wide variety of locations that would be meaningful to the families: churches, schools, hospitals, funeral homes, OPO offices, and even a post office where the honoree had been employed.

In years past, families relying on volunteers to decorate their portraits typically saw their floragraphs for the first time upon their arrival in late December, by which time they had been touched up. Now that they would be unveiled in their unrefined form, often with media present, the thought of a family's first impression eliciting disappointment was terrifying. Kathleen and the specialists kept a close eye on quality, as we had precious little time to correct major issues. Rosemont closed at five o'clock sharp, Phoenix was closed on Sunday, and the portraits shipped on Monday.

The first weekend was especially daunting, as we had thirty-seven floragraphs (one less than 2009's entire output) on the docket, twenty-seven of which were destined for finishing events. For the fifteen portraits that were being decorated by family members, Kathleen and Kari Kozuki teamed up to ensure families were thoughtfully welcomed and emotionally supported throughout their visit.

Meanwhile, dozens of volunteers were put to work cutting the mountains of everlasting and strawflower needed to cover the bird and its tail, respectively. Gee Wong worked on the head of the phoenix, carefully contouring the heroic profile with thin strips of silver leaf.

The following Monday morning, Sandra and I drove to Rosemont, where the floats sat eerily silent in their bays. Trays housing dozens of canvases were nestled into four new towers constructed by Dan Sandoval. One by one we pulled the portraits destined for shipment. Within each tray was a handwritten card from the two floragraph volunteers to the honoree's family—a response to the letter Kathleen had requested from each floragraph family to inspire their decorators.

As we packaged the card, glue, brush, and material with each portrait, we studied the artistry and likenesses to the photos. We were especially moved by the portraits of Ryan Evans, Mary Morris, Jessica Ward, and Maria Yepez, which benefited from careful application and blending of skin tones. An encore trip one week later revealed the stunning portraits of Carmen Wilber, Teresa Kemp, and Teresa's daughter Taylor, each of which employed pampas grass to make their blonde hair leap off the canvas.

The floragraph of Caroline Bryant, decorated by All-4-One— Jamie Jones, Delious Kennedy, Alfred Nevarez, and Tony Borowiak— along with Kathleen's artistically talented daughter Nicole, was a marvel as well, capturing her youthful energy. (Memorably, All-4-One punctuated their day at Rosemont by performing a lunchtime concert on a stage of wood pallets.)

Then I saw the portrait of Lena Moultrie, and panic set in. It was an utter disaster. To be fair, the original image was highly challenging. Dark skin offered few contrasting shades, eyeglasses obscured her eyes, and glare from the camera flash created islands of bright white. Despite their surely best intentions, the volunteers clearly did not have the skill to pull it off.

Lena's portrait was headed to Albany, New York for a finishing event organized by Center for Donation and Transplant. The ceremony promised to be especially emotional for Lena's mother Hazelee. Not only was this the first holiday season since her eleven-year-old daughter died of a ruptured brain aneurysm, but Lena's portrait would be unveiled and finished at the hospital where she died. I needed a solution, and fast.

I called Phoenix's art director, Cynthia McMinimy, and asked if one of her staff would be able to prepare a replacement that day, which would allow it to dry overnight before shipping for first delivery on Wednesday. Without hesitation, she offered to do the work herself. Two days later, Lena's utterly beautiful floragraph—glare and all— was unveiled and completed with four newspaper reporters, three TV news crews, and a radio correspondent present.

The third weekend of decorating, we were surprised to discover that a section of the tail we had presumed to be obscured would, in fact, be visible. The development opened an additional floragraph position, which we presented to Esther-Marie to honor her identical twin sister, cornea donor Jeni Altuna Hammerstein. The acknowledgement made for a special holiday gift before we limped into the two-day Christmas break for a much-needed breather.

36

NEW LIFE RISES

Within hours, the life that we had imagined was suddenly a reality. We are able to live a normal life free of all the restraints that dialysis places on you and your loved ones.

—JUAN PEREZ,
kidney recipient (2010 rider)

BY CHRISTMAS, NEARLY 250 media stories had aired and published in thirty-five states, driven by our broadest OPO participation and geographic reach yet. Altogether, participants from thirty-eight states and the District of Columbia were associated with thirty-eight OPOs, ten more than the previous year. In addition, organizational participation in the Donate Life Family Circle program grew nearly six fold, with fifty-eight hospitals from twenty-three states dedicating 1,091 roses (up 76 percent) and hosting twenty-five rose dedication ceremonies.

Upon our return from Christmas, Laurie, Kari, and Christina jumped into preparations for rose placement, Esther-Marie oversaw the floragraph touch-up operation, and Mike, Mimi, and Karen activated the game plan for the eleven remaining shifts.

A tremendous amount of work remained to be completed on the Wall of Names, where a hundred decorated nameplates were pinned to the foam wall. While the lettering was exquisite, the process of gluing material onto the cardstock had the unfortunate side effect of warping the cardstock strips. Each one would need to be glued to the wall with sustained pressure, then seamlessly integrated into the wall itself. The Wall of Tears required similar attention to detail, with material applied consistently to the stones and grout, plus seaweed cut into letters to engrave *mother, father, son, daughter* into the protruding bricks.

Despite the complexity of our decorating operation, we stayed on schedule with minimal stress. The RegOnline-powered volunteer scheduling process eliminated attrition issues that had vexed us in the past, and enlisting three blue-jacketed Ambassador Leads to support each shift spread the support workload to manageable levels.

On December 29, OneLegacy's family services, communications, and hospital development staff welcomed a steady stream of donor families, civic leaders, and hospital partners to Rose Placement. Following their welcome reception at the Sheraton, floragraph families arrived to place their roses. As I prepared to head to the Float Rider Orientation, I had the good fortune to meet Jeanne Ward of Washington, D.C., whose seventeen-year-old daughter Jessica was among our floragraph honorees. Jeanne eagerly reached into her purse and pulled out a photo of the two decorating volunteers proudly displaying Jessica's portrait. Recognizing one of them, I asked Jeanne to excuse me for a moment.

I walked about forty feet to Sara Faden, a Los Angeles Police Department public affairs officer and living donor to her LAPD officer husband. "Sara, there's someone I would like for you to meet," I said, then walked Sara across the apron to where Jeanne was standing. "This is Jessica's mother," I said, expecting a warm exchange of understanding and gratitude. It was so much more than that. The two collided into a tearful, sustained embrace that revealed the depth of the bond that could be formed when a volunteer honored someone in such a personal way. At that moment, I pledged to find a way for these reunions to be commonplace going forward.

After gathering myself and wishing them a good evening, I moved to the float rider orientation, which was running well thanks to new volunteer Amy Waterman, an assistant professor and transplant education expert at Washington University in St. Louis, Missouri. Our staff was stretched so thin by the four-day, nine-event schedule that I drafted Amy on short notice to lead the proceedings.

Upon my arrival, I made a beeline to Manuel Salazar, who was accompanied by Coco, his full-time assistant. The very first to arrive, he had already signed all fifty Rose Parade posters with a beautiful signature that belied the fact that he held the Sharpie in his mouth. My first impression of him had nothing to do with his wheelchair or disability, but rather his wide and warm smile. I was delighted to welcome him and assured him that we had a plan in place to for him to fully participate in all our events.

I was also delighted to see Hannah Grinnan, one of the very first recipients I met after joining OneLegacy. Born with the same congenital heart disease that had been fatal for her brother born fourteen years prior, Hannah received a heart transplant only eleven days after she was born. Ever since the Tournament accepted our application, I had been counting the years until Hannah would be old enough to ride, knowing that Loma Linda University Medical Center would surely sponsor her to represent their renowned pediatric heart transplant program.

Loma Linda also chose to honor Hannah's heart donor, Trevor, with the floragraph allocated to them. However, preparing suitable artwork for his portrait was complicated by the fact that he was born brain-dead and was just three days old when his organs were recovered. The only photo of him was grainy, with much of his face masked by a ventilator. Just as she did with Lena Moultrie's floragraph, Cynthia came to the rescue, penciling lines onto the canvas for our decorators to follow so they could reveal Trevor's face to the world.

Lena's mother, Hazelee, was one of the final riders to arrive, and it was clear that her journey from Upstate New York had been a taxing one. "I've been traveling all day, I'm tired, I'm hungry, and I miss my daughter," she said. We invited her to have dinner and meet her fellow riders, and promised her new friends and comfort over the next several days.

The next morning, the Class of 2010 flocked to Rosemont to flood the float with flowers as OneLegacy's Kari Williams and her Gala Committee—Christina, Kathleen, Sandra, and Margaret—led final preparations for the evening's event. Our move to the Pasadena Convention Center—a mere four hundred-yard walk from the Sheraton—could not have been more convenient or opportune. Guests arrived for the six o'clock reception hour in cocktail attire and the occasional formal gown, surveying silent auction items and taking photos with infectious "I can't believe I'm actually here" enthusiasm.

The spirit was amplified as the ballroom doors opened to thirty-foot gobo-lit walls surrounding fifty round tables of ten, each accented with a peacock-feather centerpiece. Following the traditional welcome by the Rose Queen and Royal Court, remarks were punctuated by memorial slideshows featuring our floragraph honorees, provoking numerous donor families to break the silence with boisterous ovations.

After All-4-One concluded a four-song set with their signature song, "I Swear," the evening climaxed with Karen's tearful presentation of the Gary P. Foxen Inspiration Award to Mike and Mimi Thompson. The fact that Mike, Mimi, and Karen—all attired in their Phoenix Decorating green jackets and jeans—were able to break away from the barn for an hour on the last night of decorating was a testament to the strength of the team we had assembled over the years

As the sun rose on New Year's Eve, I was notified that cornea recipient Cristina Margolis had fallen ill and wouldn't be able to attend judging. Her assurance that she would be better by the next morning relieved some pressure, but I still needed to fill her space. With three riders per bench, a vacancy would be noticeable. Amy's enthusiasm at the rider dinner and floragraph family breakfast—she personally visited with every single family—was perfect for the substitute role. She looked every part an official rider as she took the seat next to Hazelee, who, less than forty-eight hours since her arrival, had eased into her newfound community.

To help Manuel with boarding and offloading, he was seated between two of our strongest riders, heart recipient Glenn Matsuki and Mike Vyrostek, a football player and coach whose injured knee had been reconstructed with tissue donated from floragraph honoree Mike Craig. Seeing Mike lean down and bear-hug Manuel, who in turn steadied himself with his chin on Mike's shoulder, was a thing of beauty: the very definition of caring, trust, and cooperation.

As the judges approached, the bell rang, quiet set in, and Chris Lofthouse quietly introduced our entry to the trio. Beginning with its four opening notes, the soundtrack and structure became one.

Within forty seconds, "Hoppípolla" rose to a heavenly crescendo, the bird's flight sustained by waving and tears shared between the twenty-four riders and 250 family, friends, and sponsors ringing the perimeter. Two more ninety-second loops accompanied the judges as they traversed the circumference, initiating brief but emotional exchanges with the riders.

With the second ringing of the bell, the music gave way to a thunderous avalanche of applause, whoops, and arms raised in triumph. I had long presumed that being on the receiving end of such adulation must be a joyous moment, but as Amy later recounted, the experience was decidedly different for Hazelee. As the wave of applause hit, Hazelee burst into tears. Once she recovered, Amy turned to her right.

"Hazelee, are you okay?" she asked.

Turning to Amy, she replied: "I just released my daughter to heaven."

The spirit of Hazelee's ethereal moment carried through to a cloudless New Year's Day. For the third year in a row, the Donate Life float was preceded by an award banner: the Theme Trophy for excellence in presenting the parade theme. The Tournament's accolade was reinforced by a text message poll conducted by ABC. Asked to vote on their favorite float, ours was the viewers' choice.

Coming out of our seventh campaign, we seemed to be right on track in so many ways. We rose to the challenge of doubling the number of floragraphs. Media stories surged by more than 20 percent, approaching four hundred nationwide—no small feat in a media environment ever more challenged by the shift to online media. Our budget was in better shape than it had been in years, supported by a growing sponsorship base, an operating margin for the Family Circle, and limiting the increase in expenses to five percent, an amount outpaced by income.

Our sense of accomplishment was reinforced by the 2011 Rose Parade theme, "Building Dreams, Friendships, and Memories." As the most humanistic theme since 2005's, "Celebrate Family," the ground was fertile for a presentation conveying pure optimism and joy. Alas, my capacity to feel either was overshadowed by the emotional turmoil of my collapsing marriage. It would take contributions from my trusted colleagues to lead us into the light.

2010 DONATE LIFE ROSE PARADE FLOAT

ROSE PARADE THEME: 2010: A Cut Above the Rest

FLOAT THEME: New Life Rises

FLOAT AWARD: Theme Trophy

RIDERS: 23

FLORAGRAPH HONOREES: 77

STATES REPRESENTED: 39

PARTICIPATING ORGANIZATIONS: 119

DEDICATED ROSES: 1,891

DONATE LIFE GRANDSTAND SEATS: 591

FLORAGRAPH FINISHING EVENTS: 39

MEDIA STORIES: 347

ORGAN DONATION CONVERSION RATE, 2009: 69.4 percent[4]

DESIGNATED DONORS, US: 86,326,362[6]

37

SEIZING THE DAY

Your gift of a kidney gives me hope, inspiration, and determination to live life to its fullest. Thank you for giving me a second chance and a bright future. I live every day to make you proud!

—**ROSE DEDICATION** from California, 2011

"DREAMS, FRIENDSHIPS, and Memories," while uplifting, was also intangible. As a starting point, we considered focusing on one of the three components, or two in combination. *Memories* naturally emphasized the past, but Rivian advised caution: "We need to remember that we're here to inspire. It can't be too much of memorial." Our preliminary brainstorm came up empty, so we resolved to ask Dave, Mike, and Mimi to join our February annual meeting. We also invited Float Entries Committee chair Pam McNeely to return.

Dave launched the discussion with two abstract sketches dominated by the floragraphs. "Memories and dreams encompass everything," he explained. "It's a float that has to be sculpted, but it has to be ethereal. I was thinking of what the ultimate way would be to display the floragraphs." Rivian zeroed in on the challenge. "It's a beautiful image, but how you present it to the public in one line is difficult to imagine."

Pam brought the discussion back to practical concerns. "You gave givens: the riders, garden, and floragraphs. We want to be aspirational and triumphant. On the other side are variables: color palette, literal or ethereal, award worthiness, and camera angles. Riders on the side is a great thing. And you want the camera to make a dramatic sweep."

Attempts to make the ethereal more tangible led to suggestions ranging from jewels and art nouveau neckpieces to the Arc de Triomphe and Eiffel Tower. Dave threw in an out-of-the-box idea. "What if each of the floragraphs had its own unit? Like the Boy Scouts, only fewer so they are larger."

"Outwalkers are a variance," Pam reminded us, then added dryly, "and so is the design at this point."

Later in the day, I brought up the idea of a sculpture garden dominated by a large monument. Being that it was the only realistic idea to emerge out of our brainstorm, Dave set off to do some conceptual work.

We moved on to operational issues, foremost among them being a longstanding one: accommodating children at Rosemont. We prized the emotional healing that participating in or observing floragraph decorating afforded to children, grandchildren, and siblings of honorees. However, having them in the barn was a safety issue and opened Phoenix Decorating to liability. Kari Kozuki took the lead to make sure we were on the same page with our float builder.

Perhaps exacerbated by the pressures of the many special requests we made at Rosemont, our relationship with Phoenix was showing signs of friction. In late December, there was no iris available to use for the light blue in the Donate Life and Done Vida logos. Our crew chiefs were instructed to substitute with blue statice, which with a hue evoking Blue Man Group, was nowhere close to Pantone 278. We ultimately solved the problem, but having fidelity to our national brand so casually dismissed struck a nerve. A face-to-face meeting with Chris Lofthouse would help to resolve any misunderstandings.

We also saw an opportunity to offer additional parade seating options. Proximity to the Sheraton required seats in Old Town Pasadena, but there were few grandstands, and all had limited obstructed views. The committee sensed guests would be happy to walk three-quarters of a mile west for a clear sightline up the boulevard.

The recent campaign's individual fundraising pilot led by Stephanie Jansky had two major success stories: riders Anne Gulotta and Glenn Matsuki, who raised nearly $10,000 between them. The unwieldy Active online platform, which challenged even skilled users, was a major obstacle. Future success would rely on our ability to set up pages for riders.

As we neared the end of April's National Donate Life Month, creative development was at a standstill. In a valiant attempt to breathe life into the "Monument" concept, Dave prepared eight fully-formed sketches with seventeen-foot-tall statues surrounding centerpieces ranging from abstract people to a double-helix. Despite his valiant efforts they came across as cluttered and static. With only seven weeks until the unveiling, we were back to square one.

In one of the best examples of our collaborative approach, the committee immediately turned the page and kicked into high gear. Randa Lipman started by focusing on our success over the past three years.

"The phoenix, balloons, and stars were very colorful," she said.

"Instead of statues, you could have a little boy playing in the park with a kite," offered Rebecca Hunter of AATB.

"There may be some opportunities with kites," said Thomas. "We can connect them to walkers."

"Some of our award-winning designs communicate the joy of donation," said Amy.

"I like the simplicity of everyday things," said Ginny. "Dreams and exhilaration are related. Float riders could all be holding kites, reflecting the excitement of catching air."

"Kites could hold floragraphs, strings could be held by recipients," added Rivian.

"Kites come in different sizes. Some are huge," noted Esther-Marie.

And with that rapid-fire exchange involving nine committee members, we had generated a promising new creative direction and the consensus to explore it.

My emotional turmoil on the home front left me skeptical that something so sunny and carefree could be our answer. Tenaya, sensing my ongoing struggle to tie the kites to our cause, stepped in to author the positioning language for our 2011 float entry:

Flying a kite is an opportunity seized to share laughter, sun, wind, and the visual beauty of the moment. Through their life-changing experiences, the families of organ and tissue donors, living donors, and recipients of life-saving transplants teach us all a profound lesson: to "Seize the Day" and make the most of every moment to build dreams, friendships, and memories with loved ones.

We build dreams, friendships, and memories through life's little moments. Through the gift of organ and tissue donation, trans-

plant recipients are able to live their dreams, living donors and recipients build the deepest friendships, and donor families are comforted by the memories and living legacy of their loved ones.

Dave's first sketch, delivered within four weeks, captured the spirit perfectly. Three walkers towed a thoughtfully composed menagerie of five ornate diamond kites connected in descending size, four purple deltas, a colorful butterfly, a box kite, and three small diamonds ascending into the sky. Along each side, a long tube kite led the eye to white floragraph-laden ribbons tailing from the deltas. Within three days we approved the color rendering, ending months of languishing uncertainty. When the going got tough, our committee had truly seized the day.

38

WELL-OILED MACHINE

I gave life to you when you were born, and you gave life to me when my kidneys failed—together we shall always be as one.

—**ROSE DEDICATION** from Texas, 2010

OUR CALM, FOCUSED, and collaborative effort to rescue our float design foreshadowed the remainder of the 2011 Rose Parade campaign, which rolled out in lockstep with no major hiccups. After eight-and-a-half years of evolution, the key pieces were in place: an experienced committee, empowered committee chairs, a strong base of returning sponsors, fully developed infrastructure, and an implementation schedule that had become second nature.

The rose dedication program was the only area that required focused attention. Christina, who had stepped in to buttress fulfillment operations during the critical last six weeks leading up to New Year's Day 2010, saw first-hand the stress caused by the program's labor-intensiveness. A survey of two hundred contributors conducted by Laurie uncovered several opportunities to enhance the program. Foremost among them: streamline the program to a single package, which supported Christina's independent recommendation.

Taking the baton from Laurie, new committee chair Kari Kozuki worked with our web developer to auto-generate digital certificates and create downloadable one-sheets, replacing printed certificates and brochures, respectively. They also programmed a function allowing contributors to gift dedications to underprivileged families.

To promote first-time hospital participation, Ginny publicized Candy Smith's reprised Michael E. Creighton grants through the Collaborative listserv. The program received another boost when Dignity Memorial supplemented their four floragraphs with a presenting sponsorship of the Donate Life Family Circle, complete with 517 rose dedications earmarked for funeral homes nationwide.

As Christina and her special events committee weighed moving our orientations to the Pasadena Convention Center, we shifted our attention to onboarding the riders, walkers, and floragraph families. The float committee was privileged to sponsor a floragraph honoring Corporal Benjamin Kopp of Rosemount, Minnesota, whose mother, Jill Stephenson, has been a featured speaker at the National Learning Congress.

At the age of thirteen, Ben Kopp vowed to serve his country out of respect and admiration for his great grandfathers' patriotic service in WWII, and to vindicate the events of 9/11. Ben was deployed twice to Iraq before going to Afghanistan in May 2009. On July 10, during a firefight with the Taliban, he saved six of his fellow Rangers with the 3/75th Battalion before being shot in the leg. His leg was surgically repaired but blood loss caused trauma from which his body couldn't recover. Ben died on July 18 at Walter Reed Army Medical Center in Washington, D.C., at age twenty-one.

Ben's decision to be an organ donor was influenced by the death of his uncle, J. T. Burud, whose donation of organs six years before Ben's birth had been a source of inspiration for Ben from a young age.

Ben's heart was transplanted to a woman from Winnetka, Illinois, while his liver and kidneys went to a man in the D.C. area. Several of his friends and fellow Rangers have since visited his heart recipient to feel the beat of Ben's heart marching on.

The committee's sponsorship of Ben's floragraph was especially meaningful to Gary, who over the years consistently expressed profound respect for members of the military who gave life after giving the ultimate sacrifice. Soon after meeting Ben's mother Jill in Pasadena, Gary came up with the idea of a Fallen Soldier Donor Memorial that was unveiled at UNOS five years later.

I took great pleasure in having two colleagues named as riders. As a sixteen-year-old high school senior, Jessica Melore suffered a massive heart attack. Within hours, last rites were performed for her; she was not expected to live through the night. For the next nine months, Jessica lived on an experimental, battery-operated mechanical assist device as she waited for a heart transplant. During her wait, additional complications led to the amputation of her left leg above the knee.

Just days before graduation, Jessica received a new heart. She began her freshman year at Princeton University just three months later. She faced additional hurdles, including non-Hodgkin's lymphoma, and became a two-time survivor of the disease. Eleven years post-transplant, Jessica's personal story added depth to her role as a public education specialist for NJ Sharing Network.

Public advocacy was also the domain of Phil Van Stavern of "Phil's List" renown. A former reporter, he was thirty-eight when he learned of his need for a kidney transplant. His older brother Neil was found to be a perfect tissue match, and twenty-two years after receiving one of his brother's kidneys, Phil was respected throughout the field.

Donate Life America's sponsorship of Phil took a heartbreaking turn when Phil's fourteen-year-old grandson Nick died after a Memorial Day ATV accident. A tissue donor in his passing, Nick was honored with a floragraph, as was the donor of Jessica's heart, Shannon Eckert.

As Labor Day passed, the smoothness of the rollout allowed us to apply several meaningful touches. In acknowledgement of the support that the region's Latino and Chinese communities had provided over the years, we added nomenclatures in the two languages underneath the Donate Logo to all our volunteer T-shirts. In addition, to make our operations crew more comfortable in the cold valley of Brookside Park, we purchased lined jackets. Decorating supervisors were henceforth nicknamed "red jackets" because of the gear that distinguished them from navy-attired "blue jackets."

Kathleen's ambitious plans for floragraph families included distributing buttons depicting loved ones as mementos and conversation starters, as well as displaying honorees' photos on table card holders during floragraph decorating. Rose placement received an upgrade as well, with families treated to a personal greeting by Gary and Lois Foxen, who were stationed at the front of the queue. Together with Dignity Memorial's hundreds of roses and another 917 from forty-two hospitals, the dedication garden surpassed 2,600 roses, more than doubling in two years.

The greatest preparation went into the floragraph family brunch. With all but four of the sixty floragraph families traveling to Pasadena, Kathleen and Christina, a donor sister herself, put a great deal of thought into creating a welcoming space for people in various stages of grief. A ritual involving family members pouring colored sand into a bowl created a spirit of remembrance and unity. In addition, volunteer floragraph decorators were invited to meet the families they served with their artistic skills, creating instant bonds of friendship.

Even deeper connections were made through a series of first-time meetings between recipients and their donor families, with liver recipient Mikey Carraway meeting his donor family, and the parents of floragraph honoree Quincy Greer meeting his liver recipient, Debbie Morgan. Media interest in witnessing such profound connections unfold extended to ABC's *Good Morning America*, which covered Jessica Melore and her donor's mother finishing Shannon's floragraph together.

Two other floragraph finishing events involved officers killed in the line of duty. Tampa Police Department partners David Curtis and Jeffrey Kocab, both thirty-one, of Tampa and Kissimmee, Florida, respectively, were shot and killed on June 29, 2010, while attempting to make an arrest at a routine traffic stop. Curtis, an organ donor, was a father of four boys, while Kocab's wife, Sara, was nine months pregnant at the time he donated tissue. Sara Kocab and Kelly Curtis completed their husbands' portraits at Tampa Police Department Headquarters.

Likewise, the New Hampshire Statehouse office of Governor John Lynch hosted a floragraph finishing event for organ donor Officer Mike Briggs of Concord, New Hampshire. The thirty-five-year-old former US Marine and father of two was shot while responding to a domestic violence call.

As Christmas approached, one of our floragraph honorees offered a particularly poignant reminder of the spirit of the holiday. Cora Brittany Hill of Orlando, Florida, was born with cystic fibrosis, a genetic disease that usually ends with the deterioration of the lungs and death. She didn't let her disease stand in the way of her long-range plans. Cora pushed to graduate high school with her peers, then studied nursing while volunteering as a cheer coach for her alma mater.

On Christmas Eve, 2007, twenty-year-old Cora had a double lung transplant. She felt reborn spiritually as well as physically. Unfortunately, after enduring twenty-four hospitalizations over the next two years, undergoing another transplant was deemed too high of a risk. Faced with the certainty that she could not live without a ventilator, Cora requested that she be removed from life support on Christmas Eve so her kidneys could be holiday gifts to two strangers who were dependent on dialysis.

As the completed portraits of Cora and thirty-six other honorees returned from finishing events, Esther-Marie worked with a team led by Lynne Frutchey and her daughter, Lindsay, to touch up the portraits, which invariably lost some material during shipment.

Float decorating proved particularly challenging, as many of the elegantly entangled kites could not be accessed with scaffolding or by standing on the deck. "The volunteers did an outstanding job and they were very patient," recalled Karen. "Half the time we were over-the-top stressed." The slow-going, tedious detail work of applying one bean and split pea at a time by the tens of thousands required a flood of extra volunteers at short notice. Karen considered meeting the challenge to be a huge confidence builder. "I feel like we can handle anything."

On New Year's Day, the spirit of "Seize the Day!" was wonderfully conveyed by Ann Lopez, living kidney donor to her then-husband, comedian George Lopez. Ann walked steps behind our Theme Trophy banner—our fourth consecutive award—with a kite in tow. A veteran theater and commercial actor before transitioning to casting and producing, Ann's gregarious personality was tailor-made for the role. For five miles she waved enthusiastically to the crowd and occasionally acted as if she were pulling the float herself.

Reflecting on the campaign, Lisa Rhodes commented, "Eight years in, it seems to be working like a well-oiled machine." Comparing his experience to three years prior, Thomas concurred. "This time I was impressed with the workflow and how everything worked."

"'Well-oiled machine' is a great metaphor," affirmed Tom. "At the Float Participants reception at the Valley Hunt Club, I met an Executive Committee member. He was very animated when he found out I was with Donate Life. They are very aware of our media coverage," which yielded five hundred stories in a contracting news landscape.

"THERE ARE THREE THINGS HAPPENING SIMULTANEOUSLY IN THE BARN: A CONSTRUCTION PROJECT, A COCKTAIL PARTY, AND A RELIGIOUS SERVICE."

Ginny was more philosophical. "This is my sixth year, and I made an observation for the first time. There are three things happening simultaneously in the barn: a construction project, a cocktail party, and a religious service."

"That's exactly what is going on," said Kevin. "We want to make sure the float gets done, but we also want to give people the attention they need."

More than ever, it seemed that our experience, staffing levels, and operational prowess had finally given our entire team the capacity to engage participants on an especially deep level. Crossing that threshold set the stage for our most resonant entry to date, inspired by a parade theme that encouraged us to simply imagine.

2011 DONATE LIFE ROSE PARADE FLOAT

ROSE PARADE THEME: Building Dreams, Friendships and Memories

FLOAT THEME: Seize the Day!

FLOAT AWARD: Theme Trophy

RIDERS AND WALKERS: 30

FLORAGRAPH HONOREES: 60

STATES REPRESENTED: 33

PARTICIPATING ORGANIZATIONS: 113

DEDICATED ROSES: 2,556

DONATE LIFE GRANDSTAND SEATS: 557

FLORAGRAPH FINISHING EVENTS: 37

MEDIA STORIES: 500

ORGAN DONATION CONVERSION RATE, 2010: 71.7 percent[4]

DESIGNATED DONORS, US: 94,669,081[6]

PART FOUR

JUST
IMAGINE

39

ONE MORE DAY

My brother is currently awaiting a heart/kidney transplant. He is forty-five years old with a wife and two kids who are nine and twelve. Organ donation is certainly the gift of hope that our family prays for.

—ROSE DEDICATION from Illinois, 2013

SHORTLY AFTER New Year's Day 2011, we received an invitation from Rick Jackson, President of the 2012 Tournament of Roses. Mind you, it was not issued specifically to us, but to all float participants: "Just Imagine … " The ellipsis in the 2012 Rose Parade theme tantalized us to complete the idea with a powerful testament to what organ and tissue donation makes possible.

At our annual meeting, I framed the discussion. "There is a difference between 'just imagine the waiting list ending' and 'just imagine every life matters.' The latter is much more universal, and not so much about us. What is it that people want to imagine?" Sandra Madera was the first to speak up.

"They just want one more day," she said.

Our collective reaction was instantaneous and primal. Just like that, we had our theme. Christina summed it up perfectly: "One more day to live with their loved ones. One more day to walk with them one more time." Such an emotional idea demanded an equally powerful visual concept.

Our first interpretation was literal: a globe spinning on its axis, each revolution marking a day. The most fully-realized of Dave's first six sketches placed the floragraphs along latitudinal and longitudinal lines, with the interceding panels depicting lifestyle murals of transplant recipients. Between the lack of emotional resonance, static composition, and unflattering comparisons to the Death Star, the globe concept was scuttled.

As we searched for a new source of inspiration, we attended to the business side of our enterprise. Over the course of the past year, the Donate Life Rose Parade Float had become a separate entity within the nascent OneLegacy Foundation. Given our status as an independent entity, maintaining financial integrity reached a new level of importance.

During the last campaign, our financial performance delivered mixed results. Gains achieved with the Family Circle and the gala were offset by expenses associated with emergency volunteer needs and blizzard-induced emergency travel expenses for committee-sponsored riders. In addition, the gifting of blankets to floragraph decorators as well as a video featuring their testimonials for the Floragraph Family Brunch were both supported as meaningful enhancements despite the added expense. Looking ahead, Thomas recommended holding the line on expenses for the coming year. "We should be able to manage within what we have done in the past," he advised.

Revenue, on the other hand, appeared to be on solid ground. As of mid-February, all rider/walker sponsors were expected to renew, and all but four of the sixty planned floragraphs had likely sponsors.

In April we were surprised by a surge of interest from donor family foundations.

The Spencer Squire All-Star Foundation, the first and only donor family foundation to join our 2010 Rose Parade campaign, funded scholarships and improvements to athletic facilities at Texas A&M University, as well as a playground at Spencer's alma mater, Boone Elementary School. The next year, two more donor family foundations sponsored floragraphs: JJ's Legacy of Bakersfield, California, which arose in memory of twenty-seven-year-old Jeffrey Johns, and a Boston-based nonprofit named after facial tissue donor Joseph Helfgot.

Our 2012 campaign brought the total to eight with the addition of Donate 4 Life (Chad Jones, Katy, TX); Frankie Hernandez Legacy of Life Tournaments (Arleta, CA); In Memory of Todd Sato (Los Angeles, CA); The Kingdom Kids ("Anya" Chiemeka Ogbuji, Shaker Heights, OH); and Taylor's Gift Foundation (Taylor Storch, Coppell, TX).

The proliferation of donor family foundations was a marked contrast to the pre-2010 landscape. Rose Parade broadcast and news coverage of the Donate Life float's many reverent yet celebratory elements seemed to inspire donor families to channel their grief into good works ranging from supporting other donor families to championing causes favored by their loved ones. For many of these organizations, sponsoring a floragraph for their namesake marked their intention to honor other donors in subsequent years.

The surge of new sponsors helped cushion the departure of Astellas, which redirected their marketing priorities after their Prograf patent expired. By mid-year, their five vacated rider positions had been claimed by newcomers Carolina Donor Services, Mayo Clinic

Transplant Center, Taylor's Gift Foundation, UKRO, and eWomen Network, which also sponsored two floragraphs.

Dignity Memorial emerged as the campaign's second-largest contributor, adding three floragraphs to bring their total to seven. Upon his introduction as our newest committee member, Glenn Abercrombie described the impact their involvement in the Donate Life float campaign had on their brand and parent company. "Not only has it helped us build our brand and serve families, but it's also helped us understand more about donation," he said. "We've educated all fifteen thousand of our employees about organ and tissue donation."

In late April, Dave Pittman shared a new creative direction: clocks. Although we admired the creativity of his steampunk-inspired options, the committee focused on the most conventional design: a line of four circular clocks on each side, with lifestyle murals covering the clock faces and floragraphs occupying the hour positions. A tall grandfather clock at the rear ensured that the design "finished strong," a quality that had come to define Donate Life's float aesthetic. While the overall composition seemed sound, we struggled with the murals, feeling they would interfere with the floragraphs. Furthermore, the old-fashioned timepieces and grandfather clocks lacked visual excitement.

As the onset of May moved our pressure gauge into critical territory, Mike and Mimi Thompson called me with an unconventional lunch invitation. As much as I had come to cherish our relationship with them, it was commonly understood that Phoenix crew chiefs and clients were not encouraged to fraternize, lest sentiment intrude into business decisions that sometimes needed to be made on the decorating floor.

Within a week, we were face to face in Newport Beach. After we got past the shock of seeing each other without windbreakers and jeans, Mike pulled out a few sheets of paper showing the results of a Google search: "floral clocks." A dozen images of colorful floral gardens from throughout the world, landscaped in the form of giant, beautiful timepieces, covered the pages. *This was our answer.* Mike and Mimi cautioned me not to credit them with the discovery lest they be viewed as crossing boundaries, so their seminal contribution went unacknowledged as I shared the concept with our longtime designer.

Less than three weeks before the unveiling, Dave presented a color sketch with three floral clocks per side. "The designs are always a balance between an entertaining visual and as effective a message as possible," he explained. "You do that better than anyone in the Parade, and this does it as well. It's a decorating challenge, but not outside your abilities. And it displays the floragraphs more deliberately than ever before."

The only critique concerned the traditional grandfather clock, which didn't seem to fit with the scale or color palette of the floral clocks. Within a week, Dave had replaced it with an elegant clock tower, an appropriate counterpoint to the abstract clock at the front that would serve as our dedication garden. The final color rendering was received on June 13, only hours before the official unveiling. Within minutes, I inserted our theme into the image, answering Rick Jackson's inviting "Just Imagine ..." with an ellipsis of our own: "... *One More Day.*"

Our presentation to Donate Life America's membership brought the idea home powerfully:

Through their life-changing experiences, the families of organ and tissue donors, living donors, and recipients of life-saving transplants know intimately the preciousness of time, inspiring us to Just Imagine ...

... One More Day.

A day when donor families are reunited with loved ones, transplant recipients thrive, and living and registered donors step forward so that a life-saving transplant is available to everyone in need.

By numerous accounts, the announcement was met with goosebumps, tears, and universal plaudits, giving us hope that new sponsors would come into the fold. The expectation of additional resources inspired us to consider investing in animation, albeit only if it was minor (read: inexpensive) and meaningful.

The sun/moon dial on the clock tower was an obvious choice. It also made sense to animate the front-most clock as well, which, given its role as the dedication garden, inspired Christina to make a stunning suggestion: have it run backward.

Coming out of the unveiling, our reassessment of the rose dedication program's branding was in its final stages. It had been a year since we added "Donate Life" as a prefix, but "Family Circle" no longer reflected the breadth of participation. Many dedications honored recipients or waitlisted patients, and several organizations honored donors or recipients collectively from a single hospital or even an entire state.

Some applications of the program were downright savvy. Lauren Quinn of the Center for Donation and Transplant offered dedicated roses and framed certificates as an incentive for hospitals to fly a Donate Life flag during National Donate Life Month. Two-thirds of their forty-three hospital partners accepted the offer.

With the added impetus that "Family Circle" hadn't gained traction after five years, committee discussion segued to ideas for a more descriptive name.

"Above all, it's a garden," said Kevin.

"I like 'dedication garden,'" said Mary Ganikos, a longtime committee liaison from HRSA's Division of Transplantation.

"That's what Bob Eubanks calls it," I added, recalling his commentary on KTLA's Rose Parade broadcasts.

After yet another consensus decision, the newly rebranded Donate Life Dedication Garden inspired first-time sponsor Bacterin International to grant roses to up to three hundred tissue donor families through their OPO partners.

Joining them as first-time campaign contributors were eight OPOs from Alabama, Hawaii, New England, North Carolina, Southwest Ohio, Eastern Tennessee, Utah, and Central Wisconsin. The new wave of floragraph sponsors encouraged us to replace the numbers three, six, nine and twelve on both of the middle clocks with portraits, bringing the total to seventy-two.

As the 2012 campaign welcomed the last of our twenty-three new sponsors—bringing us to eighty-six, up 28 percent from the prior year—from out of the blue I received a one-line text from Dave Pittman:

Thinking this may be our masterpiece.

40

100 YEARS

It is quite a thing, praying for your wife to be healed, not seeing that answer, and then realizing that she is the answer to a prayer for someone who is anxiously awaiting an organ or tissue transplant.

—JARED HEIDINGER,
donor husband (2012 floragraph)

BY EARLY NOVEMBER, preparations for decorating were well under way. Karen teamed up with OneLegacy's new volunteer coordinator, Erika Ospina Awad, to ensure our decorating shifts were appropriately staffed. Volunteers experienced with beans and silver leaf were at a premium, while the clock tower would reintroduce corn husks for the first time since our 2004 debut.

Floragraph decorating preparations involved carefully choreographing each portrait to ensure our unforgiving deadlines were met every step of the way. Sponsors were required to complete a Floragraph Decorating Plan detailing the family's involvement in decorating or finishing the portrait, details about the finishing event, if applicable, and shipping information. Out of the fifty-six floragraphs scheduled for finishing events, fourteen were slated for the hospital where the honoree's donation took place.

Meanwhile, Donate Life America formally asked us to publicize their "20 Million in 2012" campaign by appending the wordmark below each of the float's logos. The initiative was a capstone of the Donor Designation Collaborative, which in 2006 focused Donate Life America's members on founding, fixing and filling state donor registries. Total donor designations nationwide had since increased from 60 million to more than 100 million.[6]

Our focus on inspiring donor designations brought new urgency to our efforts to garner media coverage. The National and Regional PR Working Groups launched with twenty-three and fifty-seven participants, respectively, and with so many veterans among them, we had high expectations for achieving placements.

Among our standout stories was that of Emily Fennell of Yuba City, California, who lost her right hand after it was crushed in a roll-over car accident in June 2006. After the amputation, occupational therapists helped her learn how to use her left hand for all tasks. She tried a prosthetic hand and a traditional "hook" prosthesis, but stopped using them because they didn't provide the functionality she desired.

She researched hand transplantation and became excited about what it could make possible, including the potential to provide more fully for her daughter, become more independent, and achieve greater success in her career. The idea of Emily waving to millions of Rose Parade spectators and viewers with a transplanted hand less than a year prior was one of our strongest story angles in years.

In late December, ESPN.com responded to a pitch centered around floragraph honoree Jovante Woods, the son of NFL Cincinnati Bengals star Ickey Woods, who was known for his "Ickey

Shuffle" touchdown celebration and leading the team to their only Super Bowl appearance. Like his father, Jovante suffered from severe asthma, a condition that never deterred him from playing football. On August 11, 2010, he had an asthma attack that led to a fatal anoxic brain injury. Jovante, who had designated himself as an organ and tissue donor on his driver's license, was able to save four lives as an organ donor and heal dozens through the gift of tissue.

Assigned to the story was not just any reporter, but eleven-time National Sportswriter of the Year, Rick Reilly. In 2007, he moved to ESPN.com after a legendary twenty-two-year run with *Sports Illustrated*. Throughout our thirty-minute interview, Reilly was deeply curious about organ donation and what we hoped to achieve through our participation in the Rose Parade. As I described our theme, design, and story, he was mesmerized. "The clock on the front of the float will move," I said. "But because it is situated within a bed of roses that are largely memorial in nature, it will run backward in time." Stunned, he involuntarily slapped his forehead.

In response to his reaction, I made a point. "That's the reaction we want spectators and viewers to have when they see us. And we hope those who've not yet made their decision will be inspired to see donation in a new way."

Reilly's story, published on December 29, captured the essence of our mission with a feast of utterly lyrical passages:

> *How can the murder of a referee in Arkansas bring joy in Pasadena?*
>
> *How can something that moves at the speed of a funeral procession make hearts race?*
>
> *How can a parade float with a clock going backward make you feel so good about the future?*

The clock that runs backward on the front of the float will remind [Woods] of his fondest wish: that time could reverse itself long enough for him to spend one more day with his son.

And for the recipients? It reminds them of time they feared they'd never get.

The Donate Life float feels like both a funeral and a christening, like heartache and heartsong.

It's a downer and an upper and a breath-taker all in one. It's one hundred feet of flower- and cinnamon- and split-pea-covered emotion. But it's helping.[7]

The day before Reilly's piece published, we joined float rider Roxanna Green and her husband, John, as they completed the floragraph of their daughter Christina-Taylor. The circumstances surrounding her donation and overwhelming media interest warranted a special, and familiar, location: the Castle Green.

Born September 11, 2001, Christina-Taylor Green developed a sense of caring and hope for others as she grew up. After Christina-Taylor's grandmother passed away, the Greens discussed organ donation and decided as a family they would all be organ donors.

"Yolanda, Christina-Taylor's grandmother, and I were active in political events and volunteering," said Roxanna. "It was only natural that Christina and my son, Dallas, join the Kids Helping Kids club at Mesa Verde Elementary to help organize food and toy drives for needy families."

Christina-Taylor also became fascinated with politics when Barack Obama ran for office. She talked to Roxanna and her grandmother about how public servants can help communities. The next year, she won a student council seat and even expressed her interest in becoming the first female president.

Nine-year-old Christina-Taylor, the granddaughter of former Philadelphia Phillies manager Dallas Green, was excited to attend Congresswoman Gabrielle Giffords' informal town hall meeting in Tucson when tragedy struck. On January 11, 2011, she died on the scene from a single bullet wound to her chest after a gunman opened fire, shooting nineteen people.

The evening she died, the Greens painfully agreed to donate whatever they could. It was a difficult decision even after discussing organ donation prior to Christina's passing. "We believe it would be next to impossible had we not done so beforehand," said Roxanna. "We will never forget the uplifting of our spirits several weeks later when we received the news that Christina's corneas saved the eyesight of two people. We knew right then that we had made the right decision and that Christina-Taylor would be proud to have helped others see."

The rose for Christina-Taylor was among nearly three thousand that were placed in the float's dedication garden on December 29. To make Rose Placement even more special, the float committee applied Gary's generous $5,000 campaign contribution to a custom tent and banner at the front of the queue. Gary and Lois personally greeted families one by one as they walked through "Gary's Gateway."

On December 30, Tenaya brought Donate Life Hollywood flair to her role as our gala committee chair. Playing a grand piano onstage was heart recipient Brad Ellis, best known as the pianist on *Glee*. He accompanied our slideshow of floragraph honorees and, in a surprise, invited the father of one of our floragraph honorees to sing our official song as the audience sang along, learning the tune for judging.

The time-honored tradition of judging was never intended to be a spectator event, so our growing ranks—now well over four hundred—created an even greater impetus for us to follow the house rules lest we lose our privileges. Thus, we devoted several minutes of the gala program to educate our guests about the etiquette surrounding the event.

The next morning, Erika's methodological approach to planning transportation, lunch, access, and seating for our guests paid off. With the garden filled and deck completed, "… One More Day" looked extraordinary as it came out of the barn for judging. For the next hour, as riders and floragraph families posed for photos in front of the float, volunteers feverishly sprayed water on the blooms to counter the wilting effects of temperatures in the eighties.

As the countdown to the judges' arrival approached the one-hour mark, a cherry-picker was positioned next to the middle clock on the camera side. There, the twelve o'clock position awaited the float's final piece: Christina-Taylor Green's floragraph. Hundreds gathered below in hushed silence as Christina-Taylor's father, John, and brother, Dallas, climbed the ladder. With great deliberation, John applied her portrait to the vessel as an emotional ovation rose from our community.

We hailed from small towns and big cities, dozens of states, and multiple countries. We represented a broad range of ethnic and cultural backgrounds, religious beliefs, and political allegiances. None of that mattered, not for one moment. There were no fault lines; they simply didn't exist. In a matter of two days, our community had come together as one. Our common purpose—honoring people—united us.

Half an hour later, the verses of Five for Fighting's "100 Years"—the other end of the telescope from "… One More Day"—filled the apron as Phoenix Decorating tested the float's audio system. In a scene reminiscent of Whoville in *The Grinch Who Stole Christmas*, members of our community spontaneously linked hands, joining one by one until our float was encircled. Seeing the moment unfold, Chris Lofthouse asked us to reprise the gesture for judging.

As the bell rang, silence enveloped the apron, and Chris introduced the judges to "... One More Day." With the opening notes of "100 Years," our circle opened to welcome them in, then melted into the perimeter. The judges gradually made their way from the sunny side around to the shade, striking up emotional conversations with our riders along the way. Then, to our surprise, they made a second circuit, doubling the time usually afforded to a single float. Finally, the bell rang, and a thunderous roar arose from inside and outside the barn.

OUR COMMUNITY HAD COME TOGETHER AS ONE. OUR COMMON PURPOSE—HONORING PEOPLE—UNITED US.

In another break from tradition, the judges remained in place, huddling for a minute between the float and barn doors. They then turned to face our makeshift auditorium and one of them spoke for the trio. "We are going to circle one more time," she said. "But this time we are going to applaud you." As they did, our community returned their extraordinary salute in kind.

The next morning, as "... One More Day" made its turn at media corner, the Judges' Special Trophy banner—our fifth consecutive award—formally conferred what we, and the broadcasters, already knew: our 2012 Rose Parade entry was truly special..

KTLA's Bob Eubanks highlighted the dedication garden as a "Rose Parade tradition," with Stephanie Edwards adding that the clock moving backward "serves as a reminder that life is precious

... too precious even to waste one minute." ABC added a special segment on floragraph honoree Katie Enos of Westford, Massachusetts, featuring her parents Ed and Marion and Donate Life floragraph volunteers Sherri and Sarah Lamon, who had the privilege of preparing Katie's portrait for finishing.

That afternoon and the following day, twenty local Ambassadors volunteered to serve as storytellers at the Post-Parade float showcase, introducing thousands of attendees to the Donate Life mission and the value of one more day.

2012 DONATE LIFE ROSE PARADE FLOAT
ROSE PARADE THEME: Just Imagine ...
FLOAT THEME: ... One More Day
FLOAT AWARD: Judges' Special Trophy
RIDERS: 28
FLORAGRAPH HONOREES: 72
STATES REPRESENTED: 37
PARTICIPATING ORGANIZATIONS: 133
DEDICATED ROSES: 2,559
DONATE LIFE GRANDSTAND SEATS: 583
FLORAGRAPH FINISHING EVENTS: 55
MEDIA STORIES: 719
ORGAN DONATION CONVERSION RATE, 2011: 72.9 percent[4]
DESIGNATED DONORS, US: 101,380,994[6]

41

JOURNEYS OF THE HEART

*Your loved one's heart has saved not only my husband
but our little family of four. Whoever you are, wherever
you are, thank you from the bottom of my heart.*

—**ROSE DEDICATION** from California, 2012

IN PREPARATION FOR our annual meeting, basic measures pointed to a major tipping point: 86 sponsors (up 28 percent), 750 guests (30 percent), 160 hotel rooms (14 percent), and 675 media stories (35 percent). We also saw a 4 percent increase in sponsorship revenue despite Astellas's departure. However, our financial performance reflected a continuing struggle to keep pace with our rapid growth.

Although revenue had risen by almost $100,000, we still had a deficit of about $30,000, or 4 percent of expenses. It was time for tough decisions, beginning with the elimination of complimentary tickets—a $50,000 line item—that had been historically included in sponsorship packages. On the revenue side, all floragraphs were priced at $3,500, eliminating the two lower tiers originally instituted to attract OPOs with small operating budgets. We also set an ambitious revenue target of $80,000 for the Dedication Garden.

Our creative approach was challenged by the 2013 Rose Parade theme's appropriation of the final book by Dr. Seuss, *Oh, The Places You'll Go!* The author's whimsical visuals seemed a mismatch for our message, but then again, his stories explored serious themes such as discrimination *(The Star-Bellied Sneeches)* and the environment *(The Lorax)*. Fidelity to the parade theme demanded that we consider how Dr. Seuss would treat a subject like organ donation.

Dave's first round explored compasses as a central visual. While visually interesting, the sketches lacked the dominant elements and floragraph integration that made "... One More Day" so captivating. But compasses could point to emotional milestones of the donation and transplantation experience—such as hope, love, gratitude, and transformation—along one's "Journey of the Heart."

Continuing the brainstorm, Christina suggested a roller-coaster—a metaphor for the high and low points of the donation and transplant experience. It also had the potential to be inspirational and fun, with floragraphs placed along the track. Both concepts warranted exploration.

While we rallied around the theme "Journeys of the Heart," a breakthrough design was elusive. Dave's study of hearts and how they could convey emotion through shape and materials included a rollercoaster track in the shape of a heart. Even more, the Seussian parade theme invited an abstract design; rooting ourselves in reality was entirely optional.

The next round took advantage of that freedom, with stunning results. Five sketches toyed with various combinations of asymmetrical hearts surrounded by interconnected, looping pathways. Over the next three weeks, Dave combined the whimsy of Seuss with the soaring, hopeful quality that had come to define our Donate Life's Rose Parade brand.

For the third consecutive year, the official rendering arrived on the eve of the unveiling and was received to acclaim. A week later, Kathleen's presentation at the American Association of Motor Vehicle Administrators (AAMVA) meeting elicited a collective "aww" from the audience, who also appreciated her dedication of roses to fallen troopers.

As June's sponsorship tally showed extraordinary momentum— seventy-two commitments totaling 93 percent of our $450,000 revenue goal—float construction hit a wall. Our unconventional float design was proving extremely difficult to execute. Phoenix operations director Sean McMinimy struggled for six weeks to engineer the mechanism for two of the fragile hearts to retract and reengage. Ultimately, it was determined that the hearts could not interlock as originally designed. They would need to be independent, and powerful electromagnets would be required to lock them into place.

Another component that went awry was the migration of our participant, guest, and event registration processes to an online platform. Since our debut, we had relied on paper forms and an Excel spreadsheet to organize hotel and event ticketing needs for our participants, partners, staff, and guests. The system had changed very little over the years, but as our guest list and event schedule grew, transposing and updating so much data had become ever more labor-intensive.

Cvent, the registration software used for most of our industry conferences, seemed able to combine our participant information sheet, floragraph planning form, and event ticketing process. However, after considerable effort and expense, it became clear that our multitude of participant categories and parties, ticketing options, and event parameters proved too complex to program into a system optimized for individual registration at single events. Resorting to our tried-and-true system cleared the way to onboard our riders.

Leading the contingent were two brothers whose family was immersed in the world of kidney disease: 2006 World Series MVP and former Angels shortstop David Eckstein and his brother, Rick, a hitting coach for the Washington Nationals. Rick awakened one morning in September 2010 knowing at that moment that he was going to donate a kidney to his brother, Ken, one of four immediate family members who had kidney transplants. Two months later, his premonition came to pass.

David planned to be a living donor to his sister if she needed another transplant. "Throughout my life and career as a professional baseball player, knowing the daily struggles of my family has always been a driving force for me to never take a day for granted," said David. "I felt it was my obligation to always do my best, and when the time comes, I will be proud to add kidney donor to my list of achievements." David would add "Rose Parade participant" to that list on New Year's Day as he and Rick joined thirty other riders from seventeen states and Canada.

The contingent also included Carolyn Henry Glaspy (Cincinnati, OH), who made the decision to donate the organs of her son Chris Henry of the NFL Cincinnati Bengals; heart recipient Larry Johnson (Baytown, TX), a Grammy-award-winning bassist; Leilah Dowsari (Loma Linda, CA), who in 1986 was the first female newborn to receive a heart transplant; and Vicky Nguyen (Los Angeles, CA), who'd lived all but two of her twenty-eight years with a liver transplant. Vicky was a familiar face at Rosemont Pavilion, having earned her red jacket after two years of decorating.

Among our floragraph honorees was Elizabeth Ann Logelin (Minnetonka, MN), whose sudden death at age thirty the day after giving birth to her first child inspired her husband Matt to write the *New York Times* bestseller, *Two Kisses for Maddy*. Also honored was tissue donor Alfredo Diaz (Ontario, CA), who served as a Tournament of Roses volunteer for more than twenty-five years; tissue donor Eric Barlament (Brillion, WI), whose wife Kari rode the inaugural Donate Life float; and Gary Foxen's lung donor, Mary Frances DeFerrari (Lafayette, CA).

Days after the mid-October announcement of our floragraph honorees, the final road test of our fully art-directed float exposed new challenges translating our ambitious design concept to finished form. While the eight deck-mounted hearts were playful, colorful, and beautifully shaped, the looping curves of the "rollercoaster track" lacked a smooth quality and had some variations in thickness. In addition, the art direction bypassed gradients in favor of sudden color transitions, and the actual size of the floragraphs—which were minimized in the rendering—threatened to disrupt the overall design.

On New Year's Day 2013, "Journeys of the Heart" had the potential to be perceived as inspiring, whimsical, ambitious—and jarring. Regardless, it would certainly be memorable.

42

CATALYST

To be blessed with good health made it an easy choice to help my friend, Georgia. She needed one kidney and I had two.

—**ROSE DEDICATION** from Kansas, 2010

HEADING INTO DECORATING, the elimination of complimentary tickets from sponsorship packages was having its intended effect. We weren't out of the woods, however, as continued growth—the number of guests and hotel rooms were up 10 and 17 percent, respectively—had the potential to increase costs during the intensive month of December.

As Erika and our Ambassador Leads welcomed our first decorating shift, our seasoned float crew went over the work plan for the day. Led by Mike and Mimi Thompson, ours was a veritable all-star team. Kevin Monroe joined Karen as a green-jacketed assistant crew chief for the first time. Supervising the floor in red jackets were Esther-Marie Carmichael, Ginny and Andrew McBride, Mary Ganikos, Gee Wong, Bob Bruno, Vicky Nguyen, Dan Sandoval, and Tina Vanderhorst. Kathleen Hostert, Pam Charron, Debbie Martin, and Joy Weller donned red jackets as floragraph supervisors.

Guided by veterans both inside and outside the barn, our operations ran so smoothly that we were able to support mid-month opportunities that would have been unthinkable in years past. On December 17, Donate Life California and the California Peace Officers' Memorial Foundation (CPOMF) honored twenty-nine fallen officers and their families in a ceremony in Sacramento. Christina and I made a road trip to the California State Capitol, transporting event infrastructure and assisting with the presentation.

The Sacramento event reflected the Dedication Garden's growing importance as a catalyst for Donate Life organizations to affirm their relationships with donation partners. The Roses for Registries program sponsored by the Order of St. Lazarus acknowledged motor vehicle agencies from all fifty states and the District of Columbia with 157 dedicated roses and companion certificates.

The Dedication Garden's most visible tribute was for all intents and purposes invisible, and intentionally so. On December 14, America was shaken by the shooting at Sandy Hook Elementary School in Newtown, Connecticut. The next day, we were inspired to honor the twenty-six adults and children who lost their lives so suddenly and senselessly. Shortly after noon on December 29, Karen and Kari Kozuki solemnly nestled twenty-six personalized red roses—twenty buds for the children, protected by six full blooms representing the adults—in the upper-right of the heart-shaped garden. Rivian reached out to only one media outlet, *The Newtown Bee*, so they could inform the shattered community of our tribute.

Over the next two days, record attendance at the floragraph family breakfast (440 guests), gala dinner (525), and float judging (475) primed "Journeys of the Heart" for a spirited Rose Parade appearance. At 5:45 a.m. on New Year's Day, we made our way from the Sheraton lobby to board our bus. That is, we would have boarded it, if only our bus was there.

Expecting a quick resolution to the matter, I called Fast Deer, the company we had used for years. To my relief, they assured me the bus was right around the corner. I looked up the street, eagerly awaiting the sight of a large coach turning the corner. Several minutes passed, and still no bus. I called a second time. "It's ten minutes away," I was assured. Again, time lapsed, and still nothing. On my third call, I was told the bus was at least twenty minutes away. "How does the bus keep getting farther away?!" I exclaimed to the agent, albeit in much more colorful language.

It was now 6:00 a.m., and breakfast was waiting at Vons. We had thirty-six people who needed to eat and get to the float. No coaches or shuttles were available. Cars would not be allowed past key security checkpoints. The was only one option.

"We're going to have to walk," I announced. Asked how far it was, to keep everyone calm, I lowballed it. "Half a mile." It was twice that.

We marched as a unit, maintaining a brisk pace. Fifteen minutes in, Rick good-naturedly offered a piggyback ride to Sue Sprague. We made it to Vons by 6:25 a.m., and just in time. As our contingent partook of the generous spread and took our traditional photo in the flower department with the Vons employees, it was clear the exertion had taken its toll. Several riders were in no condition to walk the last quarter-mile to our float. I explained our conundrum to the store manager. Before we knew it, four Vons employees volunteered to drive anyone who needed a lift. We were saved.

By the time we gathered for the lineup photo, the morning's drama was behind us. We had bonded as if in wartime, the weather was glorious, David and Rick were waving up a storm from their perch in front, and Phil Collins' "You'll be in My Heart" filled the air. We were home free, or so I thought.

On my way to pick up the riders, I received word that one of our floragraphs was missing. By the time we were all reunited at the post-parade lunch, the mystery had been solved. In the early-morning hours, as our float was being moved from Rosemont to the parade formation area on Orange Grove, tree branches knocked six exposed floragraphs to the street.

While placing the portraits back on the float, the Phoenix crew inadvertently transposed two of them to opposite their original sides. Even worse, the most severely-damaged floragraph, with a third of the face missing, didn't make it back onto the float. It was found on the deck of the float at Post-Parade. For the affected families, the exhaustive effort we put into making sure floragraphs could be viewed by their loved ones from the stands were for naught. Although the families were understanding—one mother even remarked, "There he goes again!"—the thought of their disappointment at such a climactic moment was devastating.

My disappointment was offset, however, by a moment of serendipity. Early the morning of New Year's Eve, as I was interviewed live by KTLA, the reporter asked me about the dedication garden. To dramatize its special nature, I picked up a rose and read the message tagged to the vial:

"In memory of Betsy Niles. She loved, gave, gifted. She gave strangers the gifts they needed: another chance at life. Betsy lives on in our memories and hearts, and in the lives of others who live on with her gift of life."

To my surprise, on New Year's Day I received an email from the author of the dedication, Dan Sarnowski, a dedicated volunteer for the NJ Sharing Network, asking how I came upon picking the message he had written to the love of his life. I replied:

Dan, thank you so much for reaching out to me! What are the odds that I would not only select that rose among the many, but that the individual who contributed the dedication would actually see the interview from across the country? As we were setting up for the interview, I wanted to share with KTLA's many viewers a dedication that expressed the qualities of our most poignant messages: love, remembrance and pride. I looked at about 25 of the dedications that were within reach, and when I read yours it really touched me. I could feel your love of Betsy then, just as I did reading your email. Thank you for allowing the float to be a vessel for such a heartfelt message. It is a true privilege.

Despite such fulfilling moments, as well as equaling the prior year's extraordinary output of media coverage, it was hard not to feel like our 2013 Rose Parade campaign was a letdown. Our ambitious design was challenging to execute, finances remained an overarching concern, considerable resources were wasted on the abandoned migration to an online registration platform, our float hit a tree, and we had to get to the float formation area on foot.

Looking ahead to our eleventh campaign, I resolved to get back to basics and the spirit that motivated Gary to envision our participation in the first place. The 2014 Rose Parade theme, "Dreams Come True," was a perfect starting point.

While ruminating on the notion of "dreams," I kept hearing Mandy Moore's voice as Rapunzel in the charming Disney animated film *Tangled*. Threatened by dozens of ruffians in a tavern, she implores upon them to find their better nature. "Have some humanity! Haven't any of you ever had a dream?" Rapunzel's is simple and meaningful: to see lanterns rise into the sky on her birthday.

As I related my inspiration for the eleventh Donate Life Rose Parade Float, the committee was ready to return to the approach that had garnered five consecutive awards.

"Now is the time we step up the design," said Rivian.

"Focus on the integrity of the design," Tom implored, channeling the lessons learned from the prior year. "If it is exciting and inspiring, the messaging will take care of itself."

Dave's first three sketches depicting "lantern festivals" were far too busy, but the promise of the concept was easily apparent and approved for further development. Unlike the previous year, our energy was focused in a singular creative direction.

Over the next four weeks, Dave narrowed the lanterns down to five—street, Japanese, paper, metal, and Chinese—each elegantly suspended at varying angles as if buffeted by the wind. Refinements focused on two of the lanterns, the form of the deck, and combinations of colors and materials. Animated flames flickering in two of the lanterns added a subtle and graceful expression of Donate Life's eleventh Rose Parade float entry: "Light Up the World."

On New Year's Day 2014, that was exactly what we would do.

2013 DONATE LIFE ROSE PARADE FLOAT

ROSE PARADE THEME: Oh, The Places You'll Go!

FLOAT THEME: Journeys of the Heart

RIDERS: 32

FLORAGRAPH HONOREES: 72

STATES REPRESENTED: 39

PARTICIPATING ORGANIZATIONS: 126

DEDICATED ROSES: 2,893

DONATE LIFE GRANDSTAND SEATS: 693

FLORAGRAPH FINISHING EVENTS: 59

MEDIA STORIES: 639

ORGAN DONATION CONVERSION RATE, 2012: 72.5 percent[4]

DESIGNATED DONORS, US: 108,963,015[6]

43

LIGHTING UP THE WORLD

Don't think of organ donation as giving up part of you to keep a total stranger alive. It's really a total stranger giving up almost all of them to keep part of you alive.

—MORGAN DACHIS,
donor sister (2009 floragraph);
original author unknown

EARLY ON, WE RESOLVED that our 2014 campaign would shine a light on living donation. Eight living donors were part of 2007's "Giving from the Heart," but over the last six years only seven living donors were selected to ride. Their limited participation was understandable: living donation didn't apply to tissue banks, and OPOs were restricted from engaging in living donation-related efforts. Furthermore, because of its inherent risks, living donation discussions were typically confined to a closed circle of kidney patients, their family, and friends.

In recent years, however, living donation had become more visible thanks to the success of kidney chains—a series of transplants involving incompatible pairs of donors and recipients, but who are compatible with each other. We agreed that living donors would be most visible as walkers, which would also reinforce the key message that people could lead fully active lives with only one kidney. Having them walk alongside a recipient-only rider contingent—including some of their own recipients—would also make for powerful storytelling that supported California's new living donation initiative.

During my tenure as president of Donate Life California, we collaborated with Gov. Arnold Schwarzenegger and Steve Jobs to pass SB 1395, the Altruistic Living Donor Registry Act of 2010. Two years of collaboration with the state's leading kidney transplant programs led to Living Donation California, the nation's first online resource for living donation education and referrals. Its May 2013 launch provided the perfect opportunity to invite media-savvy living donors and recipients to join our campaign.

In June 2004, after eight years on dialysis, JePahl White received a kidney transplant. Five years later, after his transplanted kidney went into full rejection, his wife LaKishia was determined that he wouldn't have to wait another seven years for a new kidney. Because she was not a biological match, LaKishia continued to research possibilities and learned about paired exchange programs.

On September 27, 2010, JePahl received a kidney from Jessica Jurado, whose mother received a kidney from another donor as part of the chain. LaKishia, in turn, donated her kidney to a person in Pennsylvania. At the Living Donation California launch event in Sacramento, we invited JePahl, LaKishia, and Jessica to join the Class of 2014.

A week later, I was charged with preparing an exhibit booth at the Healthcare Association of Southern California (HASC) annual meeting of hospital and healthcare executives. Our objective was to engage hospital CEOs so that they would, in turn, motivate their charges to fully support donation processes in their facilities. However, the environment—a strolling dinner and wine tasting among exhibitor booths—was not conducive to getting their attention, let alone quality interactions.

Having exhibited for years at the AOPO and AATB meetings, I had seen firsthand how my colleagues were moved—some to tears even—by the opportunity to handwrite a rose dedication. I wondered: *how would hospital CEOs react to the same opportunity?* Within weeks we put that question to the test.

On the exhibit floor, our Donate Life Rose Parade Float booth stood out from the pharmaceutical, IT, and human resources vendors that lined the aisles. Colorful banners framed dozens of long-stem roses, rose vials, dedication tags, and Sharpies. As the CEOs and their spouses passed by, their curious glances were converted into eager participation by a simple question: "Would you like to be part of the Rose Parade?" Dozens of handwritten dedications were proof that they did.

A month later, I tested the concept again with an exhibit at the California Association of Physicians Groups annual meeting. Once again, the Rose Parade, and the opportunity to be a meaningful part of America's New Year Celebration, sparked conversations with ease. I was then struck by a possibility: *what if OPOs nationwide could offer this experience to every one of their hospital partners?*

We had roses to spare, as the float's deck—a large planter with well over five thousand blooms—was basically one giant dedication garden. Filling it would take an extraordinary amount of effort. Fortunately, I had some open bandwidth, thanks to my executive assistant Annie Kure, assuming most of the onboarding and coordination of participants and guests. At the AOPO annual meeting, I tracked down the leaders of the Donation and Transplantation

Community of Practice—the successor to the Collaborative—and George Bergstrom of the American Hospital Association (AHA), all of whom eagerly signed on to the "Hospital CEO Roses" concept. Eight weeks later, a letter jointly signed by the leaders of AHA, AOPO, and the Eye Bank Association of America (EBAA) was emailed to 4,800 hospitals nationwide:

We are contacting you to offer an extraordinary opportunity for you and your hospital to be a meaningful part of one of the world's greatest traditions: the Rose Parade.

One of the trademarks of the annual Donate Life float design is a "Dedication Garden" filled with thousands of roses, each placed in a vial carrying a unique, personal message from an individual, family, or organization. In appreciation of your hospital's support of organ, eye, and tissue donation, we would like to offer you a complimentary opportunity to handwrite a dedication on one of the rose vials. Yours will be one of thousands of rose dedications from hospital CEOs across the country to be placed in the Donate Life float's Dedication Garden for the world to see.

In the coming weeks, your office will be contacted by your organ procurement organization or eye bank to schedule a time for you to write your dedication, as well as discuss ideas for sharing this ceremonial act with your staff and local media.

Owing to their more intensive relationships with hospitals, OPOs were given first choice of which to approach; eye banks would have free reign among the rest. Altogether, fifty OPOs and four eye banks requested more than three thousand vials, with sixty days to have as many as possible signed and returned by the Thanksgiving deadline.

In the meantime, a series of press releases formally announced our float participants. Two walkers were inspired to donate by seeing stories about donation. Upon seeing the Donate Life float in the 2013 Rose Parade, Kelly Wright (Newport Beach, CA) resolved to give one of her kidneys to a stranger. Through Facebook, she met a father of two in Massachusetts who was spending twelve hours a week on dialysis. Three months later, the transplant was a success.

Years before, Phillip Palmer (West Monroe, LA), news anchor at ABC7 Los Angeles, read a story about NBA star Sean Elliot, who had received a kidney from a living donor. The concept of living donation was entirely new to him, but he knew he wanted to give to someone, some day. Years later, after his co-worker and friend (and 2008 rider) Dale Davis suffered kidney failure, Phillip stepped up to be his living donor.

Palmer had been a fixture at the Donate Life Run/Walk for several years, so it was only fitting that he was joined in the Class of 2014 by three members of the Hostert family, who started the event in their home in 2003. Thirteen years after Craig Hostert—one of thirty riders from nineteen states and Taiwan—received a kidney from his wife Kathleen, their son Justin followed her footsteps within the last year.

Our final count of eighty-one floragraphs motivated Kathleen and OneLegacy's Ann Wennerberg to organize a formal training session for volunteer decorators. Not only was our resident expert

Lynne Frutchey able to pass along her time-tested techniques, but the exercise also allowed us to prepare twenty portraits for finishing events scheduled as early as November.

Altogether, sixty-three portraits were completed at local decorating events in thirty-three states and the District of Columbia, with eight of them the subject of multiple finishing events—one for each eyebrow. Notably, the portrait of Mike James (Bowie, MD) was finished at the Georgia State Capitol Building in Atlanta, Georgia, while the floragraph of Daisy A. Lobos (Lanham, MD) was completed at the El Salvadoran Consulate in Washington, D.C.

In a bittersweet tribute, one of our floragraphs honored longtime Donate Life Run/Walk and float volunteer Marianne O'Quinn of Fullerton, California. Her brother Bill's living donation of a kidney allowed her to continue her career as a teacher and vice-principal before her death after a fall at home was followed by the transplantation of her lungs, liver, and corneas.

Two new donor family foundations came aboard, bringing the number involved since 2010 to twelve. The Michael-Gene Kids Basketball Foundation of Melbourne, Florida, formed in memory of floragraph honoree Michael-Gene Robert Futch, provided meals, gifts, and leagues for underprivileged children. Josiah's House, a Tennessee-based nonprofit ministering to boys living in destitute circumstances in the Dominican Republic, honored their namesake, Josiah Berger, with a memorial floragraph portrait and a generous presenting sponsorship of the Dedication Garden.

Following through on our vision to make the entire deck a dedication garden required keeping close tabs on our 7,740-rose capacity. Throughout October and November, Facebook was peppered with posts showing hospital CEOs handwriting dedications in front of staff and media. By early December, Elisse Glennon of NJ Sharing

Network returned signed vials from all fifty-four of their hospitals. New England Donor Services (90 percent of their eighty-three hospitals) and Sierra Donor Services (83 percent of their fifty-four hospitals) stood out as well, while twelve more OPOs with more than forty signatures contributed mightily to the total of 1,200 vials, or one-quarter of all hospitals involved in organ, eye, and tissue donation.

In addition, forty-eight hospitals and organizations dedicated more than 1,400 roses to donor families and transplant patients. Families handwrote dedications at many of the three dozen rose ceremonies, including eight in Arkansas and four in Missouri. In the closing days, after taking Roses for Registries and other sources into account, we filled the remainder of the garden with tributes to the nation's 1,842 pediatric transplant candidates.

On December 29, hundreds of families and participants placed 535 roses in the dedication garden over the course of eight-and-a-half hours. The following morning, after orienting our float riders to their decorating shift and checking our progress from the previous night, I was on a tight schedule to make it to the floragraph family breakfast. As Randa and I headed to the parking lot, the Phoenix Decorating guard stopped us at the gate and directed us to two visitors.

A woman with a look of desperation held a tuck-top box she received from Huntington Hospital, which had honored her husband's gift of life at their rose ceremony earlier in the month. At the time of her husband's hospitalization, she had made a relative the primary point of contact. Thus, she was made aware of the ceremony only after the fact, and she retrieved the package only the day before.

Standing tearfully next to her teenage daughter, she opened the box to reveal a tagged vial, which looked utterly empty without its companion bloom. Also in the box was an invitation to place it on our float—yesterday.

"We're going to be late," I said to Randa, who smiled approvingly and waited with the family as I returned to the barn and explained the situation to Karen and Esther-Marie. Without hesitation, they quickly swept the dedication garden clean, and picked out the most beautiful rose they could find, and greeted the mother and daughter with open arms.

As Randa and I made our way to the Pasadena Convention Center, we contemplated how meaningful our participation in the Rose Parade had become to our community. Shortly after noon, dozens of donor families were welcomed to breakfast with hand-painted, heart-laden tile artworks, a perennial gift presented by Aaron Gilchrist of sponsor Bridge to Life. Soon thereafter, our guests blended small jars of colored sand into a glass vase, creating a microcosm of what the Donate Life Rose Parade Float had become: a vessel, radiating the love poured into it by thankful, generous, grieving, and proud people whose journeys of the heart brought us together.

That evening, the current edition of the Powerhouse show choir concluded our gala program with a four-minute medley of songs from our first ten Rose Parade entries. Their opening refrain of Pachelbel's *Canon in D* recalled our debut on New Year's Day 2004, when lung recipient Eunice Gibson Sutton steeled for her ride down Colorado Boulevard with a sincere wish: "I hope they don't just see us as something pretty. I hope they see us as symbolic."

A decade later to the day, our lantern festival was greeted by five miles of standing ovations, warm waves, and blessings as it approached from the west. Eunice's aspirations, and ours, had been fully realized, and then some.

2014 DONATE LIFE ROSE PARADE FLOAT

ROSE PARADE THEME: Dreams Come True

FLOAT THEME: Light Up the World

FLOAT AWARD: Theme Trophy

RIDERS: 42

FLORAGRAPH HONOREES: 81

STATES REPRESENTED: 40

PARTICIPATING ORGANIZATIONS: 132

DEDICATED ROSES: 4,582

DONATE LIFE GRANDSTAND SEATS: 872

FLORAGRAPH FINISHING EVENTS: 73

MEDIA STORIES: 430

ORGAN DONATION CONVERSION RATE, 2013: 71.3 percent[9]

DESIGNATED DONORS, US: 117,108,378[10]

EPILOGUE

I STEPPED INTO THE conference room and took a seat facing OneLegacy board member, Dr. Tom Rosenthal.

"How did you do it?" he asked with genuine curiosity.

The preceding pages have gone a long way toward finally answering that question.

It began, of course, with a vision of an organ donation-themed float in the Rose Parade. The basic recipe—a modest budget, a float design and builder, volunteers to decorate, and people to ride—would have simply raised awareness.

We aimed much higher. We felt a deep sense of responsibility to inspire millions of people to choose to be donors. After all, every donation opportunity had the highest possible stakes. Each "yes" meant that someone, or many people, would live, or live fully, one more day.

Searching our way forward, there were few guideposts, and checkpoints arose along the way. Staying true to our mission relied on asking ourselves fundamental questions:

What will touch hearts and move people to action?
How can we honor those affected by our cause?
How will we make participation easy and meaningful?
What could the float make possible?
What would Gary think?

Our mission was also propelled by extraordinary people with a deep commitment to service. Year after year, our committee, operations team, and volunteers subordinated sleep, health, and family time to further our shared purpose. As we staggered into each New Year, we were all thankful to have been part of something of such meaning and magnitude.

My final contributions in an official capacity focused on creative development for Donate Life's twelfth Rose Parade float entry. I hope its theme, "The Never-Ending Story," is a harbinger of things to come.

REFERENCES

1. Burroughs, T.E., Hong, B.A., Kappel, D.F., and Freedman, B.K. "The stability of family decisions to consent or refuse organ donation: would you do it again?" *Psychosomatic Medicine* 60, (1998): 156–162. www.ncbi.nlm.nih.gov/pubmed/9560863.

2. OPTN database as of March 2008.

3. Donate Life California 2007 media campaign overview, 9/12/07.

4. Israni, A.K., Zaun, D., Rosendale, J.D., Snyder, J. J., and Kasiske B.L. "OPTN/SRTR 2012 Annual Data Report: Deceased Organ Donation." *American Journal of Transplantation* 14, no. 1, (January 2014): 167–183. http://onlinelibrary.wiley.com/doi/10.1111/ajt.12585/full.

5. "Honoring Donors," UNOS, www.unos.org/donation/honoring-donors/.

6. Donate Life America Donor Designation Collaborative Data Summary, Q3 2013.

7. Rick Reilly, "The Parade of Life," ESPN, (December 29, 2011): www.espn.com/espn/story/_/id/7400059/rick-reilly-donate-life-float-rose-bowl-parade.

8. Klein, A. S., Messersmith, E. E., Ratner, L. E., Kochik, R., Baliga, P. K., and Ojo, A. O. "Organ Donation and Utilization in the

United States, 1999–2008." *American Journal of Transplantation* 10, (2010): 973–986.

9. "OPTN/SRTR 2013 Annual Data Report: Deceased Organ Donation," American Journal of Transplantation 15, no. 2, (January 2015): 1–13.

10. Donate Life America 2014 Annual Update.

11. OneLegacy data.

12. Malek, Sayeed K., Keys, Brandon J., Kumar, Sanjaya, Milford, Edgar, and Tullius, Stefan G. "Racial and ethnic disparities in kidney transplantation," Transplant International 24 (December 2010): 419-424, doi:10.1111/j.1432-2277.2010.01205.x.

ABOUT DONATE LIFE AMERICA

DONATE LIFE AMERICA (DLA) is a 501(c)3 nonprofit organization leading its national partners and Donate Life State Teams to increase the number of donated organs, eyes, and tissue available to save and heal lives. DLA manages and promotes Donate Life˙, the national brand for the cause of donation, motivates the public to register as organ, eye, and tissue donors, provides education about living donation, manages the National Donate Life Registry at RegisterMe.org, and develops and executes effective multi-media campaigns to promote donation.

On average, twenty-two people die each day—almost one every hour—because the organ they need is not donated in time. You can help the million-plus people needing organ, cornea, and tissue transplants each year by registering your decision to be a donor. One donor can save eight lives through organ donation, restore sight to two people through cornea donation, and heal more than seventy-five others through tissue donation.

Make LIFE possible. Register to be a donor in the National Donate Life Registry at RegisterMe.org.

ABOUT THE AUTHOR

BRYAN STEWART is a marketing professional and nonprofit leader whose people-first approach has vitalized organizations, furthered causes, and inspired millions.

His pioneering leadership of national, statewide, and regional initiatives contributed to dramatic increases in organ donation rates over the course of a decade. His marketing, communications, and branding expertise has benefited more than a dozen for-profit and nonprofit organizations, including Donate Life America, Donate Life California, and the Association of Organ Procurement Organizations.

Bryan is a vice president of corporate partnerships at Premier Partnerships, a leader in sponsorship representation specializing in sports stadiums, entertainment venues, leagues and teams, iconic landmarks, and municipal programs. His role draws upon his experience instituting the Donate Life float into the Rose Parade as well as his roles at Major League Soccer, the Bud Light Pro Beach Volleyball League, and Paramount Pictures.

Bryan has been interviewed by scores of national and regional news outlets, including CNN, CBS Early Show, History's Modern Marvels, USA Today, and ESPN.com.

His marketing, communications, and branding expertise has benefited more than a dozen for-profit and nonprofit organizations.

Bryan is a skilled graphic designer, aspiring singer, and received a writing credit on Star Trek: The Next Generation.

Raised in Oklahoma and Northern California, he has a BA in political science from UCLA, resides in Pasadena, and marvels at his daughter Sophia, an emerging writer.

FLOAT COMMITTEE MEMBERS

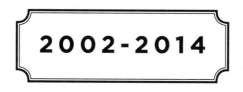

2002-2014

Glenn Abercrombie	Thomas Asfeldt*
Kari Barlament	Rivian Bell
Dave Bosch	Esther-Marie Carmichael*
Christina Courtney	John Dean
Steve Ferkau	Gary Foxen*
Mary Ganikos**	Jacki Harris
Kathleen Hostert	Julie Humeston
Rebecca Hunter	Stephanie Jansky
Anne Keshner	Kari Kozuki
Karen Libs*	Randa Lipman
Sandra Madera	Glenn Matsuki
Ginny McBride	Betty McNamara
Jennifer Moe	Tom Mone*
Kevin Monroe	Rudy Morgan
Andrew Mullins	Erika Ospina Awad
Lisa Rhodes	Renee Rhodes

Stephanie Schmitz

Bryan Stewart*#

Tenaya Wallace

Amy Waterman

Laurie Wolowic Wright

*Minimum four years of service. #Chairman *Served all 12 years
**HRSA liaison*

PARTICIPANTS AND HONOREES

2004 PARTICIPANTS

RIDERS

Patricia Abdullah

Brent Axthelm

Kari Barlament

Dionne Brown

Sara Castro

Eunice Gibson

Mike Jones

Barbara Lawrence

Sharon Maupin

Catalina M. Perez

Gerald W. "Jerry" Prose

Brittney Andrews

Darlene Aymerich

Gene Battaly

Carissa Carmichael

Patricia Elizarraraz

Kathy M. Gibson

Chris Klug

Phat Mach

Kenneth P. Moritsugu, MD, MPH

Patricia K. Perry

Ryan Zinn

2005 PARTICIPANTS

RIDERS

Lynn Allred

Tim Eluskie

Derrick "D.J." Floyd Jr.

Maggie Green

Nimfa S. Melesio

Chyrrel Mock

Cathy Olmo

Mary Palmer

Analia Quintanar

Britney Ruegsegger

Tammy Schlesinger

Ellie Tomczak

Nancy Eluskie

Derrick Floyd

Eleanor Green

Reg Green

Susana Melesio

Dick Mock, PhD

Kelly Olmo

Deborah Quick

Liliana Quintanar

Kacey Ruegsegger

Dan Tomczak

KODAK HONOREES

Christina Bueno

Nicholas Green

Tory Howe-Lynch

Richard LaRue

Kim Kimble Gast

Zenaida Hoh

Stephen M. Jokela Jr.

Patricia Madera de Waldie

2006 PARTICIPANTS

RIDERS

Robin Barrett

Gail Brooks

Mike Blood

Jackie Colleran

Myriam Correa-Sherman

Gary Foxen

Karen Garber

Kathy Hasan

Lyda Kroening

Avery Livingston

Tae Park

Nicole Brook Stoe

Mary Ann Venturelli

Kurt Wiltcher

Ilene Feder

Christine Galán

Edith Gonzalez

Kade Howard

America Leyva

Albert Paduano

Colleen Sasso

Sahra Torres-Rivera

Erika Wells

2007 PARTICIPANTS

RIDERS

Sheri Bergstrom-Casey

Robert Bonner Jr.

Bill Dawson

Charity Guergo-Ramos

Keith Karzin

Jennifer Ling

Kevin Monroe

Brenda O'Donnell

Erica Rangel-Báez

Dan Sandoval

Emile Therien

Tyson Wood

Norman Biondi

Fannie C. Brown

Susan Giess

Kelli Jantz

Rachel Lentz

Tammy Mitchell

Camille Nighthorse

Shannon Payne

Marvin Reznik

Rev. Fr. Elly S. Tavarro

Donna Warren

2008 PARTICIPANTS

RIDERS

Jan Barney

Isabel Stenzel Byrnes

Nikki Cortez

Paul DiLorenzo

Dawn Giese

Alvin Grant

George Hill

Kelli Jaunsen

D.J. Lampert

Bennie Marshall

Jill Miller

Jesus Nava

Tom Berryhill

Tracy Copeland

Dale Wade Davis

Ron Geddes

Claire Goudeau

Ozzie Herrera

Bill Ismer

Jesse Kolb

Sarah Felice Lopez

Indra Michaca

Monica Montgomery

Daniel Ronco

WALKERS

Rachel Ball

Jeannie McGuire

Terry Murray

Arthur Stone

Laurie Wolowic

Josie Flores

Mike Moore

Eva Perez

Missy Tipton

FLORAGRAPH HONOREES

Elizabeth Aguilar

Tanya Austin

Kasey Burleson

Hernán Aispuro

Sarah Braun

Erin Choe

Raymond Costlow

Nicholas Ermak

Cecil Evans Sr.

Ana Maria Flores

Dan Gromada, Jr.

Jemil Jamison

Juan Juaregui

Johnny Lopez

Katie Moore

Allen T. Murray

Stephanie Pasquale

Dennis Rivetti

Jacob C. Smith

Robert Somerville

Heather Spindler

Nicholas Stone

Michael Wolowic

Julie De Rossi

Jonathan Eshenour

Christopher Field

Steven Ginoza

Paul Hickey

Karlynn Johnson

Gretchen Lofthouse

James McGuire

Melanie Moore

Lisa Marie Odgers

Trinity Pereira

Johnathan Sim

Terry Lee Snow

Dana Spencer

David Starr

Ransom Tipton

Brian Rand Wos

2009 PARTICIPANTS

RIDERS

Lily Allen

Jim Carter

Melody Connett

Julie DeStefano

Lauren Donkar

Sergio Gomez

Debbie Kowatch

Bonnie Lundy

Mary Brown

May Chen

Joe Darga

Susan McVey Dillon

Steve Ferkau

Gaston Gonzalez

Theresa Lozada

Eric Miller

Kim Morsching

Denice Russell

Randi Swersky

Mandy Trolinger

Jose Zaragoza

Dave Murphy

Andrea Spraggins

Hooshang Torabi

Audrey Vasquez

Merle Zuel

FLORAGRAPH HONOREES

Sharday Badillo

Dustin Bauer

Matthew Bemis

Evan Burke

Andrew Colligan

Jill Connett

Jennifer Cushman

Leslie Ebert

Rachel Escue

Kelly Kline

Anne Laumer

Curtis Lovegren

Michael McVey

Micah Miller

Frank Paliswait

Alexis Porta

Paul Price

Hollie Stanyon-Fouts

Gene Ushiroda

Dalton Barnes

Edward Bax

Johnny Brown II

Anthony Charron

Bud Collins

Michael Corea

Quentin Dachis

Riley England

Ernest Goh

Jessica Kupczak

Shay Ledbetter

Victor Lozada

BJ Miller

Kelly Nachreiner

Emily Porche

Cody Prewitt

Jason Ray

Christopher Trevizo

Johnny Ysais III

2010 PARTICIPANTS

RIDERS

Steve Bond

Carter Bryant

Mina Gonzalez

Anne Gulotta

Lili Ibanez

Cristina Margolis

Nikki McKenna

Joshua Nelson

Joann Nixon

Juan Perez

Manuel Salazar

Debra Thompson

Patrice Broussard

Dolores Benton Evans

Hannah Grinnan

Tim Heffernan

Sunny Luna

Glenn Matsuki

Hazelee Moultrie

Tyla Newbold

Matthew Ogle

Wendy Rodgers

Jeremy Starr

Mike Vyrostek

FLORAGRAPH HONOREES

"BJ" Bill-Junior Falefasa Ala'ilima

Steven Alvarez

Andrew Benedict

Caroline Elizabeth Ball Bryant

Virginia M. Camacho

Andrea Carney

Cameron L. Chana

Mike Craig

Lee John Davis

Thomas Dunn

Ryan Evans

Alfredo Alvara

Timothy Baptista

Brandon Anthony Brown

Christy Bueno

Jack Cardinal

Perlita Carrillo Celis

Katie Coolican

Michael E. Creighton

Brian Matthew DeBoer

Andrew Faiez Ennabe

Annie Sarah Fleming

Trevor Frisch

Nicholas Green

Jeanette Altuna Hammerstein

Jaslynn Faith Hernandez

Jack Dean Hook-Van Hecke

Stephen M. Jokela, Jr.

Bradley S. Jordan, Jr.

Teresa LeAnn Kemp

Eric J. Knotts

Paul Anthony Lopez

M.G. Miller

Jesse Miller IV

Mary Kathleen Morris

Christopher Nixon

Bronson Parsons

Mario Pinedo

Tarrence Regan

Mike Roman Reyes

Kenneth W. Sapp

Mitchell Thomas Schloesser

Erika Desireé Schwager

Robbie Sisemore

Brandon L. Spight

Timothy P. Susco

Joseph Templeton

Thomas Tiffany Varney V

Kyle Anthony Whitworth

Maria de Los Angeles Yepez

Kim Kimble Gast

Jay Gulotta

Joseph Helfgot

Zenaida Reyes Aurellano Hoh

Jeffrey Johns

Isaiah Jerome Jones

Taylor Charlotte Kemp

Jim Kennedy

Richard LaRue

Patty Madera de Waldie

Shantel Miller

Dr. Victor Miranda

Lena Laquaia-Leither Moultrie

Philip Nixon

Ku'uleialoha Patton

Kevin Patrick Pryor

Kate Reinhart

Manuel A. Sandoval

Todd Sato

Robert Evan Schuppert

Andrew Shorter

Ronald Snipes

Spencer Patton Squire

Kiethen L. Taylor

Trever Ryan Tremayne

Jessica Marie Ward

Carmen Lee Wilber

2011 PARTICIPANTS

RIDERS

Leiauna Anderson

Irene Atencio

Michael Carraway Jr.

Valen Cover

Carl Drury

Dave Hollon

Meredith McCall

Monica O'Brien

Martin Joseph Sanchez Sr.

Jennifer Shih

Missy Sweitzer

Dee Tilton

Victor Villalobos

Norma Araos

Emma Brown

Catherine Casey

Arbeny Davis

Brittany Grimm

Jane Jorgensen

Jessica Melore

Jeff Peterson

Scott Seetin

Parker Simpson

Patricia Thomas

Phil Van Stavern

John Weakley

WALKERS

Donald Arthur

Jody Dosser

Michael "Kip" Brooks

Ann Lopez

FLORAGRAPH HONOREES

Kimberly Adams

Marco Arana

Antonio Bennett

Mike Briggs

J.T. Burud

Paul Campbell

Mia Adriano

Lindsey Baron

Donald Everett Blair

Jake Burke

Jacob Rian Campbell

Michael Carnevale

Sebastian Castro

Sasha Albert Clare

David Curtis

Jermiah Dosser

Melissa "Missy" Dawn Fields

Brian Larkin Gleason

Mandy Harrell

Cora Brittany Hill

Jeffrey A. Kocab

Jared Lamirato

Devron L. Lewis

Haley Jeannette Moore

Felipe M. Perez

Scott Patrick Phillips

Patrick Preston

Darwin Javier Rivera

David Rodriguez, Jr.

Amanda Katherine Seraphin

Taylor Storch

Taylor Lynn Elaine Tefft

Joshua D. Tolan

Thomas Vanderhorst

Keith Walton

Randall Eugene Woolen

Estephan Chavez

Steven A. Cordova

Jill Daniel

Shannon M. Eckert

Rose Anna Friguglietti

Quincy L. Greer

Franky Hazelgrove

Chad Jones

Ben Kopp

Matthew Lausch

Jim McCall

Vu Huy Nguyen

Ines Jahira Perez

Thomas A. Poliziani

Joseph Quiambao

Leon T. Roach III

Serina Dee Scheler

Andrew Paul Spencer

Zachary Sweitzer

Katya Teresa Todesco

Nicholas "Nick" Van Stavern

Kirk Walker

Christopher Blake White

Millicent (Millie) Sue Zittritsch

2012 PARTICIPANTS

RIDERS

Gaena Cho

Mary Ellen Decker

Emily Fennell

Claudia Gerlach

Jim Haemmerle, MD

Joey Ianiero

Janice Langbehn

Stephanie L. McMackin

Patricia Navarino-Winters

Arnold Perez

Anthony Robinson

Alexis Sloan

Kara Thio

Mary Wu

Susan R. Cossabone

Juan Espino

Valerie Fourtunia

Roxanna Green

Linda Henning

Cora Johnson

Lynn Livingston

Nancy Michaels

Johnny Orta

Robert Richard

Alex Rodriguez

Katherine M. Taylor

Brandon Witt

Max M. Zapata

FLORAGRAPH HONOREES

A'marion La'kari Adams

Trey Atkin

Tyrone Eugene Bowie, Jr.

Aric Brill

Kirstin Elizabeth Cantler-Booke

Lawrence (Larry) Gene Cavenah

Scott Patrick Conrad

Jeremy M. Doyle

Heath River Eiland

Eduardo Arellano

Don Boone

Daniel DeRay Brannon

Kyndall Alyse Brown

Jose Alfredo Carrillo

Christian Chamberlain

Scott Edwin Davis

Mike Dunnam

Brian Ellis

Katherine Delia Enos

Jesse Miller Gamble

Michael Deon (Rudy) Gilmore

Angela Marie Guest

Travis S.E. Hansen

Lacey Mary Haye

Sierra Lynn Heidrich

Marc Henning

Chih-Chien Hsiao

Ron Kerkvliet

Adam Long

Sybil Elizabeth McFall

Heather Nicole Miller

Patrick Shane Nunnelley

Jeffrey C. O'Rourke

Roberto DeJesus Perez

Thomas A. Pettit

Hailey Rath

Clint Adam Rivera

Paul G. Rossmeissl

Jayce Ray Sheffield

Elizabeth Sutherland

Rie Tanaka

Jeffrey R. Topping

Tommy Weiss

Mariah West

Jovante Woods

Stella Espino

Janeen Marie Ganahl

Christina-Taylor Green

Jose Gutierrez

Brandon Ross Harney

Krista D. Heidinger

Eric Michael Helm

Jordan House

Andrew Clay Johnson

Elijah R. Lee

Merle Manganiello

Melanie Ann Miers

Erica Marie Stewart Mullins

"Anya" Chiemeka Ogbuji

Christopher Paturzo III

Dylan Peters

Lisa Marie Pond

Nicole Lynn Richardson

Francisco "Paco" Rodriguez

Alicia Jeannette Sabaugh

Ryan Cody Stuck

Drew Swank

Amanda Thompson

Julio Villegas Jr.

Shawn Wero

Kimberley Rochelle Williams-Ibarra

Melissa Michelle Yarosh

2013 PARTICIPANTS

RIDERS

John Beers

Valerie Vandervort Boyer

Ernesto Bravo Chavez

Michele Shanahan DeMoss

David Eckstein

Jonathan Finger

Carolyn Henry Glaspy

Emily Henwood

Maria Knowlton

Vivian Lefferts

Amanda Missildine

Patricia Marie Nelson

Charles C. Okeke

Caitlyn Persinger

Kevin Riepl

Susan E. Sprague

Neal Bira

Chase Caspersen

Troy DeJoode

Leilah Dowsari

Rick Eckstein

Alfonso Garcia

Joe Gutierrez

Larry E. Johnson

Peter David Lang

Kelly Luchini

Amy Nash

Vicky Nguyen

Sue A. Pasewald

Mark E. Reagan

Claudia Sanchez

Denien Vittorio Wilde

FLORAGRAPH HONOREES

Anthony Ray Alvarez Jr.

Eric James Barlament

George Becker

Nicholas John Bogie

Matthew E. Bowers

Brittany Nicole Cail

Elliot Carbajal

Ryan Joseph Converse

Gabriel Barajas

Robert H. Barrentine

Maraleius Birdsong

Danny L. Bost

Ben Breedlove

Brian Scott Campbell

Andrea Renae Cleveland

Shelby Cooper

Dale Alan Covington

Salustiano De Jesus

Alfredo G. Diaz

Michael S. Doherty Jr.

Carissa Foushee

Mary Jo Gase

Jorge A. Gonzalez

Christopher Hershberger

Troy Andrew Jensen

Kristen Joe

Zackary Tyler Kallem

Dalton Chase Lawyer

Deanna Mauer

Jaret Toshiro Minami

Corina Marie Murrieta

David Martin Nelson Jr.

Robert A. Novak, Jr.

Tyler Plummer

Joshua Keith Robertson

Scott Santana

Evin Joel Shoap

Johalan Antonio Sinohui

Jessie Starnes

Taylor Storch

Darlene M. Uecker

Sandra Mariana Velazquez

Thomas Walls

Quinn Vittorio Wilde

Lexie Davis

Mary Frances DeFerrari

Jason Michael Dodds

Jesus Fernandez

David Lee Fox

James (Jimmy) E. Ginter

Jeremy Henwood

Quinn Alec Hoover

Jason Jiaa

Michael N. Kallal

Terence Kennedy

Elizabeth Logelin

Todd Davis Miller

Landon James Cole Mitchell

Elijah Nabua

Molly Noble

John Nuñez

Tony Radulescu

David H. Rodriguez

Alexis Lucia Scanlin

Holland Dru Shoemake

Justin D. Sollohub

Mark Starr, MD

Fabian A. Trujillo

Delany Alexandra Van Wert

Ryan Robert Viator

Ryan Lee Webster

Maegan Ariana Yeakley

2014 PARTICIPANTS

RIDERS

Julie M. Allred

Edward A. Bonfiglio

Faith Carlin

Yang-Chuan Chang

Nita French

Craig Hostert

Matt Katsarelis

Nefeterius Akeli McPherson

Richard Perez

Sherri Plair

Linda Ramos

Arthur Joven Reye

Jerry L. Sexton Sr.

Amy Nicole Tippins

Gregory J. Welsh

Melissa Bensouda

Kim Burdakin

John Cervantes

Dan Cuda

Brian Keith Gilliam

David Jenkins

Katharine Lawrence

Debbie Morgan

Sue Herrick Pilon

Harry Rambo

Connor Randall

Sharon Runner

Madison Shinaberry

Ana Maria Villalobos

JePahl White

WALKERS

Jeff E. Carter Jr.

Teresa M. (Terie) Cota

Kathleen Hostert

Kevin Lucien Noyes

Kathy L. Vochoska

Karen Willis

Michael Cervantes

Justin Hostert

Jessica Jurado

Phillip Palmer

LaKishia White

Dr. Kelly M. Wright

FLORAGRAPH HONOREES

Keegan Atley Adkins

John Akers Jr.

Jeff Ballard

Kaitlyn Berg

Kevin Ellis Boyles

Julio Enrique Buenano

Teresa Lynn Cassavoy

Christian Chamberlain

Rita Cihak

Noah Michael Davis

Melissa Ditta

Kevin Patrick Dobson

Andrea Rae Dominguez

Christopher Thomas Duffy

Andrew Endo

Jorge A. Fernandez

Krysta Hankee

Jesus Alejandro Hernandez

Mike James

Jantz H. Kinzer Jr.

Nick Leath

Adam Fletcher Lively

Ena "Po-Po" Lue

Elijah Cole McGinley

Marianne O'Quinn

India Kimberly Phillips

Cheryl Lynn Denelli Righter

Gilbert Frank Rivera

Annie Rachel Ahern

Bryce Ian Autry

Jay Bennevell Banion

Josiah David Berger

Garrett M. Brockway

Benjamin Bynum

Angel Nathaniel Chacon

Yo-Sam Choi

Keegan Scott Clinger

Theodore "Teddy" Blaine

Deterding Eitan James Djiji

Robyn Doiron

Michael Drozd

Dr. Michael Edelstein

Carlos Garcia Escobedo

Michael-Gene Robert Futch

Evan J. Hauk

Cory Scott Horton

Terence Kennedy

Sean LaPersonerie

Chin-Te Liao

Daisy A. Lobos

Darwin Mathwig

Leslie R. McLendon

Jonathan E. Peter

Travis James Rhodes

Fernando Rivera

Dylan Anthony Rotellini

Jaidyn Kiara Rothermel

Anthony "AJ" Salisbury

Tyson Lee Schreiber

Patrick Shillings

Lareanz Simmons

Jerry L. Spinks

Kameron Shigeo Lanaki Steinhoff

Audrey Jade Hope Sullenger

Rex A. Tickles

Joshua Thomas Waleryszak

Christopher Walters

Lindsey Denae Woodward

Paul John Young

Richard Allen Ruble

Joshua Christopher San Pedro

Todd Semon

Robert Sills

Howard S. "Howie" Smith, MD

Christine K. Springer

Patricia Streich-McConnell

John Talbot

Erich Richard Vogel

Joseph Keith Wallace

Zachary Wildhaber

Noah C. Worthington

PARTICIPATING ORGANIZATIONS

ALL ELEVEN YEARS

AlloSource

Cedars-Sinai Comprehensive Transplant Center | *Los Angeles, CA*

Donate Life America

Donor Network West | *Central and Northern California*

Gift of Hope Organ and Tissue Donor Network | *Illinois*

JDI Communications, Inc.

Life Alliance Organ Recovery Agency | *S. Florida and The Bahamas*

Lifeline of Ohio | *Southeastern Ohio*

Lifesharing | Greater San Diego area

Mid-South Transplant Foundation | *Western TN, Eastern AR, Northern MS*

MTF Biologics

OneLegacy | *Greater Los Angeles area*

RTI Donor Services

TRIO Ventura County/West Valley Chapter

Unyts | *Greater Buffalo area*

Washington Regional Transplant Community | *DC, metro area*

SEVEN TO TEN YEARS

American Association of Tissue Banks (AATB)

AOPO

Astellas Pharma US

Center for Donation and Transplant | *Northeastern NY, Western VT*

Children's Mercy Hospital and Clinics | *Kansas City, MO*

CryoLife

Cytonet (now Promethera)

Donate Life California

Donor Alliance | *Colorado and Wyoming*

Donor Network of Arizona

Finger Lakes Donor Recovery Network | *North-Central NY*

Gift of Life Donor Program | *Eastern PA, Southern NJ, Delaware*

Huntington Hospital | *Pasadena, CA*

International Transplant Nurses Society

Iowa Donor Network

LifeCenter Northwest | *Washington, Alaska, Montana, N. Idaho*

LifeLink Foundation | *Southwest Florida, Georgia, Puerto Rico*

LifeShare of Oklahoma

LifeSource | *Minnesota, North Dakota, South Dakota*

LiveOnNY | *Greater New York metro area*

The Living Legacy Foundation of Maryland

Loma Linda University Medical Center | *Loma Linda, CA*

Louisiana Organ Procurement Agency (LOPA)

Mendez National Institute of Transplantation Foundation

Mid-America Transplant Services | *Southeastern MO, Southern IL, Northeast AR*

Midwest Transplant Network | *Kansas, Western Missouri*

The Military and Hospitaller Order of St. Lazarus of Jerusalem

NATCO

Nevada Donor Network

New England Donor Services

NJ Sharing Network Foundation | *Northern New Jersey*

Phoenix Decorating Co.

Providence Health and Services | *Los Angeles County*

Renal Support Network

Sallop Insurance

Sierra Donor Services | *Greater Sacramento area*

Tennessee Donor Services

UC Irvine Health | *Irvine, CA*

UCLA Health | *Los Angeles, CA*

UNOS

FOUR TO SIX YEARS

Alabama Organ Center

American Liver Foundation

Greater Los Angeles Division

American Medical Bill Review

Antelope Valley Hospital | *Lancaster, CA*

Arizona Hospital and Healthcare Association

ARORA (Arkansas Regional Organ Recovery Agency)

Baptist Health Medical Center Little Rock | *Little Rock, AR*

Bridge to Life

Buddhist Tzu Chi Medical Foundation

Centerpoint Medical Center | *Independence, MO*

Community Healthcare System | *Munster, IN*

CORE (Center for Organ Recovery and Education) | *Western PA*

Dignity Memorial

Donate Life Run/Walk Committee | *Orange County, CA*

Freeman Health System | *Joplin, MO*

Hartford Hospital | *Hartford, CT*

Health Promotions Now

Houston Methodist J.C. Walter Jr. Transplant Center | *Houston, TX*

In Memory of Michael E. Creighton

Indiana Donor Network

Intermountain Donor Services | *Utah, Southern Idaho*

James Redford Institute for Transplant Awareness

JJ's Legacy | *Bakersfield, CA*

Joseph H. Helfgot Foundation

Kansas Eye Bank and Cornea Research Center, Inc.

Kentucky Organ Donor Affiliates (KODA)

Lifebanc | *Greater Cleveland metro area*

LifeCell Corporation (now Allergan)

LifeNet Health | *Virginia and Eastern West Virginia*

LifePoint | *South Carolina*

LifeShare Of The Carolinas | *Western North Carolina*

Mercy Hospital Joplin | *Joplin, MO*

NRG

Penn State Milton S. Hershey Medical Center | *Hershey, PA*

Phillips 66

SightLife | *Washington, Idaho, California*

Spencer Squire Charities | *Allen, TX*

St. Joseph Hospital Orange | *Orange, CA*

St. Joseph's Hospital Health Center | *Syracuse, NY*

United Organ Transplant Association (UOTA) | *Inland Empire, CA*

Upstate University Hospital | *Syracuse, NY*

Vons

Washington Regional Medical Center | *Fayetteville, AR*

Wisconsin Donor Network | *Eastern Wisconsin*